The Collected Poems
of Miriam Waddington

The Collected Poems of Miriam Waddington

—

A CRITICAL EDITION

VOLUME 2

Edited by
RUTH PANOFSKY

University of Ottawa Press | OTTAWA

u Ottawa

EDITING MODERNISM
in Canada

The University of Ottawa Press acknowledges with gratitude the support extended to its publishing list by Heritage Canada through the Canada Book Fund, by the Canada Council for the Arts, by the Federation for the Humanities and Social Sciences through the Awards to Scholarly Publications Program and by the University of Ottawa. The University of Ottawa Press also acknowledges with gratitude financial and editorial support from Editing Modernism in Canada.

Copy editing: Trish O'Reilly-Brennan
Proofreading: Johanne Muzak
Typesetting: infographie CS
Cover design: Johanna Pedersen
Cover art: Open Window, 1951, by Ghitta Caiserman © National Gallery of Canada, Ottawa

Library and Archives Canada Cataloguing in Publication

Waddington, Miriam, 1917-
[Poems]
The collected poems of Miriam Waddington / edited by Ruth Panofsky.

Includes bibliographical references and indexes.
Issued in print and electronic formats.
ISBN 978-0-7766-2145-6 (set).--ISBN 978-0-7766-0824-2 (v. 1 : pbk.).--
ISBN 978-0-7766-0823-5 (v. 2 : pbk.).--ISBN 978-0-7766-2154-8 (pdf).--
ISBN 978-0-7766-2153-1 (epub)

I. Panofsky, Ruth, editor II. Title.

PS8545.A18A17 2014   C811'.54   C2014-902886-5
                                      C2014-902887-3

MIX
Paper from
responsible sources
FSC   FSC® C100212
www.fsc.org

PREVIOUSLY PUBLISHED POEMS
(CONTINUED)

Advice to the Young

1
Keep bees and
grow asparagus,
watch the tides
and listen to the
5   wind instead of
the politicians
make up your own
stories and believe
them if you want to
10   live the good life.

2
All rituals
are instincts
never fully
trust them but
15   study to im-
prove biology
with reason.

3
Digging trenches
for asparagus
20   is good for the
muscles and
waiting for the
plants to settle
teaches patience
25   to those who are
usually in too
much of a hurry.

4
There is morality
in bee-keeping
30   it teaches how
not to be afraid
of the bee swarm
it teaches how
not to be afraid of
35   finding new places
and building in them
all over again.

1972

Ending

The big winds
of the world
have been called up
from sleep   they are
5   cross   shake thunder
and rain over the
city   spit out
teeth of ice from
their angry mouths.

10   I stand alone in
the great ante-room
no use now
even to be afraid
there is no one to
15   be afraid to anymore.

1972

Gift: Venus 24 Degrees in Virgo
For Edmund Haines

Ceremony:
a carved smiling
lazuli in a church,
brass pipes and
5   trumpets.

Caves, sounds,
chains, wires, loops,
saws, a ruffled
slow weave, waves

10   of cruel cruel
Kansas City
touching
like wheat those
tunnels, the
15   downrush of icy
birthwaters the
skipdip

of rolypoly
coasters, reckless
20   hair flying
unpaved dusty roads
the lemony glitter
in-and-out
waterfold, fishjump
25   the glyph, high
rush to fullfall

moontime and the
empty squares
of Madrid
30   filling with roses,
blowing
with white linen;

and me
saying goodbye
35   what gift could
anyone ever bring
you now except
to start
all over again.

1972

In Small Towns

Unreal as the
shifting fields
of winter
was your crossing
5   my threshold;
it must have been
in a dream dreamed
by children that
you came very
10   imaginative light
and delicate, fitful;
not at all like
those prairie towns
we lived in or maybe
15   yes, delicate like them
in a landscape of ink
and flat paper
all those fastidious
township plans and
20   lot surveys penned
through with paths
leading to the very edge
of maps dwindling
into distant archives.

25 It is all managed
    with tentative lines
    sketching the future
    speculating about
    the past, it is done
30 with apparitions
    of sixteen-year-olds
    finding themselves
    suddenly in the
    Silver Slipper Cafe
35 surfacing sharply
    from a haze of
    lost times in
    the small towns
    of Manitoba.

    1972

New Religions

I have been
converted to
all the new
religions
5   I agree that
the perfect
age to die
is fifty.

The perfect
10   control to have
is coolness and
love is the
perfect eskimo
to take to
15   the eternal
igloo; I have
discovered that ice
is the perfect
medium for
20   foretelling
the future.

There isn't
a bulb left
in the garden
25   there won't be
a single hyacinth
next spring
April will be
blueless.

1972

A Space of Love

By the gravity
of your eyes
I fell into a
space of love
5   your rosy voice
became the air
of my songs the
fires of ritual
destroyed darkness
10   and fell like
a rain on the
kingdom of unlisted
cities and your

presence flowered
15   there your presence
towered there your
presence circled
the eagles of light.

1972

Dreaming of Mister Never

In France I dream
more than in other
countries; last night
I dreamed you came
5   into my city into the
towered winter of
Besançon you commanded
my presence and once
again I awaited you.

10   I sat silently
while you talked
(have you ever
asked me what
I think?) when
15   you got up to leave
I followed awkwardly
in your footsteps
balancing myself in
the bumpy troughs
20   of snow.

I watched your
receding figure
grow smaller and
smaller and in my
25   dream I stood on
the road for a long
time watching the
snow fall and waiting
for your return.

30   I awoke to a dawn
        full of the old
        torment a world of
        endless wednesdays;
        in my real life
35   I am still waiting
        still searching for
        the dreamless country
        you have never heard
        of where you can never
40   find me again.

        1972

Finding Amos in Jerusalem

He gave me
golden stones
when I wanted
stories he gave
5   me silence
for my blindest
furies;

He withheld
his presence he
10   hid his face
I hunted the
city for his
hiding place
and dug in the
15   rubble for his
smallest trace;

He was here he
was there he was
always nowhere
20   whether dragging
the weight of
a beggar's feet
or folded away
in a stranger's
25   frown; yet everyone
swore they had
seen him pass not
an hour before.

Above the market
30   or under its roofs
I listened for
the sound of those
ancient hoofs
for ghostly wheels
35   in the narrow streets
splashing blood of
boys with the curse
of Greece while
Egypt's hate
40   burned a fiery path
to Damascus Gate.

He hid from me
in an olive grove
in a cold green pit
45   by the Nablus road
on a January day
in the winter sun;
he called from the
bunkers he shuddered
50   in caves and sent out
a whisper from layers
of stone: *God is Almighty*
and God is One while the
blue song of Islam told
55   of brothers betrayed
then fell broken-winged
from love's scaffold.

I buried its
presence I throttled
60   its voice I turned
my back on the ache
of choice; my brain
was frozen my heart
was chilled my bones
65   were emptied and then
my eyes filled with
the seeing of Amos:
through walls of fire
and stones of gold from
70   the long shelves of silence
the Jewish graves rolled;
they cried against exile
two thousand years old
from the heart of grief
75   on a January day
of the Nablus road.

1972

Imitations

I wish I were
a dog asleep
in the orchards
of Sicily or a
5   statue of a
smiling Gallic
poet under the
towers of Avignon
something that
10   dreams the blue
skies of Manitoba
that imitates the
white levels the
endless defeats
15   of snow

1972

Snowfences

the snowfences
                        of winter
icemounds
                        three horses
5   in a field   a sky
                        blue
as kindergarten paper
it only
            needs
10   a red strip
pasted on
                        to make a sunset.

me in Toronto,
                        local
15   Greenland   lake Ontario's
glacial shores
(why
            don't you answer
my letters   write me
20   about star-apples
                        banana trees
the drought in Mandeville?)

here
            no lowburning
25   hubbub
of voicesound   no
                        humming
of birdtails   no long
minutes
30   of colour   no
exploding seeds   no
black sunlight   no
loud.

                here
35   only soprano
                                whiteness
                driving to lectures
                                past snow
                and the fences
40   (all the same
                remember
                    my song).

        1972

Tapestry II
For Helen Duffy

Rags, beads, birds'
nests, straw scratchings,
summon them—the uniform
of life's fools, love's
5   fullnesses, dresses
for the carnivals
of custom.

Ship's lady
launcher of blue lakes
10   assailer of snow
shake out the quilts
of summer, scatter
my cuttings over
the ocean's propellers
15   and from cages of water
scoop me up, salty,
newborn.

Then plant me
flower or button or
20   any three-pointed thing
sow me unknotted and
flowing into Mary's
wind of Easter above
her garden of ironies
25   fantastical, foaming
with flags.

1972

Totems
I want to whittle
a new totem pole
out of a poor little
Manitoba maple and
5   turn all its faces
to the sun

I want to plant
it on the prairie
staring at the wind
10   and snow saying to
the wind: *do your*
worst and to the
snow: *mind your*
mittens, don't fall
15   *off the world naked*
into the wind you
might turn to ice
or what's worse
nothingness

20   I want my totem
pole to watch over
the fields against
the floods droughts and
the spoilers of space

25   I want the fields
and the totem pole
still to be here
when I come back a
whispering sun-ghost
30   or the flickering
shadow on the
hands of lovers
a thousand years
from now

1972

Little Prairie Pictures

1
The whisper
of shape
or the colour
of quiet
5   against no
boundaries.

2
Through trees
of space
distance leans
10   in closer.

3
White is folded
but not in squares
it has climbed
its own ladder
15   to the sun.

4
The forest
has turned
to stone the
lake sinks
20   into mirage
we leave
no footprints.

5
There is
no sun
in these mute
25   places only
unlighted dumbness
a kind of
blind glimpse
a brush of
30   what is left
when nothing
is left.

6
Slopes of
lateness
35   tilt the world
when the world
is tired
and sleeps
quietly
40   on its own axis.

7
I like
the soft hush
that circles
this sleep.

1972

Dead Lakes

The dead lakes
of Sudbury
those passive
unstirring waters
5   without splash
without fish
without waterbugs
without breath.

The slag fires
10   of Sudbury
spill molten metal
on summer midnights
and the low lakes
of Sudbury
15   press deep into earth
under the towers
of shivering
mines.

I look down
20   in the dead waters
of Sudbury and
I think of Flaubert
with his crystal
Frenchness with
25   his one sentence
a day with his
passion for clarity
like the passion
of fish for a
30   living element.

And I search
for the living water
in the dead lakes
of Sudbury
35   and I search
for a living element
in the dead places
of my country.

1972

October 1970
Under what illusions
should she live when
from the tropical time
of flowers, heat and
5   filaments of vine,
humming birds, clipped
and eclipsed in budding
sentences and brilliant
sunshine lipped on
10   snowy scrolls of sea,
the stranger turned away
and left her a winter
of questions?
The dream ends here.

15   He came again in autumn
when young girls wore
purple daisies tangling
through their hair and
school-crossing guards
20   in phosphorescent shoes
clattered the white lines
and held up stop signs:
the markets in the suburbs
were loud with apples when
25   they broadcast the news
of quarantined Quebec
and freedoms left to lose
in civil Canada.
The place is here.

30   She still remembered
      her own escape
      from the man in the long
      coat who followed her
      for months in deepfreeze
35   country; she had to rend
      her clothes in mourning,
      cross an ocean, flood
      her skin to find a space
      rhythmic enough to
40   run in, she had to
      fill her ears with a
      lake of accents deep
      enough to drown all
      dishonest voices.
45   *Their words are here.*

      Those blanching nights
      hid terrorists and lovers,
      they made him anonymous
      of greying middle age;
50   no longer real he seemed
      another continent, a legend
      once dreamed by a girl
      in a northern city as
      she traced her scrolls
55   on frosty window panes.
      Their names are here.

This was the time she
waited for; she had
no house where he could
60   live, no needs to fill,
no wish to give; she had
started to learn a new
language and moved in
a constant astonishment
65   of changing sounds; words
came and went, maps hung
and fell, edicts were issued,
violence grew, yet she knew
That peace was here.

70   She watched him leave;
his footsteps levelled
out in rain: and now
she treads dead names,
imagines distances—
75   absent-mindedly she reads
her country's history
in her own pulse and vein,
feels herself a blade of grass
in fields, in provinces;
80   and sometimes she hears
October dumbness
composing a refrain
for all its citizens:
The dream starts here.

1972

Rivers

I wasted my life looking
for dammed-up rivers
and old stone quarries
to swim in; all for the
5   sake of gravel, the dry
burn of sun, even the
taste of yellow water
foaming from clayholes.

I forgot that I never
10   liked the stillness of
lakes the windless weather
of cities until you came
on your way back from
the province of deltas
15   the accent of wheat still
heavy in your voice.

You came from the swampy
borders of dry riverbeds,
dragging seaweed into the
20   house, shedding dry blades
from the ancient grasslands,
and in your eyes I saw,
pebbly, dark, mysterious,
all the rivers of my life.

1972

The Bower

Love in your breast
will you build me a bower,
love in your hand
will you make me a nest,
5   and for my joy
will you raise me a tower
and make your heart
my flower?

For you my breast
10   will be no bower,
my hand will never
make your nest,
and for your joy
I'll raise no tower,
15   nor make my heart
your flower.

The autumn wind
will build your bower,
Algonquin lakes
20   make you a nest,
sorrow itself
will raise you a tower,
and death, death will be
your flower.

1972

Voyagers
This is my last song
to you, I am getting
ready to leave to
learn a new language
5   to accept my fate
of ten provinces and
the junction of two
rivers, something small
poor with not many
10   people and a lot of
dry silence

but bless me as I
bless you and remember
our oceans
15   remember our continents
don't ever forget
Henry Hudson
adrift
in his birchbark canoe

1972

Lot's Wife

In your eyes
I saw suffering,
it was my own suffering.

Through your lips
5   I felt kisses,
they were my own kisses.

My hope reached
tall as the world,
it was your world.

10   The pillar broke,
light crumbled,
my heart turned
and turned to salt.

1972

Renunciations

I

A morning
beset with sound
salt-and-peppered
here and there
5 with grains of
sound

all my seeing
has disappeared
there are just
10 trees and

there is just
morning I open
my eyes and there
are your eyes

15 riddles

2

Here I am
it's morning
and your body
is sealed
20 anonymous as dead
snow songs

but I don't want
to hear that
music again
25 orphic songs are
for statues not
for living people

I want
your beard every
30 living hair of it
alive against
my neck why
doesn't your
body unseal
35 your mouth?

3
If my hands
could sing like
wheat touch
like ocean
40 they would
you everywhere

1972

Motions
You are
the lullaby
in this
arctic house
5   a subtle
motion from
sleep
maybe the hand
on my heart
10   a dark glitter
from the god
of snow

You are
the sun on glass
15   iridescent ships
on greenland seas
with cargo
of dancers
turning wheels
20   of ice

Frost breath
in my ears
long arms
of wind
25   wrap me in air
lift me
small person
up up
into the cradle
30   where I began

And you
are the lullaby.

1972

Beau-Belle

I'm in love with a clerk
from Trois Rivières
who trills his r's
and slicks his hair;

5   He's smooth as a seal
his smile is jolly,
though my name is Miriam,
he calls me Polly;

He sends me greetings
10   on golden cards
and mails me snapshots
of snowy yards;

I'm *mauvaise anglaise*—
this he forgives,
15   between us two
it's live-and-let-lives;

He's in his city,
I'm in mine,
we meet at Easter
20   on Bleury and Pine;

He calls me Polly,
I call him Patrice,
he says *Madame*
à votre service;

25   And I say Monsieur
dis-moi tu,
tu es poupée
and I love you.

1973

Divinations

1
You are new as
the uncoiling fern
springtime in a pot
of green paint.

2
5   Do you ever feel
your mortality or do
all your lovers
die from your kisses?

3
When you stop
10   looking in mirrors
a fairy godmother will
come and your heart
will surely heal.

1973

Forest Poem

I am alone now
in the tall forest;
I tread the water
of your absence.

5   More bitter to me
than salt is the
world emptied of
your meaning and

Who will now kindle
10   the lights for me
or wrap up the evening
in its white shawl?

1973

Legends

1
Blinded I
kiss your mouth
in bazaars of
ice, saloons of
5   snow, in the dark cave
of winter, glad
that your eyes
are open.

2
I move
10   through the grassy
lands inside
your lovegiving.

3
And search the
dark for your
15   face among a
thousand faces,
they enclose
the night in
a half-circle;
20   the birch bow is
in the hands of
the bone hunter.

4
You step forward
you circle
25   half of me and
become an ancient
arrow in the
trough of rivers
shattering the
30   sun into a thousand
windows of
rain.

5
Even the
rain today
35   is full of
quivering
light.

6
I taste the sand
of summer
40   in your mouth;
wide beaches
roll back
the covers of
my life.

7
45   Your body
becomes
its own legend
of fire.

8
And I become
50   the legend of
earth
asleep in the
stillness of
earth.

1973

Lovers III

Sam promises: *lose* 20 *lbs*
and it's Dior-Givenchy all
the way (meantime a weekend
in NY in some splotchy dark
5   hotel should keep her happy,
put her in the mood—not like
his Gladdie-pie who sold the
family manse for 30 silver
condominiums without the wave
10   of wands or bat of eye or single
kibitzing goodbye—)
Oh what a tatty daddy to offer
his leftwing ladylove such
ulcerated sweets! Yet Sam's
15   a certain style of lover,
a hemm-er and a haw-er, sugarless,
and instead of being a sigh-er,
Sam is alas, a cough-er:
noisy and acidulous
20   in passion's market-place,
he bids on his success
and makes the lowest offer.

1973

Past the Ice Age
All of a sudden
I was empty spaces,
flexible snow
wrapping the air.

5   All of a sudden
I was ropes of night,
crickets of song
under cellar stairs.

I was a lap of
10   strawberries a stand
of cornflowers a
glassful of ice

And I wanted to
live a long time
15   just to hear
the new music
in everything.

1973

Charlottetown

It rains a lot
in Charlottetown
a queen city with
English corners
5   and streets cut
on the bias
a lady of a city
with an English
accent with a lace
10   cap and wooden
white houses like
buttons on her
black old bosom.

1973

The Dark Lake

Our ghosts still sit there
on the stone bench in the garden
they are eating lunch under the statue
and they stare straight ahead
5   into the dark lake of the trees.

Our ghosts have noticed something
in the dark lake of the trees
it is a different season and they are
not the only ones in the garden,
10   this year the people are not kind.

Our ghosts sit there and stare ahead,
this year the people are not kind;
their eyes are fixed
on the lake of the dark trees
15   they do not see each other.

They sit on the stone bench
they do not see each other,
each one is looking inward and
each one is continually taking
20   the photograph of his own ghost.

1973

Downtown Streets
There are still people
who write each other
intimate letters who
sing their personal arias
5   to an audience of white
paper; is it pain they
score, bursts of light they
note after a dark illness,
a childish jump, or some
10   mongrel dance-step in the
icicled rooms of snow?

Sometimes I still stand
outside a lighted window
on downtown streets (just
15   as I used to thirty years
ago) a woman sits at a
table writing intimate
letters, she is asking, *do*
you really like the smell
20   *of my perfume,* she is saying
next time you come it will
be winter the season of
mandarin oranges.

Standing there under
25   the window
I think I can hear
the sound
of her ghostly pen
moving across the page,
30   I think I can hear it
singing
in the downtown streets.

1973

Spring III

a loaf of bread
a jug of wine
and thou . . .

Here in this
complex province—
torn country
the bread we eat
5   is snow and
the wine we drink
is a Friday wind
blowing in from
somewhere
10   north of zero:

the thou in
the drowned fields
of my youth is the
darkening snapshot
15   of my dead husband
sitting among the
gravestones
in a Jewish cemetery
in Montreal.

1974

Absences

My father is dead
his wisdom is gone
from the world.

My husband is dead
5   his strength is gone
from the house.

His boat is lost
his oars are broken
on a northern sea.

10   My bed is cold
my clothes lie empty
on a far shore.

1974

Harvest
Every man
has a right
to his dream,
mine is a crop
5   of books so I
cultivate my papers
as if they were
lands, I plough
them and furrow,
10   sow words like
seeds, tend phrases
like plants,
thin them and
weed.

15   When summer
is over I
bring them
into the house,
their leaves shine
20   and glow and
all winter long
they burn me
with their dark
green fire.

1974

National Treasures in Havana

In the south
circled by
round sun-faces
she stares; but
5   dreams of snow
and hears
the ice-songs
buried in dead
guitars.

10   The palm-dove
sings and sings
from the marshes
and for her
the drowned quays
15   unlock their hoard
of salt songs.

A man's voice
rides in on the
dark waves,
20   flows through the
curtained light
in a webbed net
of sound:

I love you he
25   sings, *with all*
my heart with
all my heart;
the words break
and scatter
30   over the water
until even the
silence
sings and the

Stillness
35   celebrates the
evening which
falls from the
sky's crevices
and fills the
40   empty streets
of Havana:

We love you,
sing the empty
streets of Havana,
45   *with all our*
hearts, with
all our past,
our slaves, our
dead poets, and
50   *starved children,*
we have declared
silence a national
treasure.

She listens and
55   circled by
round sun-faces
dreams of snow;
she hears the
ice-songs in
60   dead guitars.

1974

Ten Years and More

When my husband
lay dying a mountain
a lake three
cities ten years
5   and more
lay between us:

There were our
sons my wounds
and theirs,
10   despair loneliness,
handfuls of un-
hammered nails
pictures never
hung all

15   The uneaten
meals and unslept
sleep; there was
retirement, and
worst of all
20   a green umbrella
he can never   .
take back.

I wrote him a
letter but all
25   I could think of
to say was: do you
remember Severn
River, the red canoe
with the sail
30   and lee-boards?

I was really saying
for the sake of our
youth and our love
I forgave him for
35   everything
and I was asking him
to forgive me too.

1974

This Year in Jerusalem
Other years Hannah
the woman who cleans
offices in Jerusalem
cursed the white sun
5   of Jerusalem because
it was not the green
sun of her village
in Poland.

This year that same
10   Hannah has something
to curse about; she
curses the Egyptians
and Assyrians who
killed the son she
15   brought to Jerusalem
from her village
in Poland.

And at dawn this year
the cats of Jerusalem
20   don't come any more
to the steps of the
post office to wait
for morning and the
charwomen to come
25   to work and feed them.

This year
even the cats know
there are too many
enemies.

1974

Tourists

For travel
they buy the style
and luggage of
the country:
5   plastic shopping
bags or canvas
holdalls for their
greyhound trips;
they wear pants
10   and sweaters,
the latest
in sunglasses,
but their eyes
their eyes are
15   imprisoned in their
own legends.

They leave
bouquets of wonder
at all our historic
20   sites, yet their
eyes their eyes are
tranced and still,
and still elsewhere.

1974

Two Trees
We all know
the tree of life
its tassels and
flowers,
5   its strong root
that sings and burns
in the centre
of everything.

But what of
10   the tree of death
that has been waiting
all winter,
waiting and sleeping,
sleeping and waiting,
15   in the centre
of everything?

In spring
it will burst
in a richness of
20   leaves
they will whisper
and sing: *come*
come, come.

They will whisper
25   and sing,
whisper and wait,
then cover us all
with their rich
dark shade
30   in the centre
of everything.

1974

Wives' Tales
When I married
my English
husband my Jewish
father said:
5   he'll get drunk
come home and
beat you,
you'll starve or
feed on green
10   pork stew—
well he didn't
and I didn't.

And my mother
being more
15   practical said:
if at least he
was a professor—
well he wasn't
and I was or
20   became.

Furthermore,
my mother said,
with a marriage
like that it's
25   plain curtains
for simple
you—

Well it was
curtains
30   in a way for a
while for me;
but for him
it was curtains
too and for him
35   forever and for
always.

1974

A Monument for Mister Never
I dreamed a mountain
of roses
roses made of silver
roses made of stone
5   black roses
heroic roses and
roses growing human
bone on bone
from a rose body
10   without a thorn.

1975

Poets Are Still Writing Poems about Spring and Here Is Mine:
Spring

You're an ice-thing
a landslide, a whale,
a huge continental
cold nose-ring
5   dragging the world
by the tail into
a universal grandstand
before it ever thought
of being born.

10   Maybe not: maybe
you're more like
a fern all curled up
in a juicy green bud
that any minute now
15   is going to burst out
of the loamy seams
of this workaday lazy
earth into a fresh
fernfan.

20   You'll be festive
with lacey little
pinked edges cut
out with God's own
zigzag scissors and
25   his million laughs,
you'll be cagey
and cunning and
you'll brush your
fingery fronds fond
30   as whiskers against

everyone's bare
legs, and you'll touch
us all with little
barbs of hot prickly
35   light, and we'll be
dyed green by the
crowds of wildly
cheering fernfans
sitting in the packed
40   high galleries of summer.

1975

Friends II

The postman is no kibitzer,
he gravely deals with fate,
brings bills from Eaton's
and regrets from Volvo:

5   their warranty won't cover ...
also: Domtar won't re-roof.
Re fellowships: *your letter*
comes too late: re poetry:
sorry, but we're overstocked

10   *with women's verse* (forever)
the very hex and curse the
sow's ear in the purse of
literature since ever time began
and Adam was a man and Eve

15   was also-ran.

And here's news from Leo,
my own gentleman, back from
Spain at last to find the snow
piled high and downtown traffic

20   stopped; the union still gives
trouble, committees stall,
so does the bi-and-bi, while he
for one would like to see
the language issue dropped.

25   Bad news, bad news, on every side!
Would you believe that Leo's tailor
died with Leo's measurements
inside his head? We never know
what's apt to happen and although

30   money isn't everything, how will
things be, where will they go,
when us, our generation, win or lose,
fed up with curbing hell, at last
drops all the reins and everything

35   busts loose?

Don't worry Leo: uneasy only lies
the head that wears the crown;
let strikes rotate from coast to
coast and post offices automate,
40   let ferries stop, make them, the people
wait while railways alternate;
we're out of it, or will be, pretty soon.
Think on these words dear Leo,
(they weren't written on the moon
45   but on this dear planet that spins
us silly): *death comes to everyone.*
Yrs. truly, Trilby.

1975

By the Sea: For A. M. Klein
His grief it fell and fell;
he mourned that his brain
could never be like new—
a seamless whole again.

5   He polished it with spit
and sealed the cracks with glue,
he pinned it to the air—
yet away it flew.

He caught it in a net
10   of silken words and wit,
but his broken brain
was fragmented and split.

He quilted it with grass
and anchored it with ships,
15   he sailed tilting words,
they foundered on his lips.

He dropped a silver line
into the tides of verse,
and found his broken brain
20   had hooked it to a curse.

So he called the angels down
from balconies of sky,
they emptied out his life,
they would not let him die.

25   Then someone drained the ponds
in his unlettered land,
and strangers hid the road
beneath a mile of sand,

Apollo's golden ear
30   was sealed against his cries,
his lonely broken brain
was barred from paradise.

His grief it falls and falls
on green fields and on white,
35   he rocks his broken brain
that never mended right,

And sings his silent song
to earth and tree and stone;
we hear it when we hear
40   the rain beat on the stone.

The rain beats on the stone:
but how many recognize
his broken brain, his fear,
are nothing but our own?

1975

Husbands

My husband had two wives,
me and she, but me was legal.
Signed, sealed, and twice
delivered, I cookered,
5   cleanered, polishered spoons,
floors, and children; her wasn't
so she at nine drove up the
hill to hospital and job.
Well, now she's in, I'm out;
10   still childered, cookered,
cleanered but somewhat
tarnishered, I drive and drive
to live my loveless life
and swear to boss and job
15   my faith forever.

And that old termagent, my
tongue, is queen of nothing
now; has lately split, run off,
and begun to play it safe.
20   It likes to lie there low,
a frozen log in ice awaiting
spring's bright crack-up
to let go its drift of grief
and garbage; but my brain
25   stays loyal and knows its
loves and hates; endlessly
it calculates why him and me
and she did equal minus me;
and no matter how I add, I'm
30   left with nothing now except
to wonder how was lost the rich
and gleam (by grace of course
unearned) of love, and love's
dear increment.

1975

London Night

There was nothing
to remember;
only the beating
of your heart
5   and the beating
of wings on the
windowpane
and all the sorrow
that being a woman
10   asleep
beside a man
can bring.

Were they
angels
15   of the city or
Blake's chimney-
sweeps or were they
birds of London's
summer night?
20   There were no
angels in that
room there was
no fluttering
of wings.

25   There was only
an old woman
shaking her head
and sighing at
the years that lay
30   heavy in her
lap tangling
words and tying
them in a jumble
of cruel knots
35   and ragged torn
strings.

I slept uneasily
and dreamed of
Caedmon and his
40 angel: in my dream
I stood and sang
into an empty
city and there
was no one to
45 remember, no
mythic heroine,
no legendary
king.

Then I woke
50 blinded by the
darkness
of your arm
across my eyes,
imprisoned
55 by its heavy
locked gate
and chained
to a thousand
iron rings.

1975

Artists and Old Chairs
For Helen Duffy

A puff of wind
a stretch of sky
a rush of air—
and Helen
5   who commands the stars
and planets
now commands
a chair.

Old and whiskered
10   its stuffings
thinning—
it wakes up
one morning
on the junkman's truck
15   alive and even
grinning.

Whoosh and thump!
It lands
in Helen's garden
20   with a mighty bump;
and there among
three birds two
squirrels five
marigolds an orange
25   cat and this
old friend,
the chair decides
that life's not over yet,
it's not the end.

30   Helen's garden
      is nice, the company
      likewise: three
      birds two squirrels
      five marigolds
35   an orange cat and
      this old friend
      are quite enough
      to make the chair
      forget
40   the leaky huts and
      muddy humps of
      the world's worst
      garbage dumps.

      The chair
45   looks on benign
      and sees
      the scarlet runner
      climb and
      turn somersaults
50   on its own vine;
      sees also how
      it tickles windows
      here and there
      and how
55   its curly tendrils
      defy all gravity
      to lean on
      simply air.

That's why the chair
60 decides
that nothing dies
or ends,   .
it only changes,
especially
65 when artists bring
their loving looks
to rest upon old things
and there discover
in such unlikely places
70 as rocky earthbound faces,
the eternal lineaments
of the transforming lover.

1976

The Dead

The doubly dead
are harder to
reach than the
others like my
5   parents who were
always there
until they died
of time in their
own time;
10   but the doubly dead
who first went away
and then died,
like my husband—
those dead are
15   harder to reach:

Yet it was he
my dead husband
whose shadow
I glimpsed today
20   as I drove along
the sinking hills
and rising rivers
of the Gatineau;
and it was he
25   my dead husband,
who rose and called
to me from the
high rivers and the
drowned hills.

30   And it was he
      my dead husband
      whose face I saw
      for the last time
      before he turned
35   and walked away
      into the darkness
      that lies invisibly
      across summer.

      He walked away
40   taking himself and
      our married years
      into the darkness,
      the same darkness
      that looks out
45   at me now from
      the eyes of our
      two sons.

      1976

Tallness and Darkness

Wherever I travel
home has always
been your tallness
and darkness, but
5   was it tallness or
darkness that made
it more home and
why did I need both?

Your darkness is
10   pure Egypt; pyramids,
my little brother
Moses with his straight
brows and far-sighted
eyes; your tallness
15   is the other part,
northern steppes,
prairies,

My blue-eyed uncle
coming to Winnipeg
20   from the cruel snows
of White Russia, later
raising celery
on Point Pelee, then
crossing an ocean
25   to lose himself in
the cold salty desert.

He is buried there
in a remote grave
without a marker,
30   he is sleeping there
under the restless
snows of Mount Hermon;

Those snows are
still always packed
35   tight around my heart;
when your darkness
descends the snows
melt and everything
hurts and grows.

1976

Notes of Summer
Love still lives
in a place
where the wind stands
and fiddles for
5 north country dances,
where the rabbits run
across morning lawns
their paws diamonded
with dew,
10 where the forsythia
bush studs with
flowers the golden
tiara of April
and the violins
15 everywhere
fill up with the
long grazing notes
of pastured
summer.

1976

Old Chair Song

Knots and crosses,
thread and leather,
.cut your losses
stitch a feather.

5   Knots and crosses
dot your i's
baste your losses
with your sighs.

Mend what's broken,
10   make old new,
forms are false
but shapes are true.

So flash your thimble
push your luck,
15   if you win a chicken
lose a duck;

If you find a chair
that's old yet new,
it might teach you
20   how chairs grew

From knots and crosses
silk and tweed,
so close your eyes
and twist a bead;

25   Ask a riddle,
turn your head,
and you might learn
to raise the dead.

1976

Naive Geography
Miami is one big yellow
pantsuit where the ocean
is louder than the sighs
of old age; Chicago is
5   a huge hot gun sending
smoke into the sky for
1000 miles to Winnipeg;
New York is a bright sharp
hypodermic needle and the
10   Metropolitan opera singing
Wagner on winter afternoons,
and my own Toronto is an
Eaton's charge account adding
to the music in a Henry Moore
15   skating rink; Montreal was
once an Iroquois city huddled
around a mountain under a
cross and is now the autoroute
to an Olympic dream; everything
20   has changed all the cities
are different but Manitoba
oh, Manitoba, you are still
a beautiful green grain
elevator storing the sunlight
25   and growing out of the black
summer earth.

1976

Winnipeg and Leningrad

That far terribly
northern city
I see when
I close my eyes
5   is it Winnipeg
or Leningrad?

Both have the same
skinny church standing
alone like a black cello
10   in the snow and you
can see the same
half-dozen people
on skiis or snowshoes
making their way
15   across the same flat
white park.

What's missing here
is the 18th century
architect who built
20   these houses with
their stucco fronts
and lace balconies,
also those 19th century
idlers squinting up
25   at the sun from behind
the curtains of their
second storey windows
on the same cold
Saturday afternoons.

30   The iron gates
      of the summer gardens
      are locked the snow
      piles up its cushions
      on empty benches and
35   the frost wraps itself
      like a bridal wreath
      around the lighted
      smoking street-lamps.

      It is all
40   so much the same,
      I can't tell
      if this far terribly
      northern city is
      Winnipeg or is it
45   Leningrad?

      1976

Old Wood
Without smoke
that is how
good old wood
burns
5   that is how
I want to live
to give
fire without
smoke to be
10   fire

1976

Real Estate: Poem for Voices

> Life begins enclosed, protected, all warm
> in the bosom of the house.
>
> —Gaston Bachelard

Alone in a house
between two cities
she was living
the story of centuries;
5   note this: that year
birds outroared
the traffic
YOU BETTER BELIEVE IT

A flowering
10   snail
one breast one
hand and the
shadow woman,
a stamenless calyx
15   in a garden
of grasses
WE COULDN'T CARE LESS

That year the
summer hours fell
20   just short of
twilight in a
spring of humid
dawns and cuspidors,
and there was
25   nothing to suggest
lilacs or the
smell of syringa
ALL THAT BULLSHIT

The hours
30 continued to be
empty as sucked-out
honeycomb and
transparent as
dragonfly wings
35 or bluebottles
making their speedo-
whizz getaways
(watch out for
those dragonflies
40 they're really
darning needles who
sew your mouth up)
WHAT BOOK DID YOU
READ THAT IN?

45 The hours
˙continued to be
bland and mean
as city neighbours,
their car exhausts
50 everyone's serenade,
their dogdroppings
everyone's carpet,
their lawnmowings
everyone's banquet
55 SO LET THEM EAT GRASS

Half-woman
purpling in the
shadow of the
shadow woman,
60   if you could only
tell fortunes or
read oracles or
have a good car-
washing husband
65   WHY DON'T YOU GO BACK
WHERE YOU CAME FROM?

It is completely
irrelevant to ask
what is your house of ·
70   spruce saying over
and over again and
what is the message
of pine over and over
again and what is
75   the burden of beech
over and over again
and how about the
agony of elm over
and over again
80   GO HIRE A HALL

And if it's answers
you want
cheerful answers
if you insist,
85   the developers
have changed the
by-laws, you must
start packing
now this minute;
90   if you refuse and
are still here
tomorrow they'll
take and shoot you
HURRY UP TIME
95   IS MONEY

One hand
one breast
a shadow woman,
maybe one
100   is better than
none, who says
a snail needs
a shell a bird
its nest we must
105   fight to stay
alive we must
fight fight
THAT'S ALL RIGHT
DON'T MENTION IT

1976

What the Angel Said

Caedmon dreamed
that an angel
came to him and
said: *sing* and
5   he awoke and sang.

I dreamed that
a man in a white
shirt sewn with
stars rose out
10   of the scrolls

of the snowy sea
and the angel
turned to me and
said: *love* and I
15   awoke and loved.

1976

Grand Manan Sketches

1

The island
lies in perpetual
August you have
to expect storms
5   and hurricanes
also strong
sunlight slanting
across triangles
of rock glossy
10   and black as
seals

Here even
the rocks
are alive and
15   intelligent

2

In town
I entice monarch
and other butterflies
by planting milkweed
20   among the flowers

In Grand Manan
I don't need
such enticements, the
butterflies, monarch
25   and swallow-tail,
crowd in skimming
through spruces
drinking the daisies
and dipping their
30   wings into the
rosy flames of the
fireweed

3
Nothing
burns them
35   in this bright
light everything
moves to water
except me
who am motionless
40   stunned to stillness
covered with
gold dust

4
Look how
I am hanging
45   like a bird from
midsummer
golden
in sky space

5
And look
50   how I am
burning
burning away
the distance
of water of
55   sun of
island

1976

Ecstasy
The pale net of her hair
blowing in spring
will not
shut out the world
5   nor will the green knee
of season
bend to his will;

These two
separated by a field
10   of growing wheat
and several cities
still incline to each other
and from their distance
merge
15   slight and brief
as clouds touching

1976

An Unliberated Woman Seen from a Distance

I suppose I am
thinking of wooden
houses in Moscow
because I want to be
5   like Tolstoy's Natasha
I want to burn with
love and don't want
to remember your
silence or those
10   cold stormy kisses
that swept me aside
like a wind

1976

Profile of an Unliberated Woman

I was a dish
to be eaten off
to be broken
I suppose to
5   fall wherever
I fell I wish
I had been
more (or less)
breakable I
10   was blank
white un-
patterned
and I had
only the usual
15   contrariness
the irritating
resistance of
all inanimate
objects

1976

The Things We Talked About

After seven years
when I saw that
between us everything
was going nowhere
5   my one-sided
devotion suddenly
ended.

When we first met
we used to talk
10   about art, later
we talked about
artists and
finally we talked
about his arthritis.

15   Of all the things
we ever talked about,
the one I enjoyed most
was his arthritis,
it at least was
20   personal and my
devotion had never
been to his mind,

It had been to
his dark rosy face
25   and his black eyes,
the like of which
were never before
and will never again
be seen on this earth.

1976

The Secret of Old Trees
For Tobie Steinhouse

If I could just divine
the secret of old trees,
how to be
their vertical silences,
5   or if lying low
how to embrace
their caged green light,
their space,
or even let us say—
10   how to baste the grass
with pine needles and cones,
and then when it is done,
to serve the world up
as a delicious dish
15   of warm roasted earth
rolled in four-leaf clover,
and for dessert to drink,
like every summer comer,
from a giant loving cup
20   the liquor of the sun.

1976

Snow Stories

When I was a child
I loved to hear
snow stories: how
travellers lost
5   their way and after
freezing became
warm, fell asleep
in the snow and
never woke up.

10   Or else travellers
were chased by
wolves on a snowy
night in December,
and a snowstorm
15   blinded them and the
wolves howled and
they lost the road
and never found it
again.

20   This Christmas
the snow story is
almost the same;
we travel and lose
our way, we fall
25   asleep and cannot
wake up, we are
under a spell cast
by the lies of winter.

We have let the
30   wolves of Chile
howl us off the road,
we stay asleep, we
do not stop for other
travellers, the light
35   hurts our eyes and
the truth gives us
a headache.

The potentates
of oil, the kings of
40   tar, the ministers
of sand and all the
presidents of wrong
entertain us every
night on television;
45   but we are still
mesmerized

By the snow stories
of childhood, gullible
to the fake gestures
50   of a foreign poet,
no one talks to his
neighbour anymore,
the heart of the world
is dark and cold.

55   The hearth of the world
is dark and cold,
this is a Christmas
no fire can warm.

1976

How I Spent the Year Listening to the Ten O'Clock News

Last year
there were executions
in Chile
bribes in
5   American no
transit for Jews
in Austria
and lies
lies everywhere.

10   The children
of Ireland are
also in the news,
they have become
hardened street
15   fighters some of
them murderers,
I ask myself
where will it
all end?

20   Of course
the interests of
Canadian citizens
(read corporations)
must be protected
25   at any cost no
matter how many
good men are
shot like dogs
in the streets
30   of Chile or
how many poets
die of a broken
heart.

They claim
35   the world is
changing getting
better they have
the moon walk
and moon walkers
40   to prove it,
but my brain
is bursting my
guts are twisted
I have too much
45   to say thank
God I am too old
to bear children.

1976

Morning on Cooper Street
Eight o'clock: morning
on Cooper Street,
October sun falls
through half-fans and
5   anchors, lights the
stainedglass transoms
of rooming-houses.

The smell of yesterday's
frenchfries hangs outside
10   the quicklunch: across
the street the humming
machinery of the Sealtest
factory is forever churning
milk into cartons (you would
15   hardly believe this is a
scene in the seventies in
Ottawa the nation's capital.)

Except that the cars
are already parked
20   thick as rats outside
Mamma Mafia's cafe and
the bicycle repair shop
is open too (I wonder
if they really fix
25   bicycles and whose),
I pass a spastic man,
two old ladies with
shopping bags and a
dozen sleepy people
30   coming out of the rooms
of their rooming-houses.

They teeter, list, and
drift, spindly and dazed
in the morning traffic,
35   they are precarious as
the houses they live in,
and condemned to the same
development, a future
that has no room for
40   old things, no place
for living people.

I look around, listen,
take in these new omens
and old dangers; I'm
45   superstitious, I carry
amulets and lucky images:
I'm remembering
a clump of mushrooms blazing
yellowly in the woods
50   safe somewhere far
far away across the river.

1976

The Wind in Charlottetown

Early morning;
and the wind
is awake, he
lays his hands
5   on the shore and
his head on the
gulf lap of
red sand, of
pine needles.

10   The wind
murmurs love to
Jerusalem and love
to Charlottetown,
it makes no
15   difference to him
whether he's in
Jerusalem or
Charlottetown;

As long as he
20   can weave his
hands in and out
of the seasons,
as long as he
can knit up the
25   dogwood and drape
the forsythia
on the bosom of
old lady world.

His voice is
30   ancient and layered
like stone with
the grief of
Jerusalem and the
crying of birds on
35   the prairie wastes,
and his voice is
as old and sad
as the lament of
the folksinger

40   Alone and adrift
on Prince Edward Island.

1976

I Take My Seat in the Theatre

Look—
it's carnival time
in market square!
Here come
5   the musicians,
drumbeats, noise,
agitation:
the clatter
is deafening.

10   And here come
the masked dancers,
hands flying—
windmills:
heads rising—
15   towers: and hats
dipping, circling,
laced with
little windows,
motions
20   that lean out
of winter,
motions in a
medley of broken
mirrors reflecting
25   summer.

Beyond their masks
the dancers
are dancing out
the most ordinary
30   rituals; they
lunge, plunge,
spar, dodge,
(by day the chief
dancer is clerk
35   in the village
store) but here
he's bad-man tiger
against good-man
elephant, he's
40   stripe against
circle, sinister
against simple.

And now
one of them
45   shoots a silver
arrow into
the dust; tiger-man
folds his hands
over his heart
50   and drops dead among
the sunflower seeds
in market square.

Without warning
the princess
55 runs in; hurray!
All is well on
this side of
her rosy mask,
she holds a
60 bouquet and she
hangs a tinsel
wreath around the
neck of good-man
elephant.

65 Drumbeats; noise;
agitation;
the clatter is
deafening; the
ending is only
70 the return to
all the beginnings,
and no one sees
or looks
at the dead man
75 still lying in
the dust of
market square;

Except me
who am the people,
80   always
summoned from
everywhere to
watch everything,
I stand around
85   and gossip
with neighbours
in the dusty square,
until night
falls
90   and the drumbeats
fade away and
stop forever.

1976

Afternoon on Grand Manan

I sit at a table
on a small island
off the New Brunswick
coast doing nothing
5   thinking about
nothing.

It is Thursday
afternoon the light
on Swallow-Tail
10   comes and goes puts
away darkness and
like a good housewife
sweeps the sea,
the foghorn cuts
15   the mist and
rhythmically laments
the anonymous
dead.

At the wharf
20   the fishing boats are
back they have brought
in the haddock they have
filleted the pollock
and tomorrow they will
25   untie the herring nets,
the green-bordered boats
will empty the weirs.

(All summer
a man cuts birch trees
30   for the weir poles
his stories entertain
the tourists) but
the weather-man
is the only one who
35   can tell fortunes
or make prophecies,
the rest of us
pick berries and read
our dream books.

1976

The Price of Gold

The price of gold
is the same in Merida
as in Montreal but in
Amsterdam diamonds are
5   cheaper than in Toronto
or Capetown.

A wife costs more in
America than in Egypt,
and it takes less to bribe
10   an official in Hungary
than a bureaucrat in
Ottawa but in all these

Market-places, in every
corner of the world,
15   the price of death
is a hidden sum not
for barter or bribe but
meant to inscribe

On a secret scroll:
20   unlisted, unquoted,
not written or spoken,
its worth lies beyond
the talisman token,
and each of us knows

25   His own instant of death
by that strange sudden
thinning of blood and
of breath, and each
of us knows, at last,
30   when he's in it,

Where the doors open,
how the doors close.

1976

A Lover Who Knows
The man with death
in his body knows
everything about death;
he knows how the walls
5   of laughter are
studded with skulls
in the crypts of Portugal,
he can follow
a gypsy on the dusty road,
10   and from the smoke
of her campfire,
from the smell of the
whiskey on her breath,
he can tell my fortune.

15   He has wings around
his face, love in his
eyes and he comes with
gentle kisses; he gives
me everything I want—
20   a sack full of words, a farm
north of the city,
perfect haircuts, safe-conduct
in five o'clock traffic—
but day and night he sleeps
25   in my grave and he never stops
calling me to hurry up
and come to bed.

1976

The Days Are Short

In September
the days are short,
and I think how
never did I love
my country so much
as now.

In October
the days are short,
and I think how
never did I regret
the summer so much
as now.

In November
the days are short,
and I think how
never did my words
fly south so much
as now.

In December
when the days are short—
to look for
the country of my youth,
so blindly and so much
as now.

1976

Where the North Winds Live

I long for
the transplanted
European village
the one
5   that became my
prairie city.

The north winds
lived there
they always
10   whistled me
clean
with a blow
of white polar
air.

15   They whistled
me clean and
they stripped
me bare then
they told me to
20   hurry
and gave me a
push with the paw
of a suddenly
humourous bear.

25   They gave me
a buss and a
blow and
with a spirally
flurry of snow,
30   they told me
to go from
the transplanted
village of snow,

To a land
35 where apples of gold
grow from a
golden hand,
and the touch
of a golden bear
40 warms
the summer air,
and forever
is always ever,
and forever is
45 always there.

1976

The Cave

I

Back
back to the cave
of green light
and water
5   here is the self
here is the other
here
is the sky
without father
10   or mother
here
is the fire
and fear of
the father
15   here is the
mother the bringer
of water
here
is the brother
20   the healer
of hunger
and here is
the sister the
dancer diviner

2

25 The dragonfly
in the glacier the
fish that climbed
the slippery pier
here are
30 their traces their
watery faces
lit by the fire
of father and mother
by the ashes of self
35 by the birth of
the other and all
all are shadows
on shadowy walls
the shadowy laughter
40 of those
who come after

3

In the cave of
green light
where the self
45 is the other
and the mother
is father
and sister is
brother
50 where single
is double
and the double
is neither

the heart of
55   the earth is buried
forever
and the pulses
of water must
sound here forever
60   flowing back
to the cave
of green light
and water back
to the source
65   of their shadowy
laughter

4
Now the light
widens
from a crack
70   in the darkness
and the pulse
quickens through
miles of water
revealing the love
75   beyond lover
or healer

Revealing the hand
with its signs
and its wonders
80   writing bird
beak and claw
writing
ice mounds and ages
whose writing
85   has summoned
from the caves of
green light from
the flowing of
water
90   the shadowy figures
of those who come after
and their shadowy
laughter

1976

Prairie II

The only
shadows here
are those of
angels soft
5   and ruffled as
paper flowers
in the churches
of the poor.

These shadows
10   settle like
wings on either
side of a
giant seed.

1977

Horoscopes
I was born
in winter the
December of
revolution but
5   my lovers were
all from autumn,
scorpios and
sagittarians
sourpusses and
10   vegetarians.

Now I await
the true lover
omened by stars
and promised
15   by rain,
he will come
with his bow
and his arrow
dressed in the
20   green livery
of spring.

1977

Warnings

Don't fall in love
with that face!
It looks older
and kinder but
5   it's the face
of your husband
long dead with
flowers in his
eyes and grasses
10   in his hair
so beware!
Beware of the
cruel animal
lurking there
15   (his heart is
its lair.)

Don't fall in love
with that face!
You, the stranger and
20   walker-at-leisure,
are in danger, in
danger! You'll slide
slow as glaciers
through old arctic
25   passes where ice-
palms wave their
fringes above cream-
coloured bears and
the seals dive
30   down to explore the
tusky deeps under
bluebeard's locked
door, where the black
oil gushes your death
35   from the bluest fjords
of your sleep.

It's there
that you'll drown
in the flowers and
40   choke on the grasses,
there that you'll
lose your way in
the maze of antarctic
passes, and you'll
45   freeze (how you'll
freeze!) in the
windblack meadows
of ice on far frozen
northern seas, so
50   don't fall in love
with that face!

1977

Mister Never Playing

Let's fly
be blue as air
fall off the
world weightless
5   and wayless;

Or crackle
like paper explode
into ho-ho-hey-hey
flowers and
10   rustle like

Leaves hide
from cats leap
into squirrel nests
or hang from
15   tree-swings;

Then climb
up high wires
up jim-jams
and plant red
20   and blue

Maps on the
baby continents,
then let's rock
those small
25   continents

in their blue
sky cradles to a
gentle laughing
sleep.

1977

Running up and down Mountains at Changing Speeds

Fifteen years ago
it was my pleasure to run
up and down the mountain
in Montreal; not only pleasure
5   but ecstasy, and I knew
what the word meant;
I used to open my arms
to the wind, be embraced
by a huge wave of air, then
10   enclosed in a cape of the
same air with only my head
showing and only my voice
sounding; I used to shout
to the sky: *hey look world—*
15   *world, here I am!*

And in those days
the sky did look at me
half-approving and half-
disapproving, and the trees
20   inclined to each other and
whispered: *psst there she is!*
And the wind shouted back
at me: *look who just blew in!*
and all of us together
25   raised our voices in a choir
of hallelujahs singing the
same song to each other and
to the world about the
pleasures of running up
30   and down mountains.

These days I sometimes
give a little secret run
when no one is looking,
I might even bend over and
35   pick a late dandelion or
out-of-season clover from
a south-facing ditch, and
I always stop to listen to
a bird calling another bird,
40   wondering what they are
saying with their bird-talk:
that the worm crop is good,
that we need more rain,
that someone's nest just
45   fell out of a tree, or what?

Whatever they are saying
they will never get the
chance to say about me
that it is one of the sins
50   of my old age to pretend
I'm still running up and down
mountains the way I used to.
I acknowledge my bad temper,
short breath and all my
55   disappointments: these days
I don't have the nerve anymore
to shout up at the sky: *Look,
here I am world!* These days
I'm glad of every small
60   courtesy, I rejoice when
the wind steps aside for
me and greets me quietly
with cheeks puffed down
and lips unpursed, and I
65   like it when he whispers:
*hello old friend, so you're
still here!*

1977

When the Shoe Is on the Other Foot for a Change

Fall in love?
I can't you're
too old your
body is cold,
5   your life runs
away like water
off clay your
body is dry
as old bread,
10   your hands spidery
red your lips
mouldy and grey,
your words are
heavy, unleavened
15   as lead and you
smell of death
and decay.
Get lost, shoo, vamoose,
go away.

1977

Certain Winter Meditations on Mister Never

I am still
as a bird
(the winter
shakes snow down
5   trembles
is space)

The world rises
and sinks
bewitched and
10   entranced by
cloudwands
and skyspeeds
trees lift and
turn then fall
15   to snow blindness
coiling their
silence
on spiralling
roots

20   (Where is
the swanboat of
Lohengrin of Leda
of the crystalline
Elsa who waits
25   for a name?
Who launched their
letters like ships
on the waters
hung a question
30   on sedges
then braided the
daisies to wires
of ice?)

(To love her to
35 knot her the king's
only daughter,
soon is too late
now Apollo has
caught her and sealed
40 her and wound her
around in her fate;
three stems and
a flower two wings
and a seed)

45 Stems of love
seeds of light
touch me and
tremble
they fold away
50 darkness
in the nest
of last autumn
(I am still
as a bird
55 in a world
entranced)

1978

Feasts

Beside the sandy
road and the historic
river three Indian
boys from a lost
5   prairie are eating
their lunch,
they have come here
to hunt but we
have come here to
10   cut spruce boughs
for the Feast of
the Tabernacles.

The maple trees
are burning fiercely,
15   their red and yellow
leaves ignite the
Sunday afternoon
and their redness
bites into us,
20   points us winterward
to December nights
lighted only by
snow trees from
the Gatineau.

1978

Holiday Postcards
I meant to send you
a postcard but the
farmer came out of
his dell and went
5   commercial the scene
changed old Mother
Goose was forced out
of the fairy-tale
business nursery
10   rhymes were *passé*
too tame not enough
blood hyperactivity
or brain damage not
enough how shall I
15   put it old men with
young women young
men with old women
battered wives or
suicidal husbands
20   and the sharks were
after everybody.

Nature was
all disordered
the zucchini always
25   overcooked the wine
tasting of tar and
even my good friend
the wind blowing hot
and cold and never
30   knowing which way
to turn: everything
was crazy and I
couldn't find the
right kind of
35   postcard showing
what it was really
like to go on holiday
five thousand miles
from home only to
40   see that everything
was exactly the same
there as here.

That was my big
discovery the farmer
45 going commercial
kicking the cat loading
the donkey taking his
wife locking up the
house selling it to
50 developers and going
into a new kind of
retirement condominium
that was just being
built in Delphi or
55 maybe it was Florida but
honest I meant to
send you a postcard
telling about the
grass at least and
60 the flowers whose names
you know and the
ocean that was blue
and still tasted so
miraculously of salt.

1978

Lady in Blue: Homage to Montreal

Lady in the blue
dress with the
sideward smile,
I see you at your
5   easel in the field
beside your house
painting the blur
of long-ago summer
in the night-eyes
10   of children in the
dark mouths of
sleepwalkers in the
floating bodies
of rock-throwers
15   and flame-eaters.

In the soundless
streets of our French
bedlam city with
its old creaking
20   heart and venereal
stairways, its bridges,
spaghetti houses, railway
hotels and second-hand
monuments, there,
25   Lady Blue of the
saint suburbs, there,
just there you were
lost, lost under
the mountain, under
30   the snows and *calèches*,
the steep cliffs of
Côte des Neiges, there
you were lost under
the fortress facades
35   of a thousand steel-
armoured apartments.

Under the slow blonde
sorrows of your tangled
hair we are all lost,
40   lost in the distance of
endless streets in the
trackless wastes of our
vanished mother-city;
we are ghost people,
45   uneasy night-walkers
locked up in Montreal,
and we will never leave
unless your tireless
brush moves us and draws
50   us into the blue-sleeved
avenues of your still-
flowing rivery wonder.

1978

Letter from Egypt
In this country
noon embroiders night
with golden
threads
5   and the stars
leave their love
messages in
hollow skies.

The forests
10   are full of the
noise of priests
at their prayers,
but the rabbis
have all gone away;
15   they rode out
one long-ago day
on their own
nightmares.

And guess what?
20   The people all
live in the tombs,
they have chopped
down the tress
and killed the
25   caterpillars, then
they watered
the sands, poisoned
their hens and dyed
oceans the colour
30   of Macbeth's
plunging hands.

They also speak
a strange language
here, so don't buy
35   your ticket just yet;
if you come you
may not be met,
the taxis have all
gone to war
40   and the fields
are drowning in sand.

Wherever you look
things crumble and
break and even my
45   cymbals don't ring;
of course nobody
dances and the
pyramids still
aren't built, so
50   wait till you hear
that we have our
visas for home.

Until then
I don't think
55   you would like it
here.

1978

Mister Never in a Dream of the Gatineau

Mister Never is back:
top-hatted
very elegant, a gentleman
in black,
5   he steps from the circle
of night and
appears in the clearing,
stands
knee-deep in waves
10   and weaves
the golden leaves.

Mister Never
is disguised, he plays
a seventeenth-century
15   explorer;
last week he discovered
two new colonies
west of Quebec and
the province pinned
20   him with ribbons
and leases.

No wonder he clicks
the heels
of his dancing shoes
25   and makes a great leap,
no wonder he turns
in arabesques
until he is consumed
and burns
30   in foreign fires
and fears (who wouldn't
if he were lucky enough
to be a widower?)

He knows the spring
35   and the future
will ransom him,
Providence will provide
him with Paris and a new
wife but for now
40   he is La Verendrye on
the pages of our
unwritten history books,
and a painted face
on a souvenir plate;
45   *je me souviens.*

Je me souviens
fifty nine autumns humid
summers and freezing
winters: *je me souviens*
50   the emissary
from cartels unlimited
sent to dissolve
hey hey all the new
autumns and ho ho
55   innocent seasons of Canada.

In another minute
when he has buried
the night
and turned his back
60   on December, I intend
to forget all about
new licence plates
and love of country,
I will learn about
65   economics and how
to invest my money.

1978

Postcard from Underground

You send me
stems and flowers,
your letters
when opened shake
5   out seeds and
herbs but I have
gone away, deep
into the dark
corridors of
10   the earth;

And you'd be
surprised at how
entertaining the
company is: Neptune
15   who foams above me
with his beard and
trident, Orpheus
who serenades me
with the latest on
20   his harp, and there's
Bluebeard who tells
long stories about
his wives.

All the same,
25   thanks for
thinking of me;
you may hear
from me again
next spring.

1978

Unemployment Town
Even here
the children look
up from their
sandboxes to smile
5 briefly into
the camera.

The icy villages
and empty harbours
are back there
10 behind them wrapped
in the loitering
streets, washed in
the civic fountains
and the thin dreams
15 of their shivering
fathers.

It is all there
inside the camera
under the torn
20 clothes and the
forlorn gutters,
and especially
in the pieces of
old rope left
25 lying around on
roads that always
lead nowhere.

1978

Prologue

The rosy wall
the samovar the
flowered curtain,
even the calendar
and lamp remind me
of long-buried bliss:
a child's hand a
husband's kiss,
a grandmother and
her soft lips.

The house
with its glass porch
unanchors
from the leafy street
and drifts
out of the prairie city
on ocean waves of
light;
smiling its sails
towards me unaware
of icebergs, night,
and the endless war
of tides.

1978

Mister Never in the Gardens of France

Rain obliterated
the golden neon-beaded
sign of the Hotel Royale
in Lausanne but the mosaic
5   roofs of Dijon preened
themselves like peacocks
in the sun of a mustard
summer when Mister Never
walked through the gardens
10   of France picking a flower
here stepping on a caterpillar
there and ordering a dozen
escargots for dinner all
for himself oh Mister Never

15   Suddenly the street
grows dark the stones
wither the air falls
heavily I choke on
escargots

1978

Mister Never on the Toronto Subway

Send me a bouquet
of Moscow roses
and a postcard
telling about winter,
5   write that you intend
to send me an oriental
silk it's my birthday
tomorrow so raise your
arm from a stranger's
10   body on the Toronto
subway and wave me
a greeting as you leave
the platform, I have
given up expecting
15   visitors and I can't
feel your wounds
anymore.

1978

Mister Never Shows Me How to Fall off the World

His eye curved
like a scythe or
the hooded eye
of a serpent,
5   Eve's apples
were stacked in
my throat I could
not cry for help
stung to silence
10 by that hissing
hooded eye.

No more
loving myself
I stood in fields
15 of snowy music in
acres of singing
blood, rapt and
listening to the
cold tilt the
20 warm hum of the
moving world.

Then I knew
the rib of my
balance lost as
25 I walked Adamless
out on the heaving
groundswell far
out on the plank
of my sinking
30 disordered bones.

1978

The Big Tree
I dreamed
the big tree
in my backyard
was being chopped
5   down by blades
dropping from
aeroplanes sent by
the prime minister
of remote control
10   from the province
of pipelines and
the land of final
solutions.

At dawn the
15   planes flew past
my house
dropping salt
to seed rain and
spraying Zen-X
20   to dissolve
the ozone.

Somewhere
underground Lot
looked up from
25   his forge with
a red steaming
face and roared
out above the
fiery noise:

30   This is what
      comes of all
      your know-how,
      everyone will
      burn anyhow
35   and equally in
      the empty
      emptiness and

      There will be
      no one left
40   to inscribe
      even a single
      little hieroglyph
      on the age-old
      pillar of salt.

      1979

Managing Death

It is not easy
to manage death
or the thought of
death, our own or
5   that of our friends;
each friend who dies
empties the world
and leaves fainter
traces of our own
10   bodies on earth.

It is not easy
to manage death but
it is not heroic
either; it is the
15   piecemeal following
of hints, the slow
breaking of this
link or that in
the last quickening
20   flash of the iron
chain of the flesh.

It is moving through
the patchwork of light
into deepening darkness,
25   and the glimpsing against
our will of the land
that can only be known
by those who are silent
and blind.

1980

Crazy Times
When the birds riot
and the aeroplanes walk,
when the busy sit,
and the silent talk;

5   When the rains blow
and the winds pour,
when the sky is a land
and the sea its shore;

When shells grow snails
10   and worms eat toads,
when winters chase summers
on upside-down roads,

We'll sit by our fires
and warm our hands,
15   and tell old tales
of bygone lands.

1980

The Green Cabin

The year went by
in marriages and deaths,
not least do I mourn
the death of my youth and
5   the death of
the friends of my youth,
and now at last I have begun
to mourn the death
of my young mother whose life
10   was bewildered by children,
and also to mourn the death
of the young mother in me
who still wanders so
restlessly haunting the lives
15   of her children.

In this year of deaths
and marriages I mourn
the death of the lover
in me who ran to meet
20   a world full of love and
star-blessed miracles,
but now those doors are shut,
and the miserly world
has locked all the rainbows
25   in earth.

Where did the year go
with all its marriages and
deaths, its wedding cakes
and funeral flowers?
30   How did the year drift out
on elegies and sail away
to foreign harbours before we
noticed its going?
Why did we continue to work
35   after our friends and lovers
died? Some of us sculpted
statues and others composed
life-music to each small
delicate motion while the rest
40   kept on painting people
in deck-chairs staring out
at the never-ending sea.

This year of marriages
and deaths I sit and mourn
45   in the green cabin
under the spruce tree,
I hear the rain on the roof
black and dark as the heart
of November, a rain dark as
50   the heart of old age, dark
as my heart of stone that
mourns the dark stone of
age, itself a dark stone
in a dark dark age.

1980

Honouring Heroes

In April he stands
narrow-chested and tall
in a net of bare branches,
he is saying goodbye
5   before he leaves
on one of his journeys,
his forehead is as tanned
as any explorer's,
and around him are many
10   beautiful women all
with the same face.

Does he know
that even explorers
grow older and lose
15   their hair while the
beautiful women stay
always the same, young
hipless and windblown,
with the same fixed
20   empty eyes?

Sometimes he feels
the flow of his blood
shifting and shrinking,
or his heart turning grey
25   and beginning to crumble;
has anyone counted
the lands he has surveyed,
the tombs he has rifled,
or even how many lions
30   he has shot with that
mounting courage so much
admired and envied?
How many wives has he had,
and how many children
35   has he abandoned and buried?

When you go to shake his hand
you see a tiny blood speck
floating in his left eye,
so small it is hardly
40   noticeable yet you see it
and recognize it,
it is the stigma of a wound
nothing can heal,
it will grow and spread,
45   it will devour his life.

1981

Conserving
On November afternoons
the harem girls are out
walking their dogs.

They have eaten pineapples
5   and drunk white wine,
they have heard murmurings

From enchanted palaces,
they have dreamed of sultans
with turbans of gold.

10   The frost pinches their faces,
the wind teases their hair,
their eyes have the blinds down,

They don't want anyone to see
behind their shuttered eyes
15   where they are working hard

To conserve the small heat
in the rooms of their lives;
they are husbanding warmth

For their anointed lords
20   who will return from travels
at difficult sundown,

After dangerous journeys
on highways and throughways,
after hand-to-hand fighting

25   In offices and corridors;
what more can harem girls do?
They have walked their dogs

And eaten the pineapples,
they have combed out their hair
30   and buffed up their nails,

They have chopped up the day
for firewood, hating November,
and now they are burning the sultans

With the turbans of gold,
35   they are burning their dreams
in suburban fireplaces.

Perhaps the harem girls are angry,
for it is not always possible
to be beautiful or to walk the dogs;

40   And they have to work so hard,
they have to burn more dreams
than they really have

In order to conserve the heat
in the small rooms
45   where they live.

1981

The Milk of Mothers

Stars, stars,
lean down and speak:
tell me what I am
on mother earth,
5   *our planet.*

They have reduced
our winnowing skies
to ash and lava,
and set out lunar
10   onion plants with
mountain parsley;
without a word they
rolled our mother
earth, this planet,
15   in syrups of the dead.

Crumbs of recent
feudal feasts
still cling to our
nuclear shrouds,
20   and one-dimensional
graphic cows are
outlined stiff in
charcoal to mark
the shadowy shifting
25   negatives of field
and forest.

No grave
delineates the light
of absent earth,
30 and there is no one
left to hear
the cries of those
whose ashes are
heaped green and
35 pulsing in deserted
tomato fields.

Tell me, stars,
what fortune-teller
will now guess
40 the thoughts of
weather and what
wizard bind the
splintered sides
of logged-over
45 blackened hills?

Stars, the milk
of the old mothers
is thin and the
milk of the young
50 mothers is shrieking;
the milk of the
mothers runs out
from every eye and
breast and throbs
55 with the white blood
of electricity.

Stars, stars,
lean down and speak!
Tell me what I am,
60   and tell me where
is the milk of
all the mothers now
on earth, our planet?

1981

South American Nights

She dreams she is
queen of a brothel
in a wide feather-bed,
her name was lost
5   in some prison and
now they call her
     Rose Red.

She loves the cruel
prince of a burnt-out
10 war-surplus shed, his
subjects are armless
guerillas and their
camp is a starved
     river bed.

15 She dances with green
mercenaries and
garbage bags stuffed
with the dead,
she dreams she is
20 queen of a brothel
and her name is
     Rose Red.

1981

Primary Colours

1. Being Born
Be red,
a red of space
and stretch,
a flow,
5   a burst of
burn.

And now
reverse, contract,
enclose
10   to interpoint:
shift darkness
into out or in
until you have
a hearse,
15   a box, a cage,
with nets and loops
of leaves, with pods
of seeds.

Then move
20   in protoplasmic
dance
through streaming
mysteries
of cell and cellicle;
25   flow
through careful
barriers of bone
and storms
of blood,
30   past cartilage
and hinge,
past loose vestigial
wings and
dangle from torn
35   ligaments and broken
muscle strings.

Whatever
you are or ever
were or who,
40   made old or
born new,
embellish,
polish space;
rake up the
45   summer, loosen
winds,
plant seeds until
glorious at last
you hang
50   upside down from
sky's umbilicals.

2. Living
Be blue,
a blue of fathomless,
a spray of far,
55 a gleam of
absent sunlit
highs and
glittering echoings,
grab the empty
60 edge of skies,
swing wide,
and plunge
to blanching
presences.

65 Now write
your hieroglyphs
on snowman's
letterhead,
dictate
70 your glaciers to
sleeping space,
compose
an orange song
and circle it
75 with canticles
of blue;
pack up the forest
and consign
its hundred owlish
80 eyes to earth
in nailed crates
of night.

Or slide
some measured
85   two-by-fours
through open
window frames;
then wake the
dreaming dead
90   and touch
their breath
with stars.

Before you leave,
sweep the blue
95   sawdust up
into a heap,
and with clean
brushes scatter it—
through a thousand
100   radiant doors.

3. Dying
Yellow,
who are you
yellow?
Tuwhit tuwhoo
105   I am I,
yellow and
you are you.

Yellow
you are the
110   sound's horizons,
its early
orisons unpacked
from vats
of dew.

115   And yellow,
       you are the
       golden bar
       across
       the topmost
120   star.

       You are also
       the fertile toad
       of the yellow
       swollen day,
125   you are yellow;
       the shrunken
       pearl of the
       loudly yellow
       night.

       1981

Selves

I

My old self
comes back
to visit me
more and more
5   often; at three
years old at
four years old,
at six years old.

I am three,
10   I am sitting
on a brown floor
holding a mirror
in broken sunlight,
I squint at my face
15   in the mirror it is
derelict streaked
with tears.

My hair what is
left of it is
20   ragged, the scissors
are still open in
my hand and my
tears are falling
through the spaces
25   between the sun-bars
that open and close
like shutters on
the floor.

I am crying,
30   I will be scolded,
I will be punished,
I will be ugly
duckling and my
uncle will never
35   make spinners out
of buttons and string
for me again.

My mother will stand
towering over me,
40   made of huge marble,
a naked statue,
like the one on the
postcards people are
always sending us
45   from the Louvre.

2

I am four years old;
my mother among
the picnic things
is calling: Mia, Mia,
50   Mia! I hear her but
I wait till she turns
her back, I am there
all the time right
under her nose buried
55   in last autumn's leaves.

As soon as her back
is turned I jump up
and throw off the leaves,
I run north, Kildonan
60   Park is empty as a
theatre on Monday
morning and the tall
elms are pillars
holding up the sky.

65   I keep on running,
      I'm heading for
      Dead Man's Creek,
      I run past notches
      cut into the bark,
70   I plunge through
      mushroom dust and
      fern jungles, I blanch
      I am afraid, what if
      I meet a giant or
75   a witch, or worse—
      what if I meet the
      dark chloroform lady
      who waits behind the
      door of the cupboard
80   in my room, or most
      terrifying of all
      the Selkirk avenue
      streetcar conductor
      with the big loud
85   buttons?

      3
      At six years old
      I can still hear
      my mother's voice
      calling, Mia, Mia,
90   but I don't care,
      she doesn't own me,
      I'm running away
      going to the forest
      still heading for
95   Dead Man's creek,
      still looking for
      buried treasure.

Suppose I get there
and am the first to
100   find it, what then?
Three boys once went
fishing from the banks
of the Red River they
found a dead gopher
105   and started to bury it,
they dug a hole and
found treasure, an iron
box full of gold coins
left there by pirates
110   or other explorers.

I find only
a handful of dandelions,
but I feel
just as rich.

1981

History: In Jordan

Long ago
you drowned
in the lake
of my sleep.

5   I buried you
in a tomb
in faraway Egypt,
in Cairo's crumbling
city of the dead.

10   You don't remember;
you have forgotten
the long paved streets
and the burst water pipes
of Jarash.

15   As for the amphitheatre
and the Nubian actress
who was homesick for Crete,
you kissed her in the wings
where the wind was
20   the only voice.

The wind and
the silence
and the bent grass
that grows
25   between the stones.

I too have forgotten
that time.

1981

How Old Women Should Live

Old women
should live like worms
under the earth,
they should come out
5   only after a good rain.

Or be the kind of worm
that lives in flour
and has stood too long
and when discovered
10   is thrown away in disgust
by the good housewife.

Or be a wood-worm
that patiently winds
its journey through
15   history's finest
furniture like those
old women we see
in the corridors of
nursing homes.

20   Or they should be
constructive like the
silk-worm who lives
on nothing but a box
of mulberry leaves in
25   hot China too far away
to bother anyone.

The wisest old women
imitate the glow-worm
who is never seen by day
30   with all its grey worminess
and shrivelled feet,
but shines wise and warm
only after dark.

Old women should be
35   magical like those worms
in transition and chrysalis
from egg to butterfly;
even decrepit old women
can turn into butterflies
40   in the third existence
promised to us all.

And remember that worms
are fussy about where
they live and what they eat;
45   they like warmth, darkness,
and good nourishment and
sometimes when it suits them
they like to come out in
all their loose nakedness
50   to crawl in the sun.

1981

Old Age Blues

This is an age
where you have to
expect disasters;
in summer the roof
5   leaks in winter the
balcony collapses
under the weight
of snow and the
furnace also gives
10   up the ghost, coughs
and sneezes, finally
explodes in a fury
of old age so
sing, sing the blues.

15   Even worse: the man
you thought would
marry you marries
someone else (lady
your house is more
20   than 20 years old
you've been getting
a free ride no repairs
all these years) and
your youth is more
25   than 20 years away so
sing, sing the blues.

Also, move along:
can't you see that
the sidewalks are
30   crowded and the
throughways are
throbbing with the
rutting young and
jumping with No
35   Exit signs? They
say that old wood
burns slowly but
old wisdom never
made anyone's heart
40   burn brighter so
goodbye now and
sing, sing the blues.

Here I go, flying
high, disguised as
45   a fairy godmother
whirling and twirling
my old-age wand;
just watch me—
I'm about to turn
50   a million glittering
cartwheels in milky
outer skies and I'm
rolling in stars,
rolling all the way
55   up to eternity and
I'm singing
sing, sing the blues.

1981

Portrait of the Owner of a Small Garbage Can

The woman who
lives alone has
only a small-size
garbage can to put
5   out Monday mornings,
very little garbage
and very few leaves
to rake; the leaves
fall in profusion
10   only in yards where
children play.

The single woman
is lucky if the sun
shines on her and
15   the wind blows
through her hair,
the touch of the
wind the touch of
the sun even the
20   bite of frost is
the closest she
will ever come
to knowing love.

Instead of kisses
25   what she gets are
lonely dinners in
vegetarian restaurants,
under the sugary
lights of the icy
30   chandeliers in a
chain eating-house
she dances every
night with a different
steak made of nutmeats
35   and eggplant.

She walks back
through the streets
of an empty Toronto,
her tongue feels
40   deep-fried, her glass
slippers hurt and
she has lost the
telephone number of
the fairy prince.

45   At home she goes
upstairs and lays out
next day's clothes,
then she fills
a hot-water bottle
50   shaped like a toad,
sighs pearls and
goes to bed.

1981

Committees
All the outpatients
of Toronto have
overnight become patrons
of life; they have been
5   elected to committees
on longevity, they sit in
special clinics studying
their horoscopes convinced
there is a science as
10   well aṣ a strategy to this
business of outwitting the
scowling doctor of death.

1981

Old Woman in a Garden

There she is
kneeling in the garden,
an old woman
planting tomatoes,
5   sifting the earth,
breaking the clay,
her face half-hidden
by a red garden hat.

There she is
10   old woman in a garden,
satisfied with the sun,
not wondering
how long he will stay,
knowing
15   he can't go away
or die like
the others.

He won't
grow up or go
20   away he will always
be yellow-eyed
and young
with a honey tongue
and a bee-striped smile,
25   he can't go away,
he is here to stay,
and every morning
he brings her
a breakfast tray
30   with a cupful of light
and a saucer of day.

There she is
kneeling in the garden,
an old woman
35   in a red garden hat;
what is she thinking of
as she scratches the earth
and plants her few
small seeds?

1981

Celebrating Mavericks
Go little words and fly,
round up the mavericks
all those stranger-words
and make of your flight
5   a moving wing of sound,
a deepening of the
ever-darkening light.

Advance, but curb the
changing words with reins,
10   bells, fringes, tassels and
soft bandages; with them
you'll bind angels, jokes,
gabby citizens, seed-lists,
and people raking leaves.

15   Then, little words, expand,
be horticulturists, invent
new cabbages, grow roses, name
gentians for their blue and
coax low nasturtiums into
20   giant forest trees, lay out
rich gardens for the starving
world—water and fertilize.

Having done your work
lie down to rest in shade,
25   let ministers of sleep
lull you to dreaming and
when you wake find yourself
a marcher on parade,
an eternal member of some
30   other-world procession,
a golden cipher
in God's motorcade.

1981

The Transplanted: Second Generation
Some day my son
you'll go to Leningrad,
you'll see grey canals
under arches and bridges,
you'll see green and white
walls of winter palaces,
you'll visit the towered
prison across the river
and smell the breath
of dead revolutions;
perhaps you'll even hear
the ghostly marching of
sailors in empty avenues
and catch the ebbing sound
of their wintry slogans.

You'll remember
that Jews could spend no
nights in Leningrad when
it was called St Petersburg;
Jews moved with documents
shuffled and crushed like
paper; the Yiddish writer
Peretz was met by his friend
Anski at Leningrad station;
he delivered his lecture
to a crowded hall then spent
the night in a suburb
twenty miles away.

Some day my son
30   when you are in Leningrad
you'll see those palaces
and turning fountains,
you'll stare at pendulums
of gilded saintliness,
35   count kingly treasure-hoards
in glass museum-cases;
then you'll remember
Nova Scotia's pasture lands
its clumps of blueberries
40   and our August mornings
on hidden lakes at the end
of logging roads.

And some day my son
just there in Leningrad
45   across those distances
you will feel my Winnipeg:
·   its lakes of fish its skies
of snow and its winds of
homelessness will stir
50   something in your blood;
then you will hear forgotten
languages and you will read
the troubled map of our
long ancestral geography
55   in your own son's eyes.

1981

The Visitants

At night you think
of your friends the dead;
they sing to you
in a choir of stone voices
5   and you want to tell them
old stories more ancient
than you mortally know,
all that you fleetingly
surmise shimmering
10   through the hole
in the foliage of the
nearest tree.

Oh those voices of stone!
Those earth-stained voices
15   those murmurings in wood
those singings in grasses
those soundings and turnings
on the pathless prairie;
my father groaning and
20   Gabriel Dumont staring
blindly into the camera
of his own fate.

Those anguished visitants:
they come to dissolve
25   the emptiness,
they come to console
your cries they come
with their firefly lanterns
to lead you amazed
30   through their blazing
gateways of stone.

1981

The Secret-keeper
In memory of Marvin Duchow

Long ago one April
you whispered and gave me
a secret to keep
of time and of music.

5   I pondered the secret,
and wrapped it in sleep,
then I put it away
forty years deep.

When you died I awoke
10   and pulled up the blinds,
I parted the clouds
and looked out into May.

What was the secret?
It was about being
15   young and about being
old and also about

The dying of Yeats
who came to Montreal and
sang of golden nut-trees
20   and of silver pears.

In June you came to visit
and played Mozart under
my window and in July
we met again and walked

25   On the royal mountain
with its fiery cross
and daytime blaze
of ponds and children.

You asked me why I knew
30   nothing about Bach but
I had no answer and stared
dumbly at swallows flying.

In August I stayed home
and when I looked up from
35   weeding the garden I swear
I heard Beethoven humming.

In September it rained:
there were storms in Europe
and Jews were in a hurry
40   to pack their belongings.

The rest of the world
was busy listening to the
overture of the death camps
in the music of Wagner.

45   In October there was no sun,
people said they had never
known the streets so empty
and the hospitals so full.

In November a miracle:
50   the azaleas flowered again,
we lighted lamps and had
second thoughts about leaving.

December was full of laser
lights and people picking
55   bouquets of pink sugar roses
off tall wedding cakes.

January was freeze-up time,
our father winter came and
wrapped us snugly in the fugues
60   of his cold white beard.

We slept through February
and only woke up when the
postman brought us valentines
stamped and postmarked *Death*.

65   In March we shovelled snow,
and then it was April again
after the thumpings of winter,
and the false alarms of spring.

Now at last I have found
70   what you gave me to keep,
the secret is simple,
and its music is this:

Dark night; pestilence.
A scabby apple tree.
75   Distorted song; its murmur
stilled; your death.
An empty field.

1981

When We Met

When we met
the first time it was
really the last time,
we spoke to each other
5   in the lost tongues of
our parents' Europe;
whose piano did you play
that spring afternoon
in the shadowed house
10   near the mountain
and whose song was
I singing entirely
to myself?

Was I my mother?
15   Were you your father?
Did we meet on a street
in Odessa or a birch forest
on the Volga or was it at
the artificial lake I dug out
20   in miniature and planted round
with tall buttercups for trees
behind an old hotel
in Winnipeg?

Why did it take me
25   so long to find our
lost languages,
to learn our songs?

1981

In a Summer Garden
In memory of Morris Surdin

The musicians
who sang to us are dead;
they left us sitting alone
under the pear tree
5   in the scalding afternoons
of August; all at once
they emptied the garden
of sound and everything
stopped; even the wasps
10   hung motionless.

We still hear them,
those musicians who sang,
suspended they move
through the widening rings
15   of their silence until
they float in the leaves;
laughing and rosy-faced
they climb up to the sun
and turn the key of C
20   in the door of the sky,
they stand on a threshold
of clouds and throw down
capfuls of sound, rich
and shining as cherries.

25   The musicians who died
are still singing and laughing,
they are whirling and dancing
in the spiralling wind
to the tune of new songs;
30   their notes shiver the clouds;
their voices are saying
they want us to sing.

1981

Elegies for a Composer

1

Now there is only
the whisper of grass,
gentle under the flight
of your song's swallow.

5   Now there is only
the motion of earth that
sleeps under the mountain
beyond your song's sorrow.

2

You have crossed
10   into the world
below the frost line,
you have gone to join
the effigies of
our immigrant parents
15   who lie frozen
into statues under
fields of snow.

They lie there
and wait for us
20   under the wild sage
of their summer,
they look out at us
from the hundred white
eyes of the stinkweed
25   that grows so modestly
on the prairie.

Muffled by mouthfuls
of earth their voices
sing to us in the lost
30   tongues of our childhood,
they sing to us
the buried truth
of ourselves.

3
Why did it take us
35   a lifetime to hear
through the strange
accents of our parents
our own songs?

4
Now you are dead
40   and your song is
digging its way up
through the garden;
it emerges slow and
glistening with the
45   earthworms who labour
so earnestly for every
new planting.

1981

Bulgarian Suite

I

Shall we sing of the graves
in the forest of tombstones
in the museum village
of Kopriv-shtitsa, shall we
sing of the pity in the eyes
of St Trofim on the charred
icons or shall we sing
the unfathomed the fateful
discords of death
in the museum village
of Kopriv-shtitsa?

2

On spring nights
you can hear the
echo of the battle
fought on the bridge
a hundred years ago
in the museum village
of Kopriv-shtitsa.

On spring nights
you can smell the
whispering fear of
the informer and on
spring nights you
can hear the faraway
sound of his horse's
hooves as he rides and
rides into the dawn
of his betrayal.

3
And always
30 when spring shakes out
its apple blossoms
on the museum roofs
of Kopriv-shtitsa
you can see the mother
35 who waits still and
dumb as stone in the
forests outside the
museum village of
Kopriv-shtitsa.

40 She sits there
among the daffodils,
a statue in the forest;
locked into her stone
body with her hand under
45 her chin, she meditates
and waits for her son
to come back from the
battle he fought
on the bridge outside
50 the museum village
of Kopriv-shtitsa.

4
She waits for her son
who never comes home
from the Turkish prison,
55 her son sits there
writing his testament
his renunciation and his
farewell with his own
heart's blood.

60   His heart is
        red as a flower
        and death flowers
      . in his heart until
        out of his heart's
65   blood the red flower
        bursts into death,
        death that blinds and
        burns the mother.

        She sits still and
70   dumb as stone in
        the forest outside
        the museum village
        of Kopriv-shtitsa,
        she meditates among
75   the lichens and mosses;
        locked into the stone
        of her statue she never
        stops waiting for her
        son to come home.

        5
80   Inside the museum
        we file past mouldering
        archives, we stare at
        long lists of names in
        cyrillic alphabet but
85   the letters are mute
        and motionless, they stay
        enshrined in their
        glass cases.

We scan row after row
90 of faces in photographs
as if looking for a
brother, an uncle, or
a dead grandfather,
we recognize no one;
95 there is no face here
that speaks to us—
there is no sign.

There are only the
tombstones out there
100 in the forest;
rooted in the bodies
of long-dead warriors
they flower silently
and lean into a future
105 full of questions.

6
Death flowers and
meditates
and the stone woman
in the statue
110 sits and grieves
for her son and
his ragged armies.

7
Sometimes they step down
from their photographs,
115 all the ragged young men
from the peaceful villages,
you can hear their ghosts
riding out on the wind,
you can hear their voices
120 singing into the trees
rising above the darkness.

8
The past is always
singing and crying
in the green light
125   of the forest outside
the museum village
of Kopriv-shtitsa,
the past is always
singing and murmuring,
130   the past is reminding
us to never forget
the battle outside
the museum village
of Kopriv-shtitsa.

1981

Wake-up Song

Lay aside your grief,
old child, infant lady,
in the land of unbelief
grief is the kind of fury

5   That morning will not bury,
and night cannot erase,
for grief is the weaker side
of anger's double face.

So close accounts at last,
10   the ill that's done is done,
change the worst to best,
for so must every one.

Now lay aside your grief
and wake the sleepy world,
15   old child, infant lady—
its yawn is purest gold.

1981

Winter Storm

Nothing is half-mast
or half-measure in a
snow storm everything is
.caught in the whirling
5   carnival and everyone
has a turn in the crazy
kaleidoscope of winter.

The tow-trucks are out
with all their pricking
10 lights and little flags
of colour; winds clown
sirens hawk wheels
somersault and burst
while snow-plows furrow
15 country paths across
the city fields.

At last night comes
with all its raucousness
and scraping shovels
20 and sings the world
to sleep; it reaps our
darknesses and props
their falling sheaves
with next spring's
25 seeds and sorrows.

Yet we are ignorant,
and travelling light,
rock ourselves to warmth
in scattered rooms and
30 tents, in feathery
high-rise nests; until
like a Moses miracle
the dawn arrives:

Loud with commands
35   and promises it stuffs
our crumpled sleep
into a huge knapsack
packed for travel—
then zooms away
40   in search of new hotels
and seasons
on distant arctic stars.

1982

Questions

Why do I still dream
of lovers, hikes along
the Gatineau and
autumn bonfires beside
5   Fairy Lake?

Why do I think
of the cindery
canal paths beside
Ottawa's driveway the
10   rosy tulips of spring
and the leaves ankle-
deep in September?

And when walking
across Laurier Bridge
15   blind as a sleepwalker why
do I keep glimpsing
myself aged sixteen?

Aged sixteen: and why
do I keep seeing
20   the man who became
my husband walking
towards me

In a future
that lies so far
25   behind me?

1982

The Visitor I
With the golden fleece
for cover
he pours blood
into a bowl.

5   In the corridor he finds
a cracked basin
to catch the falling rain
from the hat-brim
of Jason.

10   He steals
the golden fleece
and wraps
its weeping folds
around his wolfish
15   face;

Then he flies
stinking
into red night
to do his murder;
20   war.

1982

Song II

Paint me a bird upon your wrist
Or paint me wheat to walk among,
Feel me space and light and mist,
Sketch me meadow-rise and song.

5   I am the rising song, low voice,
Hear me in your quiet sleep,
And in its boundaries do keep
The letters of my love; rejoice.

Rejoice in your uncoloured mood
10   And draw me falcon as you will,
Or paint me flying wheat until
My words fall headlong in the wood,

And light upon your darkened sleep
With loving tone and lover's rue,
15   For I am I and you are you,
And this is all that we may reap.

Draw me falcon, paint me bird,
Erase my poem, love my word.

1986 (composed 1958)

Women

For a thousand years
in a thousand cities
we have lived in
images dreamed by
5   others, we have been
lamp-lighters in houses,
bulb-changers in
apartments, spinners
of wool in tents, weavers
10   of linen in cottages,
and foreladies of
nylon in factories.

We were always
the floor-washers and
15   the jam-makers the
child-bearers and
the lullaby-singers,
yet our namelessness
was everywhere and
20   our names were written
always in wind, posted
only on air.

Now the winds blow
old images off the
25   mind's pages and we
are no more the face
in the picture but
the hand making the
picture, we are no more
30   the watery song above
the wind's waters but
the source of the waters
flowing back to the waters.

Our voices have healed
35   from the fever of silence,
they bring from the waters
the health of the morning,
we are mapping adventures
by the light of the future,

40   We are carving our names
in time's forest of stone.

1986 (composed 1976)

Magic

Red shoes, red shoes, on my slender feet;
Night and I alone here in the cobbled street,
And all the mad gaiety of red-slippered feet.

The young wind tugs at my fly-away gown
5   And whirls me high through the tall-gabled town,
And my tangled hair comes tumbling down.

Red shoes, red shoes, what do you seek,
Past the narrow docks where the old boards creak,
And a low-moored ship sways its gloomy peak?

10   Will we find the wizard waiting in the dawn,
Standing with a mountaineer belt buckled on?
Oh where has the blue-eyed wizard gone?

Red shoes, red shoes, through the market square—
The dark towers bend sharp roofs to stare!
15   Is the brown wizard man still waiting there?

I passed all the stalls to the last empty row;
Oh where do the blue-eyed wizards go
When the moon is crusted with late spring snow?

Red shoes, red shoes, no one here to meet!
20   Only night and I in my gay-shod feet,
And the warm red echo clinging to the street.

1986 (composed 1936)

Partisans II

There is the soft murmur of wheat
Stirring in the earth
Pushing up through the winter
Is the sweet sound of wheat,
5   The good promise,
And the burnt cities
Can hardly believe it.

Last year there was an eerie rolling
To the earth in these parts,
10   Unnatural heaving and the long murmur
Of our buried people, not dead,
Was in our ears, and quick as fire
Travelled their words to us,
Their murmur their outcry
15   Was the light in our blood, the torrent
Coursing through our veins, and we had courage.

There were guns among the sunflowers
Moving like hosts of ravens through the green,
The tanks ploughed our earth with a long wound
20   Through the deep grass and even the roads
Were quiet and waiting for something else
Except women and children asking, 'Mother, where are we going?'

Where they went no one can follow,
And what they suffered no one can expiate,
25   Their memory is our anger and our decision.
And now spring is coming like a romantic letter
From the beloved, and now wheat is stirring
Under the shell-shocked earth,
And soon sunflowers will be nodding their bold heads
30   Against our native sky which still remains
Vast and indestructible as our anger.

1986 (composed 1944)

Three Prose Poems: Little Allegories of Canada

1. Ontario Cellars

So you are afraid to be a husband she said to him. Come in then and be
my child. We will live happily ever after. She shut the door behind him
and opened the closed world. The north wind came howling down from
the Rouge hills with Pickering in its claws. The echoes all sighed
Oshawa Oshawa and the lake of Kawartha rose up and drowned the
voices of the Indians. The dead stirred one last time in their community
graves. The underneath room of the earth rocked and seethed in a
wedding dance.

The sun shone in the middle of the sky and apple trees bent their
branches to the earth. Faraway now he could hear her say: are you still
afraid? And before he could answer she said in a light blonde voice:
come, now you will be my child.

The earth opened and touched him. He walked into its cavern like
a sleepwalker. A trapdoor opened under his feet and he fell deep into
an Ontario cellar. Here beside the stacks of New Testament Bibles
were heaps of carrots, all gold, bins of potatoes, all nickel, and bags
of onions, all carved out of solid ivory. On the walls the mould shines
with gold.

He hears her say: this is the heart of the world. Now you will be my
child forever. And high above them beyond the trapdoor he hears the
apple trees bending their branches to earth. And the wind never ceases
to sing into the darkness, into the locked centre: *now you will be my child.
Now you will live ever after.* The mould in Ontario cellars shines with gold
forever.

2. Montreal: All French Speaking Here

25   What do people do with foundlings? They open their front doors on
Christmas morning and say: look someone's gone and left a baby on
our doorstep. Would you just take a look at its red hair? And: oh it's
a boy they say it's a boy.

Then they say: I've always wanted a little baby. But whatever shall
30   we do with a baby? Who will look after it whilst we're away at work?
Do you suppose it was Jaime from over Fullum street went and left it
on our doorstep?

The sun shines Christmas morning Sunday early in the little suburb
across the bridge. All French speaking too. And just look at that bridge.
35   Spun out of cobwebby iron silverlike, aluminum they call it. Funny
thing, once I knew a painter, artist lady and she liked to wear a pink
smock, all covered with paint stains it was. And her legs. Usually bare.
Calves high-knotted, cruel, and hard looking. I saw her at her husband's
funeral. She threw a handful of earth on his face last thing before the
40   gravediggers pulled the carpet of fake grass over him. Now why would
she do that do you think? With all the people around watching her. She
wasn't wearing the pink smock that day but not black either.

What shall we do with this foundling? I have heard they are called
Myra but some call them Moses. Down by the river we are all French
45   speaking. The city clerk won't write it into his archives and there
are acres and acres of little cradles behind the wall in the convent on
Dorchester street. The Catholic girls cry their eyes out when they see
the field of cradles and all the little babies left on doorsteps. Poor souls.
Father Noel will bless them.

50   But I'm so glad. I always wanted a little baby and this one has red
hair and it curls. Whoever will look after it whilst we are away at work?

Now don't go down to the riverbank. Didn't I tell you the bridge
fell down and the cradles floated all away? There are no more houses left
in my father's ark. Oranges and lemons the belles of Saint Clemens.
55   This is not London. We are all French speaking here but some are called
Moses.

3. Winnipeg and Ottawa

Last night Winnipeg played the love game with Ottawa in my living
room. Winnipeg just had her fiftieth birthday twenty-five years ago and
Ottawa is celebrating his centenary so if you don't know what
60   that means I can't explain it to you.

The winter as usual is snowlocked frostbound hoaryrimmed. It
clings to these cold anglosaxon walls and silvers the golden mission oak
and leather sofas and Ukrainian cushions with red roses on them and
we'll be lucky if Winnipeg and Ottawa both manage to stay alive for an
65   hour or two never mind a whole winter.

So who needs to go to the races asks Ottawa and Winnipeg answers
from deep inside her wintry flesh: I love to go to the races you can wave
so many flags. But asks Ottawa the thinker what use is it to wave flags?
Winnipeg is quelled and stilled. She is youthful for her age but what
70   use is it with Ottawa the thinker? Well she says to herself I could never
marry you you're old and what's more you're oldminded. If there's
anything I hate more than an oldminded man it's a goldminded man.
After many a summoner fades the swan.

Fades the time and she thinks of an answer. Waving flags is no use
75   maybe but people enjoy themselves when they wave flags haven't you
noticed? Ottawa pulls a long spinsterish face. A peering pearson face a
diefening sound. Were we put into this world this veil of fears to enjoy
ourselves? Winnipeg is crushed completely gravelled. She wants to say
yes yes we were I would rather marry the streetcleaner on Mount
80   Pleasant road in Toronto and go walking in Edwards Gardens on
Sunday than marry you.

She makes up her mind she will never marry Ottawa. Go paddle
your own canoe. Drown dead. Let the last goldeye die out of Lake
Winnipeg let the Icelandic fishermen reel in their lines for the last time
85   let the irises fade from Grasmere ditch and blow all the way to Selkirk's
loony bin let the last Scotch pine burn itself into the stones in those
forest fires around Lac du Bonnet I'll never marry Ottawa. East is east
but west is yeast and last is beast.

Then Ottawa says out of the purple into the blue: I'm a widower
you know getting on. You're a widow I hear getting on. If only we could
always be the age we are now. How would you like to marry me? I'm very
fond of huckleberries.

Winnipeg is in a flurry. She should have seen it coming so where
would she now be going? She's just a chary pie and much too young to
leave her mammy.

That love game. They played it last night in my living room.
Nobody ever wins but Ottawa certainly didn't lose. And if you don't
know what I mean I can't explain it to you. It's all in the grain but
Winnipeg's snowpoor heart is broken. It explodes into a million icerich
icicles snowlocked and crowflocked in a deep coffin hidden in a mound
across the built-up prairies of the world.

But Winnipeg is not speechless she forces herself to answer: I love
the mountains. And: will you take me to the races sometimes? Black and
white you can wave so many flags. June weddings are nice. The flower
girl should be all in blue. Satin shoes something new.

Last night Winnipeg played the love game with Ottawa in my living
room. If you don't know what it means I can't explain it to you. It's
a very old game but you know what? A funny thing happened to the
mission furniture and the leather sofas and the rosy ukrainian cushions.
They turned into assiniboine frost and redriver gold. Red river red
rover make the whole future over with Montreal Quebec Halifax Ottawa
Winnipeg Toronto Regina Calgary Vancouver Fredericton Red river
rover we call you all over wished and washed in the redriver gold.

1986 (composed 1973)

The Gift
Ghostly hands on my breasts
a ghostly body on my own

(Hush it is nothing
only the wind
5   blowing up
from the valley)

Ghostly kisses in my ear
stars bursting in my blood

(Hush it is nothing
10   only the wind
fretting against
the windows)

There are branches on the bed
there is snow in my mouth

15   (Hush it is nothing
only the wind
blowing open
the door)

Hands kisses branches of snow
20   blanched worlds breaking in light

(Hush it is nothing
only the wind
blowing away
your breath

25   and hush
he is bringing
you a gift
your body's
death)

1986 (composed 1984)

Aspects of Owls I

1
Certain owls are golden
you can see them
sometimes
asleep at the bottom
5   of very deep wells

It is comforting
the way they wait
for a pebble to fall
through the many
10   transparencies
that tremble
the countless arches
that rise
always in water

2
15   Owls wait
for the pebble to fall
into the absolute region
at the brink
of their stillness

3
20   It is startling
to watch the single
zigzag shiver
of motion
that both announces
25   and delivers
its own birth
from the golden point
in an owl's golden
eye

4

30   The golden eye
flickers
at the bottom
of every deep well

1986 (composed 1984)

Aspects of Owls II

1
It is necessary
to respect owls
they are aspects
of future
5   odd little fragments
of feeling

2
They are
drowsy messengers
they send us downy
10   letters and soft words
they whisper
of our lost seasons

They write us
about the white weather
15   of the nineteen-thirties
sealed now
under canals heavy
with plutonium

They write us
20   about twentieth-century
skating rinks
flooding the fields
with vapour

Also about deserts
25   of frozen ash
heaving
with the blind cries
of the unborn

3
Under the feathers
30 of this new darkness
the unborn lie
and the owls sleep
their uneasy days
wrapped in our own
35 endangered sleep

4
Somewhere perhaps
muffled rumours
and faint traces
of the golden eye
40 flicker
in the bottom of
an old well.

1986 (composed 1984)

The New Seasons: Light and Dark

1
In winter
we tread dead names
in all our cities,
mornings
5   we imagine origins
and read
our country's history
in our own pulse
and vein.

10   In spring
we find ourselves
in blades of grass
in fields in provinces,
and listening
15   we hear
old prairie winds
composing the refrain
of secret legacies.

2
In autumn
20   we stand on banks
of asphalt
as the night descends
and wonder
will this city space
25   survive
to hear our rivers sing
of daylight and clean water
above the roar of words
and flooding numbers
30   that issue from machines?

3
It may be
citizens will endure
to march like Birnam Wood
against the whim
35   of buttons the mindless
push of levers and
the vanities that seethe
in board-rooms;

Then citizens
40   will calculate with ploughs
the contours of each corner
of this earth,
and they will plant
their wheat and flowers
45   and raise
the flag of life
to celebrate our love
of country
and declare ourselves
50   rooted and revealed
in place.

1986 (composed 1984)

The Angels Who Sweep I

1

The angels
with the red lanterns
and frost-veined wings
are sweeping the night
5   from the snow cities,
they are sweeping drifts
from the forest paths,
they swing their lanterns
over the tops
10   of sleeping mountains.

Like picture angels
they almost fly.

2

Other messengers
with suffering eyes
15   and shaved heads
come from the moths,
from the dry nests
beyond the borders
of dark snow cities.
20   They sit in libraries
pretending to read,
their tongues are tied
and heavy with cold,
their heads on thin stems
25   flutter and nod,
their faces shrivel
to powdery dust,
they have no names.

Like old fences
30   they almost fall.

3
In my backyard
two lions prowl,
they have stepped down
from museum posters
35   of bright Jerusalem,
in my workroom
the dolls desert
their clever houses
and the pretty girls
40   who used to smile
from the tops of old
chocolate boxes
blacken their lips
and comb the mice
45   out of their hair;
they don't shop for
groceries anymore,
on Fridays they have
nowhere to go.

50   Like friends who turn,
they almost walk away.

4
The cruel stepmother
brassy and empty-breasted
meets with her cabinet,
55   she briefs the weather,
summons the winds
calls up the floods and
hastens the hurricanes;
at night she talks to us
60   on television; she smiles
into our living rooms,
while her secret army
chloroforms and gags us.

To the grinding of words
65   we almost sleep.

5
The white cats
go into the ravine,
the poplar trees
are bitten to the ground,
70   the sun hangs in the sky
like a naked bullet,
it scalds and deafens
the air.

6
The cherry tree flowers
75   and grows eyes,
its fruit is soft,
pale and big as apples,
the centre whitens
and withers.

80   The leaves stink
anger and helplessness.

7
A dove sits on a post
on the throughway,
a wispy flag
85   blows in the wind;
elsewhere perhaps
a green branch sleeps
in an old trunk
under the glacial shield.

90   The angels
        with the red lanterns
        continually sweep the snow
        from the rivers and
        they sweep the snow
95   from the glaciers,
        they are tireless
        in their sweeping,
        but the watchmaker's clock
        ticks and ticks
100   and knows no growing time,
        no human season.

        1986 (composed 1985)

The Angels Who Sweep II

1

The silence of angels:
their words are hushed
in the murmur of snow,
when they look up
5   from their sweeping
their brooms are frozen,
caught in the stillness
of winter's mid-air.

They incline their heads,
10   they are listening
to Beethoven play
his bursting song
when prisoners first see
the blinding light
15   through their barred
and buried windows.

2

The red lanterns of angels
hang waiting in mid-air
and the bells
20   in the golden throats
of church spires
ring between silences.

3

The blessed silence
of angels; like those
25   Sunday morning silences
when we walked through
city streets that were
half-asleep and empty,
and only the smells
30   of fresh bread and coffee
drifted down with us
to the river.

4
And the streets
in those days stretched
35   across shining bridges
to the unknown prairie
and the ripening future;
unmindful
we walked on the bridges
40   and admired the lacy
fretwork crocheted from
silvery steel by some
giant hand.

5
We did not ask
45   whose was the hand,
we did not read
the specific gravity
of girders or guess
at the composition,
50   the depth of the pilings.

6
Locked in our separate
trances, we joined
the invisible procession
towards what was still
55   undisclosed; and the angels
with the red lanterns
hovered over us,
their wings brushed us
with silence and the silence
60   was the silence
of the angels who sweep.

7
In our hearts we knew
it was not really summer.

1986 (composed 1985)

Languages

Once a man came to my door
selling storm windows,
he asked me was I widow
and the answer was yes.
5   I married him and he begged me
to teach him better English
so he could drive a taxi.

After some years
we went different ways,
10   I taught people
in many schools how
to speak better English
and I forgot the storm windows
and the man who sold them.

15   Until one day
jumping into a taxi
to go to one of my schools
to teach people how
to speak better English,
20   I gave the taxi driver
directions and he turned
around to me and said:

Do you remember storm windows
and how widowed you were?
25   I'm married again
I have a little boy
I speak good English
plain for everyday;

But your English,
30   it's pretty your English
is like a flower.

1987

The Last Landscape
I follow
the sky west
to another city,
drive through a ring
5   of cardinals, a wreath
of flowering birds;
the road dips
and I descend
to the dark lake.

10   There are
no sunsets here,
only men who beckon
through armoured windows
of plate glass;
15   their gray teeth shine
they offer me
porcelain words and
paper handkerchiefs
for my broken hands,
20   they give me documents
for safe-conduct
through the glass mountain
where some say many
are still imprisoned.

25   Below us sits
the queen of snow
on a soundless shore,
she is old and wrapped
in crusted shoals,
30   she strokes the sour waves
on her lap and mutters
doughty incantations;
in her oyster eyes
the milky seas rise
35   and fall.

I taste salt and
count the dead fish
on the beach; on the road
I drive past two clay bowls
40   and a startled cow,
I travel fast I stay
inside the white lines,
I don't want to scatter
the red petals
45   in the wreath of cardinals;
I don't want the birds
to fall out of the sky
in a rain of red flowers;

And most of all
50   I want to get past the rumour
of drowned countries
and no other cities,
I'm afraid—
I'm afraid I might touch
55   the hot grinding sound,
the cannibal roar
of the planet's death
when it begins to happen.

1987

Mysteries
It is wonderful
what some people
store up and pour out
in old age,
5   poems and all kinds
of stories,
what journeys they plan,
what voyages
they set their hearts on.

10   Before starting out
on their travels
they move into new
apartments, settle
on blue tiles
15   for their bathrooms
and self-cleaning ovens
for their kitchens,
and for their bodies
they decide on a spa
20   in a country slightly
to the south of them.

How truly one can say
of such people
that they have gained
25   wisdom; myself I was
spendthrift and stored
neither money nor wisdom,
and I made no plans
to voyage out to far countries,
30   since all that needs to be seen
can be seen right here
in my own city:

Men with closed faces
selling subway tickets,
35   science centres,
children packed into
yellow buses, and sealed trucks
loaded with deadly landfill,
in short, a future
40   full of aging colonels
and empty libraries.

Also rows
of silent schoolgirls
rolling by in wheelchairs,
45   (of course there is
commerce too people
laughing and talking
and even a cherry tree
that flowers in the spring).

50   I regret nothing,
I understand nothing;
sometimes it does no harm
to let mysteries remain
mysteries,
55   no more and no less
confusing
than what we imagine
is ordinary reality.

1987

Spring Night at Home

I'm home tonight
with the chickens and goats,
there is no car in my carport
just darkness and the wind.

5   Beyond the darkness
the garden shivers with cold,
leftover frost is still hanging around
although it's spring;
look how the daffodils
10   are freezing, swollen with cold,
beaten down and battered,
(but their feet are warm
wrapped in bulby bedsocks
of earth).

15   Can anyone tell me
why the trees look blind
and shake from their canes
and their branches bunches
of curly newborn leaves
20   while the forsythia bush
in the northeast corner blazes
with yellow lamps vulgarly
advertising spring?

The japonica on the west side
25   is more modest, lies there
snug and small in its place
in the gardenbed and lowers
its red flower-nipples
to suckle the earth and
30   all the time the hawthorn tree
is busy shining its blossoms
like searchlights
into the naked night.

Isn't it strange
35   how on this night the trees
float like moon islands
through the valley,
and how across the highway
two frogs are singing
40   and losing themselves
in the hum of traffic?

And here I am home tonight
with the chickens and goats,
they're all asleep—
45   and I'm waiting for morning
so the sun can come in
and help me to feed the world.

1987

Jacques Cartier in Toronto

Do we ever think about Jacques Cartier
as we pilot our cars downtown
through a river of streets
looking for safe new harbours?
5   And do we ever think of green fields
or cows as we make our way later
through the vast acreages
of office and department store?

And do we feel the drought
10   on miles of western townships
as we water our city lawns
with green plastic sprinklers?
We read that the reservoirs
are empty that the corn is dying,
15   that even the marshes and wetlands
have dried into colourless chaff.

We shrug and go into our houses,
(the world was always hungry
and now it is thirsty too),
20   we shower and change we are ready
to board our cars and pilot them
across the city to distant restaurants,
our weekend gateways to Cathay.

Do we ever remember
25   that somewhere above the sky
in some child's dream perhaps
Jacques Cartier is still sailing,
always on his way always
about to discover a new Canada?

1988

Living with Rumours of War

Cities close early
these days
wild people roam
the empty streets
5   the garbage cans are full
the furnaces are out,
the bus carrying people
to the suburbs never comes,
and there's a tall old man
10   around who keeps wondering
why he can't get a taxi.

1991

Places

In that country
we heard distant moon music
and cuckoo cries,
in those days we filled
5   our baskets with beads
and coloured Sundays,
but in this country
there are only handbills
junk mail and free coupons,
10   they pile up in our mailboxes
and no one has time
to read them.

Instead we wait
for love-letters from
15   South America,
we speak words heavy
with corncob wisdom
and sometimes we wonder
what is so wonderful
20   about longevity when
so many are dying young,
some from hunger, others
from war, disease, and poisoned
waters while still others
25   just hang themselves.

Who is left to speak
for those who are dying?
Silently the artists
enter their workrooms,
30   slowly they carve out
nests and flowers inside
themselves in the long
darkness; outside there is
noise of civil war and
35   the fading summer.

On a distant hilltop
in the stone tower
of a capital city
carillon bells are ringing
40   their songs; homeless children,
surplus grain and rumours
of barricades, bayonets, and
broken bridges.
The rivers listen and grieve,
45   the hills hear and mourn;
as for ourselves we are
packing for a journey.

We fold our sober snows
and winter wisdom into
50   big trunks and ship them off
on pirate tankers to places
with tropical names where
black pepper grows under
the glossy leaves of never-
55   never-Monday morning trees.
Years from now
we will tell ourselves stories
about those imagined countries,
places where to this day
60   no one ever dances and
no one ever sings.

1991

The Archivist

1

Her life burst
from its chrysalis
a butterfly;
her body limpid
5   and luminous
had no wings.

Hummingbirds came,
they dived, hung,
stared, then drank
10   from neighbouring
milkweed, paused,
thanked her and
flew away.

Then someone,
15   a magpie or bluejay,
maybe an owl,
set her to turning
words around;
soon she could read
20   commas and periods,
decipher question marks
and sort through
a thousand layers of
delicate documents.

25   Sometimes old papers
crumbled in her insect
hands but not before
she had decoded their
molecular messages;
30   with just her compound eyes
and scanning antennae,
she could push all
the pieces together
so they made sense.

2

35 She was dutiful;
day and night she
crawled among papers,
her segmented legs
had no memory her
40 body bore no imprint
of ancestral flight,
or the airy dance
of wings.

Yet occasionally
45 when she looked up
she could see above her
certain marvels; almost,
she imagined, even
miracles.

50 In summer
the dust whorls
on roads dizzied her,
and the faraway sound
of snow melting on
55 mountain-tops always
cooled her.

In autumn
people in red sweaters
raking leaves on the
60 lawns consoled her,
and in winter when
she slept she heard
the wind rattling
the bare hedges.

3

65 She longed
to make a journey,
to travel though the
stillness of winter
to find spring, a pot
70 of gold, and a mother
who loved her.

But the papers
would stretch out
their arms to her
75 and call after her,
so she would always
put aside miracles
and postpone the world
for later.

80 Always she postponed
everything for later
after all the myth
of her birth and the
placenta of her destiny
85 had foretold she would
never fly but as a reward
she could live longer
than the others, much
longer, and she could be
90 their archivist, she
could record the dreams
of all winged creatures.

Nearly always
the butterflies dreamed
95   the same things, the smell
of sweetpea liquor the
taste of nasturtium trumpets,
or a tweak from the thumb of
sunlight; occasionally
100   a rosy clover would pour
a ray of petals into
her eyes and once in a while
a cabbage would fan out
its leaves to cradle her.

4
105   She recorded it all,
the nectar and the cabbages,
the slim pickings and the
fat plenitudes; she called it
a collage a paste-up of
110   the world and gave it
a permanent press with drywrap.

So she was surprised
when she saw her collage
had the double shape
115   of butterfly wings,
that it was a helix
outlined with the cold
fusion of absence, that it
had an aura, that it glowed
120   in the dark.

The helix burned
with unrelenting furious
power; she recorded
its double spiral and
125   the way it multiplied and
multiplied and never
stopped multiplying.

Then she recorded
how it killed people.

1992

The Woman in the Hall

I

There is a woman
in the hall,
she lives alone in
some upstairs room
5   in a nebulous city,
surely you have passed her
on your way to the bathroom;
and haven't you met her
coming out of the
10   communal kitchen?

Is she birdwoman or
sibyl, farmwife or
fishgutter, or is she
the buttonhole maker
15   who worked on the suit
you wear or maybe she's
the pastry decorator
who picks out the words
on the cakes your order?

20   Whoever she is
she is also Guernica
and Madrid she is Moscow
besieged and Dieppe
betrayed, she is all the
25   sombre-eyed girls in Goya's
drawings forever mourning
their soldier lovers forever
wandering through littered
battlefields forever
30   gathering fragmented faces
and gnawed-off limbs of
seventeen-year-old recruits.

2

That woman in the hall
is hunger and desolation,
35 she is the addled brain
of the crazy woman who
survived the camps
to sit out the days on the
shores of the Dead Sea
40 muttering curses and
incantations, the woman
in the hall hears the
messages from beggars
in Berlin from street girls
45 in Buenos Aires.

3

In her sleep
the woman in the hall
sometimes sings lullabies,
her hair fans out on the
50 pillow in streams of
water and babies, her many
faces are covered with rain
and falling leaves her ears
tremble with whispers of
55 lost children but she knows
concealed in the white thigh
of every woman is a mouth,
the mother of all speaking.

4

Who is this woman
60   who dreams against guns
and hunger whose words
turn into songs as they
climb into higher and
higher skies? Is she
65   birdwoman or sibyl,
is she fishgutter or
buttonhole maker or is she
the quilter in some small
town eking out life on
70   a pension? Whoever she is
she hears your messages,

5

And turns the tides
with your anger and sorrow,
her wrists throb with the
75   pulse of ruined cities,
she dreams your dreams,
and scatters her muffled
words into your sleep;
she is the ragpicker who
80   comes to warn you
of future Guernicas,
and she is the woman who
at last awakens in you
your broken promises your
85   ancient righteousness.

1992

Futures
After the spring and summer
of being twenty,
and the long sunny autumn
of being thirty,
5   we are suddenly in the winter
of being forty.

Being fifty
will be even deeper winter,
as for sixty—
10   it simply stands there waiting
for the weatherless season
of becoming seventy.

After that there is only
the frowzy worn-out path
15   to death,
or else the unlikely nudge,
the plunging shock
to a new awakening.

1992

The Snow Tramp

When it snowed
in Winnipeg
my mother would look
out the kitchen window
5   and say
I wish I was a gypsy.

She would put on
her moccasins and
sweaters, wrap a scarf
10   around her neck, shoulder
her snowshoes and go
tramping
in Kildonan park.

That evening when
15   my father came home
he found us all supperless,
he was angry and worried
but he opened a can of soup
and fed us.

20   When my mother
came home it was late
and dark; she shook
the snow from her hair
and wondered how it happened
25   we didn't know she had gone
tramping
in Kildonan park.

My father scolded,
but my mother's soul
30   was far away
wrapped like a gift
in stars and snow,
and all night long
her gypsy tunes sang
35   and danced in the wind
around our house.

1992

Instead of Lovers
I think I have
forgotten
how to love a man.

Long ago
5 in my youth
I loved many men,
touched them
with the red feathers
of my heart,
10 glided over them
with the yellow silk
of my hands
and sounded in them
the bells of my voice.

15 I embraced them
with the forest
of my arms
rocked them to sleep
on the clouds
20 of my breast and praised
their every awakening
with the whiteness
of morning.

Now I wonder
25 who plucked the feathers
of my heart,
who trampled the silk
of my hands,
who broke the bells,
30 chain-sawed the forest
and darkened
the whiteness of morning?
Are these the men
I loved?

35   As they draw nearer
I see
instead of lovers
a crowd of old men
coming to meet me,
40   they are dressed
in narrow suits of
carrion-crow black
they are making speeches
and shouting,
45   they are hoarse from
exhorting us
with their cracked old
promises of doves
and freedom.

50   They don't know
they are talking to the
deaf winds
in the space of yesterday,
to the blind snow
55   in the crevices
of aeons ago—
and as they walk
towards me each one
carries in his mouth,
60   like a dog his meat,
the body of a dead child.

This is the gift
they offer
to the women who bore them:
65   dead children.
Dead children
are the garland
they bring
to place on the grave
70   of the future.

1992

Reflections
How we photographed
ourselves
and each other when
we were young;

5   Now we avoid mirrors
and turn away
from reflecting
windows;

And these days
10   when we travel
we turn out the lights
lock up the house,

And leave our cameras
closed and shuttered,
15   safe in the darkness
of home.

1992

The Life of a Woman

The life of a woman
is never in tune
with the times,
she is born too early
5   or too late and suffers
discords, interruptions,
humiliations and
surprise endings.

With the life of a woman
10   it's like with those
green bananas I buy
in the supermarket in winter,
they never seem to ripen
or grow sweet,
15   instead they turn black,
then they wither and shrink,
reminding me of a certain
raw and passionate love
that darkened my youth;

20   The one that never ripened
or grew sweet,
but withered into a death
emptier and colder
than the freezing corridors   ·
25   of subway stations
after midnight.

1992

Knives and Ploughshares

The knife
is not a ploughshare
but a versatile instrument,
use it on your friends;
5   it works,
send it to your enemies,
they'll sharpen it,
give it to your mercenaries
as a matter of course,
10   or take it
to a dark street and plunge it
into a passing jogger,
it says nothing
political.

15   Better still
conduct an opera with it,
dance a Carmen
with the knife sharp
between your teeth
20   like a rose;
the knife—
flower of our
civilization.

1992

The New Jasons
With the golden fleece
for cover
they pour our blood
into a bowl.

5   Then in some corridor
they find
a cracked basin
to catch
the magic rain
10   that falls
from the hat-brim
of that old hero
Jason.

These new Jasons,
15   their false words gilded,
steal
the golden fleece
and wrap
its shining folds
20   around their wild-rat
faces.

Then they fly
sated on flesh
of the young and
25   banqueted
on the sacs of our dead
futures.

With teeth bared
and stinking tongues,
30   they shriek
and fly into
the world's red night
of nevermore and terror
to do their murder:
35   war.

1992

Amos

Your justice was
a mere whisper
in the armed gardens
of Jerusalem.

5   In the noisy
sunshine your
justice glittered
and was subdued.

Your justice
10   shattered
on the broken
rocks of
Jerusalem,

And was enfolded
15   in the slashed
remnants
of its ancient
light.

1992

Ulysses Embroidered

You've come
at last from
all your journeying
to the old blind woman
5   in the tower,
Ulysses.

After all adventurings
through seas and
mountains through
10   giant battles,
storms and death,
from pinnacles
to valleys;

Past sirens
15   naked on rocks
between Charybdis
and Scylla, from
dragons' teeth,
from sleep in
20   stables choking
on red flowers
walking through weeds
and through shipwreck.

And now you are
25   climbing the stairs,
taking shape,
a figure in shining
thread rising from
a golden shield:
30   a medallion
emblazoned in
tapestry you grew
from the blind hands
of Penelope.

35   Her tapestry
        saw everything,
        her stitches
        embroidered the
        painful colors
40   of her breath the
        long sighing touch
        of her hands.

        She made many
        journeys.

        1992

Gardens and Us

Thirty years ago
full of plans and hopes
we moved into
brand new houses,
5   planted smoke-bush
and yew, mountain ash
and flowering crab,
painted and carpentered,
refinished old tables,
10 laid tile for patios,
scolded the children
and enrolled them
in junior hockey and
baseball clubs.

15 The children grew up
and moved away,
the yew grew to monster
size the crab attracted
tent caterpillars,
20 the quince scattered
its bitter fruit all over
the flower beds
with spiteful cunning,
the roses and wild
25 sweetpeas were rebellious,
rampant and out of control,
the black medoc, crabgrass,
and speedwell didn't care
what happened to the lawn,
30 and settled stubbornly
into cracks and crevices
in the driveway where
the earwigs and ants
daily multiplied.

35 The refinished tables
have lasted and still shine,
they preen themselves,
have become collectible
and sought after;
40 the painted walls
are pale and smooth,
bland and silent and
the chairs don't
talk to us.

45 But we have other
serious troubles—
the sour chemicals from
the golf course drift
across the valley
50 with the wind and kill
the phlox and even that
survivor, periwinkle, wilts;
the rabbits eat up
the parsley and marigolds,
55 but the garden is indifferent
and passive, has become old
and introverted, returns us
none of the old love
we lavished on it.

60   The butterflies are gone,
        there are no more toads,
        but the cardinals
        still come, they sing
        to us at suppertime,
65   otherwise the street
        is quiet as the grave
        and so are we as we take
        our dutiful walks;
        we are practicing to be
70   future ghosts of ourselves
        who will return
        in spring to haunt
        the old neighbourhood.

        1992

Paper Boats
When we divorced,
we each divorced our youth,
sent it like paper boats
sailing to who knows where,
5   and lost our selves
in those old lovers' lanes
still winding
through our blood.

In my blood
10   the self has dwindled,
and the lovers' lanes
have faded,
but in your blood
our youth still dreams
15   and winds its way
through the remote rivers
of your death.

1992

Mechanics for Women
Late in life
I am finding out
the immortal names
of screwdrivers.

5   First there is
the plain screwdriver,
then there is
the star-shaped one
called Phillips,
10   and a few in-between ones
whose names
I never learned.

There are also wrenches,
open and closed,
15   and hammers, soft-faced
or hard-lipped,
and pliers called
needle-nosed or blunt
like fish swimming
20   through the mighty
mechanical lakes
of the universe.

Among all the tools
I love the spanners
25   best because
you can do anything
with spanners
depending on the size
of them,
30   and you soon learn
which spanner to use
when and what signs
spell trouble in the
universal joint.

35   It's all so easy
so enchanting so
original, from
the newest sparkplug
to the smallest
40   distributor cap.
Oh the wonderful
the beautiful the
absorbing folklore
of tools!

45   Yet I still find it
impossible
to change a flat tire.

1992

The Summer Girls
Under the awnings
of street cafes striped
with runaway sunlight,
the summer girls
5   in their flowered dresses
are eating their lunches.

They have only an hour
but have dreamed
for a lifetime of the
10   far snowy mountains
and green-painted rivers
that run icy cold
over sand-bars and pebbles
that flicker and blind
15   them with glintings
of gold.

They see themselves
flying and hear
themselves landing on
20   spongy marsh grasses
among Indian paint pots
of vermilion and ochre,
colours that time
with its patience and
25   patchwork has coaxed
from the stone.

They see themselves
bending like trees
in the water their
30   faces refracting the
leap of the light,
they feel their hair
loosening luxurious
and falling on shoulders
35   of August,

Far from the corridors
and clocks of their
earnings, far from
the memos that nag
40   and harass them,
out of reach of the
telephone with its
hiccups and jangles
breaking into their
45   trances, their daydreams
and longings.

When the hour is over
they rise from the tables
and turn to leave
50   their oases of canvas
the striped awning cafes.
They float and they fly
across prairies and fences
to their downtown offices
55   where the wet mouth
of the city slobbers and
swallows them.

Yet somehow the colour
of the Indian paint pots
60   trails and follows them,
and the washed rags
of laughter clothe
and caress them
the whole afternoon.

1992

In the Hurly Burly Arcade

When she was a child
she killed her mother
and married her father;
later as a young woman
5   she poisoned her lovers;
was it her fault they died?

Disillusioned with men
she entered a university
and gave herself to books;
10   gradually the books piled up
and grew tall against the
windows, they begot children
upon her, dwarfs and hunchbacks
and a single willowy girl
15   with skyblue eyes.

When she was middle-aged
her waist thickened and
her behind flattened from
sitting so much in libraries,
20   she began not to sleep well
and to have nightmares,
she dreamed the willowy one
was poisoning the sherry
or lurking on the balcony
25   among the disused summer
furniture or else
she was waiting to meet her
on the stairs so she could
push her headlong down.

30   One day she went downtown
      secretly to buy a bus ticket
      to Vancouver but when she
      got to the bus station all
      the good seats were taken;
35   most of the time she sat beside
      bushy-haired seventeen-year-old
      girls and their pale babies,
      or else men in big black hats
      who smelled under the armpits
40   squeezed in beside her.

      The journey to the coast
      took longer than she expected,
      she bought a lot of sandwiches
      in Winnipeg and they lasted
45   most of the way to Regina;
      somewhere near Rogers Pass
      they sold cheap coffee
      then the bus went through
      Crow's Nest Pass where the
50   farmers were still picketing
      for lower freight rates.

      Finally she got to Vancouver;
      Gastown was bleak and empty
      as a prairie railway stop
55   and she hadn't really had
      any adventures so she decided
      to take the ferry to Victoria
      where she found Emily Carr's
      boarding house was under new
60   management; all her friends
      were dead or living in tidy
      retirement homes.

What was she to do? The best thing
was to go back to her own city
65   and make guarded peace
with the willowy daughter.
She would work hard at becoming
invisible for the years
that remained to her; she would
70   haunt the libraries and read all
their books, she would take notes
and do a lot of xeroxing, she would
eat her lunches on benches downtown
or at McDonald's where they give
75   old women free coffee.

After all her travels
she would end up with this
small wisdom; how to find
warm places and free coffee.

1992

Mountain Interval I: Studio

We look
through the window
see tree branches
nibbles of grass
5   and traces of elk where
the antlers were rubbed;
we sniff
chipmunk and squirrel
follow
10   barrel shadows
of bear.

Then undergrowth
shoots
arrows of sun
into chrome yellow
light,
we track footprints
and fossils
in secrets of stone.

20   We wait;
in that silence
hear
trees fall, see
ghosts walk,
25   they look over
their shoulders then
turn and beckon us
up to the heights,
to the slide
30   of the glaciers.

We dissolve
into nothingness
but our old antlered
hope rubs off
35   on the tree trunks
and grows in the grasses
for children to scatter
in the seeds of their
laughter
40   a hundred years later;

Or until the last
silence
descends on
these mountains and
45   fills up the distance
with waterfalls
falling.

1992

Mountain Interval II: Pow Wow at Bragg Creek

I

I compose
grasses
turn words
on a loom
5   thread the yellow
of sun through needles
of sharp
mountain moonlight

2

I sing the flow
10   of golden streams
over ochre pathways
the fingers
of gravity in
the infinite pools,
15   the yielding of
marsh grass
to the forces
of water

3

I sing the snowy
20   smile of mountains
over hazy plains
over sweetgrass meadows
that sleep like
children under
25   skies and rains

4
My sleep is
dreamless
bound with belts
and crossed with
30   beads,
swift coyote tails
fly past with
the wind

5
I am dizzied
35   by bird faces
owl masks and eagles
in endless procession
I am deafened by
drumbeats blinded
40   by dust
and the swoop of
the dancers

6
They circle
and move
45   in their shining
numbers in their
myriad thousands,
thundering ravens

7
Dust rises
50   and falls
its clouds cloak
the dancers
until tireless
they ride
55   away into distance

8
They disappear
and are lost
on the shimmering
roads

1992

A Few Things

There are only a few things
the politicians of war
or the privateers of
free enterprise
5   haven't yet found out
how to do.

These are to have dreams
and raise children,
be kind and human,
10   let birds nest
and trees and rivers
live.

1992

Freedom Games

The stars unbutton
their tight jackets
they peel off
their silver shirts
5   and naked dive
from cloudy springboards
into widening pools
of night.

And we below
10   are fishes lost
in the murky deeps,
blindly
we swim our way
through caves and tunnels
15   of unstable water
to the wavering light.

And always
we strive to surface,
and always
20   we stretch and strain
to force
our fishy bodies upwards
in a leap
towards the height.

25   And as we leap
all of us
are silvered by
showering meteors and
shreds of shining stuff;
30   frisky in our play
we dart and turn
until we are discovered
by your telescopes.

You chart
35 and label us
and carefully engrave
our Latin names
on little metal plates
that spell captivity.
40 And so you put an end
to fish somersaults
and all our freedom games.

Then you enclose us
in watery boxes,
45 and sluice us through
the gates that keep us
prisoner
in the stone museums
of your dying states.

1992

A Man and His Flute

A man in a black coat
plays a song
on a black flute
in a concert hall.
5   He plays with his whole
body with his hands
with his trunk until
he becomes a tree and
his arm a branch;
10 his fingers are urgent
extensions that startle
the air in the leaves.

His song is obscurely
about a lemon
15 picked from an old tree
in another country then
brought home and cut
against the blue
of a winter sky.

20 The lemon and the
black flute and the man
in the black coat who
sways with the music
in the concert hall
25 takes the blue sky the
yellow lemon and the
cold sunlight of March
and turns it into an April
filled with the blueness
30 of hyacinth; winter turns
its back and melts away
in the runnelled snow piled
against frozen houses.

The man and his flute
35   play their song,
the audience is pierced
by the blueness of sky,
the audience hears
the snow melting,
40   the audience sees spring
approaching the audience
stands up the audience claps,
the audience dances.

The man and his flute
45   end their song,
a smell of cut lemon
fills the air.

1992

Orchestra

Let me sing myself
into the very centre,
the sunheart
of a flower.
5 And sing myself
out again on the
high-low scales
of wind
its majors and
10 minors.

Then sing myself
away on all those
transparent
enchantments of climate
15 where a thousand bees
are humming
under the baton
of a single hand.

1992

Autumn
(For *Lyubomir Levchev*)

When shall we visit
the garden of our friends
again?
When shall we again
5   break the walnuts
of September
and leaf through books
and argue again
about literature?

10   And when
in what year will we
again eat grapes
from the vineyard
of the poet's father
15   or drink the wine
of three harvests ago?

1992

Science and Literature

The scientist sits and worries
about very ultimate problems:
take the permeability
of the cell wall—
5   how does protoplasm move
through the cell wall anyway
and how does it know when
to start or where to stop?
That's one problem,
10   and if we knew the answer
to that we'd have
the cure for cancer for
radiation burns and even
for old age—maybe.

15   Another ultimate problem:
take the curvature of space
and how to measure it;
imagine a doughnut the
scientist says all the surfaces
20   are curved and now imagine
a ladybug trying to crawl
over that same doughnut,
you mean how are you going
to figure out those distances
25   I ask intelligently or is it
simply a matter of X+Y=Z?
After all I say defensively
I studied high school calculus
trigonometry and algebra
30   such as they were of course
in the olden days.

And I add: wasn't James Joyce
doing the same thing in different
terms when he claimed language,
35   mere words, could change the way
blood flowed and hormones worked?
No no the scientist says
that's not it at all it's a matter
of dimension what you have to do
40   is grasp the fourth dimension!
(*go and catch a falling star*).

Well I say that's really hard
you're right X+Y=Z is just
child's play compared to
45   curvature; I think James Joyce
must have skipped that fourth
dimension and gone straight on
to the fifth without doing
the proper calculations but
50   you being a scientist, you still
have to worry about ladybugs
crawling on doughnuts and
measuring distance on the
curvature of space and
55   I suppose many even more
ultimate problems.

1992

Jacques Cartier in Winnipeg

We never dreamed about you
Jacques Cartier,
Russia was very far
from your Saint Malo;
5   there were no telegrams
of congratulation from us
when you sailed down
the broad Saint Lawrence,
and you never entered
10   the minds of Winnipeg's
immigrant children.

So what was our life
those days on the prairie?
It was mornings
15   in fields of blue vetch
and on road-banks of clover,
it was games before dark,
Hiding-O-Seek and
Red Rover Red Rover.

20   Those ghostly children
still hold hands in a circle,
they turn and dance,
as their thin high voices
fall through the clouds
25   in a chorus of chanting:
Red Rover Red Rover we call
Jacques Cartier over!

You hear them and smile
and you come running over.

1992

Remembering Winnipeg

How are you Winnipeg
of the wide streets
and colonnaded art school
near the train station?
5   How are you old city
with your broken accents
Ukrainian farmers and
Jewish welders? I miss you
city of small tailors,
10   cheap stores, back lanes,
and houses with glassed-in
verandas.

How is your black earth
below the frost line,
15   and how are those ghosts
of buffalo herds and hunters,
I wonder if you still hear
the big horses ploughing
and are they still riding
20   over the prairies in cabriolets
with bells ringing
and red fringes flying?

I hear that your skies
have turned cannibal,
25   that your rivers are slimy
and your ghosts now wander
through ragged lanes
fighting with broken bottles
in the glittering midnight;
30   Winnipeg, your house is on fire,
on fire, and your children
are burning!

So summon your winds
from all the four corners
35   to fly with the news
that a storm is brewing,
and clean rain is coming
on clouds from the north
to clear all the pathways
40   of shadows and debris,
to make room for the light.

So I can say hello Winnipeg,
hello to your wide streets
and narrow rivers,
45   hello to your summer boulevards
and lazy cemeteries,
greetings and l'*chaim* to your
Siberian caragana hedges.

And good luck
50   to all the freight cars
sleeping in your railway yards,
good luck to the abattoirs
of St. Boniface, to its golden
crosses and fearsome statues,
55   *bonne chance* to Louis Riel
wherever he is and a last salute
to the haunted house on the edge
of old Fort Garry.

Shake hands Winnipeg
60   remember me in the evenings
when the mosquitoes hum,
think of me at noon
when the cabbage butterflies
hover; don't forget me, Winnipeg,
65   when the frost strums its banjo
and comes to sing under
your windows.

Goodbye, Winnipeg, goodbye.

1992

The Visitor II
One day
you realize she
may come any time now,
your friend
5   Ms. Death.

You are
digging dandelions
in the front lawn
you look up
10   and there she is
smiling and standing
against the cedar hedge,
she's dressed in leaves
loose and flowing
15   as water and her face
is vague absent and
familiar.

She's new and modern
though she lives
20   in books and sometimes
steps out of legends,
if you look closely
you'll see
she looks like you
25   only younger, more silent
and secretive, even
a little mysterious.

You dread her visit
even though you know her,
30 have dreamed about her,
and for years now
you have traced her every
move in the lines
of your own hand, often
35 you've heard her skirts
rustle in the next room
the silk of their folds
papery and dry as your own
old lady's skin.

40 She's very like you,
that motherly apparition,
as she hold out your own
arms to you as she smiles
your own smile at you,
45 a smile of doubt and
wonderment as she beckons
and calls to you.

And the worst of it is
you know you will answer her,
50 and in the next instant
you will be gone—
she will wrap you in her shawl
with the cedar fringes,
the one you were knitting
55 when she came to visit
last summer.

1992

Peace Notes
A leaf, a flower, a child,
September grapes,
red and white carnations
in the rain;
5   windborn messages
from a distant coastal
city.

1992

Untitled

The landscape sways
to the endless rhythms
of love.

1996

Noises
Late last night
someone scraped and shuffled
and sighed
against the wall
5   of my house.

I shone a light—
but no one was there
no one
no one at all.

10   Yet it wasn't the wind
and it wasn't the rain
so who was it?

Some poor ghost
I suppose
15   asking to come in
from the cold
and the dark.

The next morning
I found a half-eaten
20   crust against the wall
where the shuffling
had been.

It was a sign,
my ghost was lonely
25   but at least
she wasn't hungry.

2003

Songs of Old Age

1

There are leaves
all over the house,
red ones and green ones
of spring;
who is trailing them
into the house anyway?

2

If it isn't me
if it isn't you
it must be the wind
the wild wild wind
blowing through
cracks in the door
into my tame house
into my wild unruly
wild old age.

3

The love I bore you
in my youth
lies
like a dead child
in my heart.
I never buried it
with either word
or song
and am condemned
to mourn it
still.

4
Now that I'm old
my pleasures
have become pale—
30   lacey webs
like lady shawls,
and sparse
like old men's
beards.

5
35   Since I am
an old woman alone
people ask me
don't you ever get
lonely
40   and I answer, no,
how can I be lonely
when I have
outside my kitchen door
a great company
45   of snails and slugs
beetles and bugs
and four square feet
of summer earth
full of birth
50   that blooms and death
that grows?

6
When I died
in April I dissolved
in clouds and returned
55   as rain
in the tear of a primula
who mourned my passing
who mourned my care.

7

Now spring
60   lights her candles
in the willow trees
for the anniversary
of my death
and the wind
65   with lips of fire
sings me a tribal
prayer.

2003

Spring Onions
Once on a bus in a foreign country
far from home
just when winter was turning
into spring
5   I sat beside a woman
who knew my language.

I didn't know hers
but that didn't stop us
from starting a conversation—
10   first about our children,
their ages and genders,
then about the politics
of the foreign country
and how stupid men were.
15   We kept our words general
in case someone who shouldn't
might overhear and report us;
but we did venture bravely
to say how everything
20   would be better and different
if only women
were running the country.

As the sun was shining
and a pink smell of
25   blossoming was in the air,
we soon forgot our children
and the stupidity of men
and began to talk about
spring onions and how
30   they made the best soup
in the whole world.

We agreed that you start
with a good-sized
experienced old onion,
35   a carrot or two, a bit of
winter parsley and of course
a potato; then you boiled it
for a while to mingle
the flavours and finally
40   you added a whole bunch
of spring onions—
the first ones of the season
that you found in the market
that very morning.

45   We smacked our lips
at the thought of that soup
with all the flavours and
colours of spring,
spring that was ending
50   the winter and about
to break into flower and
song all around us.

Before we reached the bus station
the woman turned to me
55   and said: come to my house
tomorrow evening and
I'll make you a soup of
spring onions; even the
thought of it filled us both
60   with warmth and we burst
into womanish laughter.

Did I go the next evening
to my new friend to eat
a soup of spring onions?
65   I found my way to her
apartment through the narrow
lanes and twisting alleys;
she had only two rooms—
a kitchen and sleeping room,
70   her two little boys slept
in the kitchen where she had
cleverly concealed two beds
in almost no space.

We ate the spring onion soup
75   in her little kitchen
under the red wall hangings
and slavic smells of her
apartment, and I'll never forget
how spring whirled and sang
80   around us as it burst
through the walls of that house.
Now I think how much more
pleasing her apartment was
than all of Paris and London,
85   how much more musical
her two rooms with their
singing choirs of colour,
and how they lighted the poor
shabby streets of that
90   faraway foreign city.

Every year since then
I go to the market when
I smell the first whiff of
spring in Toronto or
95   Winnipeg or Vancouver or
wherever I am, and I buy
the onions and make
a spring onion soup;
and my heart flies
100   light as a bird across
the far seas to salute
a strange woman in a
legendary country—
and I know she is also making
105   a soup of the first
spring onions that very minute,
a soup for us to share
with all good people
everywhere.

2003

The Collected Poems
of Miriam Waddington

PREVIOUSLY UNPUBLISHED AND
UNCOLLECTED POEMS—SELECTED

Reveille

Pale, sleep-tranced maiden,
Your eyes dream inward
With dusk thoughts laden,
And old secrets heard.

5   Deep, slow-stirred maiden,
The wind strays by you,
And sighs, pollen laden,
The still evening through.

White, youth-held maiden,
10   Turn your heart to the world,
And pale-blossom laden
Be your soul unfurled.

1931

Romance

You are waiting
Somewhere in the distance of the countless nights
Where the moon alone
Soars frozen through the desolate heights.

5   You are standing
Like a hard thin flame, intense, agleam,
Like a tall strange lamp
You burn your shadow through my dream.

You are alone
10   One far strange being of solitude
With a heart of power
Your face cold and pale and subdued.

You are stranger
Somewhere in the distance of the winter years
15   Alone and proud
Your dream is the song the world hears.

1932

Politics

I had a little bird house
And nothing dwelt in there
But a golden starling
In a silver snare.

5   The president's attaché
Came to visit me,
We passed the time of day
Beneath the apple tree;

Russia's two ambassadors
10   Came to visit too,
And bought my golden starling
For the Soviet zoo.

So now the little bird house
Is empty, and my care
15   Is for another starling
Caught in another snare.

[c1931–1935]

Biology Room
(modern style with a dash of Baroque—just a dash)

Shall I go modernistic after all?
Shall I go modernistic in my verse?
Dare I go modernistic in such a place
As the Biology Room?
5   How one understands human bodies
When one studies the plant cell—
How the complicated facts of human passions
Resolve themselves into their simple factors
After one has looked for half an hour or so
10   At the plant cells under the microscope.
And one thinks—
Even that sandy man with the parted moustache,
(What a precise and sandy moustache)
Even he, who stands and lectures in a monotone,
15   After all, he has a body too.
And wouldn't it be interesting to have a love affair
With a man who knew all about biology
All about the impulse of life?
Still, I dislike men who are small.
20   Nevertheless it is quite fascinating
To watch the spirogyra reproduce
Under the microscope—and to hear—"turn it high power"
From the sandy man who talks forever.
So I turn it high power
25   And gaze quite absently at the stupid cells
Who keep on confining their activities
To mere reproduction and reproduction.
And I think nevertheless, how interesting
It would be to have a love affair
30   With a man who knew biology.
Oh well—when I go to college, perhaps—
There are biology students at college.
But didn't I know a girl
Who married a biology man
35   And found him coldly scientific?
So perhaps it would be quite dull

To have a love affair with a man
Who knew all about biology.
Meanwhile the voice goes on forever—

40   "This is the gamete—the male gamete—
The female gamete—the gameteospore—"
How futile that everything
In this chanson modern of the universe should resolve itself
To the ultimate male and female.
45   Dare I go modernistic in the Biology Room?

[c1934–1935]

The Pool

O woodland pool between the trees,
Who breaks your silence with a sigh?
Who comes at night when no one sees?
No reply.

5   I come at night among the trees,
And flutter silence with a sigh:
I hear your mournful melodies—
Only I.

I wander through wet fields and come
10   To your stillness in the deep,
Where wind and stone alike are dumb—
And I weep.

Though my tears tell of my grief,
Your slow dark waters are unstirred;
15   My heart is like a lonely leaf—
Still no word.

O woodland pool, if it should be
That lovers wander here and kiss,
And murmur comfort tenderly,
20   Tell them this—

How once a girl's sorrow drew
Her weeping to your mossy cover,
With heart a lonely leaf that knew
No lover.

c1934–1935

Tea Leaves

I am alone while afternoon creeps into night;
Sitting where you left me, quite alone,
Save for the shadows in the candle-light
On the walls grotesquely thrown.

5   And I muse here, quiet, in my woman's way;
Waiting dimly for the night to start,
Gazing at the empty tea-things on the tray;
All that lingers of you in this evening grey,
Save the echo of your smile in my heart.

1935

What Is This Life
What is this life if full of care
We have no time to stand and stare?
What care I if light is green
Or what the traffic signals mean?

5   So Jack be nimble, Jill be quick,
Jump in case the traffic's thick,
And do not stand on busy street
Lest life be short as it is sweet.

[c1930s]

The Peasant's Revolt

The men forsake the plough
The women bind their hair,
Strange storm is in the air—
Spring and revolt are now.

5   The shepherd leaves his sheep,
No regret upon his brow,
The fields lie quiet in sleep
Bearing the rusty plough.

10   The horseman does not heed
His favourite's straining call—
The hay will go to seed,
No harvest be this fall.

For by that vivid impulse
15   That turns the seed to root
Long suffering at last
Bears its bitter fruit,

And the men forsake the plough
And seize what comes to hand,
20   For time of revolt is now—
The peasant storms the land!

[c1930s]

The Flying Weather

She cried out to the flying weather,
Lord, have mercy on my soul!
The sun still shone, the winter weather
did not pause, the mouse and mole

5 Found shelter in their earthly burrows;
The Lord had mercy on their souls;
The quick frost froze in spongy furrows
And trapped her in an iron hole.

She strove and struggled to stand free,
10 With, *Lord have mercy on my soul!*
Against the fatal gravity
Which pulled her to the deathly pole.

[c1930s]

Envoi
In some quiet glade
At peace be he laid.
With little green moss
Strange patterns emboss
5   Over his grave.
A star and a cross
Curiously moss.

Let no one enquire
The rage of the fire
10   That consumed him so young;
Be content that this glade
Shelters on in its shade
Whose youth was betrayed.

[c1930s]

To a Three Year Old

Child, on your forehead milk would melt
And snow would trace
In your sleep a silver penny
With an angel's face,

5   And butter freeze upon the words
That from your mind stray out,
Oh capture them, these nebulous steeds
Before they can take rout!

And prance away in sugared trains
10   Against the winter air,
While your untutored feet must tread
Still the darkened stair,

Where half seems whole and whole is hidden
In newness and unbirth,
15   Child, you have still to learn
The dangerous tilt of earth.

[c1930s]

Medea

Your prayers are answered, the bitter pill
Again is proffered; take and taste,
Let its acrid flavor permeate
The mouth which was by kisses lately filled.

5   With folded hands in classic silence closed
Sit out this thorny hour; how often
You complained in nightlong weeping
Of unfriendly fate, but now you see

You might have trusted fate with keeping
10   A wiser troth; more lasting; you have lived to be
Yourself destroyed, your woman wasted,
To know your children dead.

And still with gravelled voice
You implore the gods
15   To increase your portion;
And of bitterness
To feed you more.

[c1930s]

At the Gate

The love I bear you is peculiar sight
To see where see no others and find light
In all this darkness, to illuminate
The stranger seeking stranger at the gate.

5   Still endeavor, for if I fail, my task
Will be to answer what everyone may ask,
And all my hunger ecstasied in silk
Will flow to nutmegged honey and to spicèd milk.

[c1930s]

The Pattern
You are of me the angled ecstasy,
The careful plotted minuet,
The pattern cut and placed on me,
So recognize me swiftly nor forget

5   To trace me, throw me to the wind
Where in its space I'll multiply
To your design, and new arrangements find
For problems old in every chosen eye.

It is a purely upswing and the certain surge
10   To meet the curve wherever source does lie:
So trace me fine with slow precision's urge,
And mirror me immortal in your eye.

[c1930s]

Our Journey Was a Failure

We must drive cruelly on although we know
Our journey was a failure from the start,
And from love's burning, you a while will glow
And I, for months, will nurse my wounded heart.

5   What good avails this love to us different are
That we can only meet at outer edge?
And though we strive for nearness, attain only far
And knowing this, we substitute a pledge?

You bring no comfort though my dreams exalt
10   You higher than trees the western forests grow,
And I no ease to you through some deep fault
Though I would give my wholeness just to flow

Smoothly as blood and closely in your veins,
But world forbid, and has done from the start,
15   So let us part, you with your passionate mind,
And I will keep unchanged my poet's heart.

[c1930s]

Pleasures

In the deep pleasures of my heart
no river flows more sweet
than your name, no stop or start
impedes its motion in itself complete.

5   The dark and unending river bed
winds your name in silence, marking all
its trembling course and mapping in my head
its secret source and highest waterfall.

When to dissolution I in time must go
10   you will divide and burst the care
with which I cherished you, yet know
your soul inhabits me, in rock, in sea, in air.

[c1930s]

Journey to Winnipeg: 1940
All day she watched the fields unfold
mile on mile their emptiness,
the snow lay glittering and cold
in drifts that bore the winter wind's impress;
5   all day she sat in silence while the train
whirled her nearer to the northern plain.

The hills closed in around the tracks
like great flat waves of an advancing tide,
they bore the scraggy pines upon their backs
10   with an aloof and melancholy pride;
their sterile faces were without complaint
enduring, bare as some El Greco saints.

The train sped on across the winter plains
nearer to home and to its strange confusion;
15   our lives are motion but one place remains
immutable, held ever in illusion,
and this is home; though seven years had passed
she was returning from the world at last.

There was none to greet her at this homecoming,
20   none to say her either good or bad,
she knew return was a futile summing
like lullabies are after Scheherazade;
her journey was by deep compulsion urged
and from her mind forgotten things emerged.

25   One was of a hired man called Irish Dan
who told them stories of the Flin Flon mines,
he carried fish worms in an old tin can
and on the river strung up pickerel lines;
two years later this same Dan was dead
30   hit by a train that passed and plunged ahead.

There was a Métis girl with an alien stare
who followed her through fields and down the cliff,
hung back with lowered eyes, dishevelled hair
and spoke with tongue that found the language stiff;
35   she showed her all the secrets that she knew
where mushrooms and plump lady's slipper grew.

And so that winter in a western city
a stranger walked through cold and snow-deep streets,
familiar scenes filled her with thoughtful pity:
40   here is the shop she used to come for sweets,
and here the walk she daily took to school
through little streets, remote, adventureful.

That world was past; somewhere beyond its rim
there is a legendary river Sambatyan where
45   childhood divides from knowledge and the grim
dark brutalities in the works of men;
there people walk in sunshine, live in peace,
nor dream of bombs or spies or the police.

The Métis girl she heard had turned out bad,
50   Dan was drunk the night they found him dead,
her favorite friend committed suicide, went mad,
and lady's slipper gone, extinct, they said.
Crumbled, destroyed, the world that she had seen
caught in the tide-rush of the years between.

55   Still the Red River and Assiniboine flow
meeting a moment under the rigid ice,
·perhaps the flowers take root beneath the snow
where ginger roots diffuse their bitter spice,
perhaps next summer other fishermen
60   will come and will amaze a child again.

Perhaps it will be given to these prairies
to see the tranquil dawn arise once more,
things happen so by humorous contraries
as ships, given up, do sometimes reach the shore;
65 perhaps these frontiers, menaced by a war
may gain in peace more than they had before.

1940

Love
John Sutherland 1942

1
We breathed in each other.
Now the white alternatives of love narrow
To dark compulsion, and there is no relief
From the bitter breath of our togetherness.
5   There is no turning in this brutal corridor
Where we kiss—and from the windless cavern
Of our limbs there is no escape.
And the city seen from the mountain fades
Like that light summer world of innocence
10   Which we have lost, have left, forgotten.

2
Stand there and let me study
The line of your neck and shoulders.
Let me memorize the painful story
Of your body and this moment
15   While I comfort my heart with the moral
That love is always sad and separate and possessing.

[c1942]

Who in Their Love

Who in their love great passion's season find
Must to their minds a holiday declare,
Pack reason off to take the seaside air
And other promenades for judgment find.

5   It is with love as oceans, overwhelmed
By vastness we are to smallness given,
And rush with all our rivers into heaven
While true self sails emptied and unhelmed.

[c1940s]

At Court

The unrelenting judge had a strong mother,
In higher court he had an older brother,
When he came to office, inherited a chamber,
Furnished with precious things in jade and amber.

5 The boy he judged, his mother was a liar,
She raised but never quenched the fire,
Dazed and confused he one night swung a hammer,
Stilled inner noise, and so resolved the clamor.

The judge reads only charges, not boys' faces,
10 Is not concerned with homes, or schools, or places,
He weighs each assault strictly by the book,
And is not influenced by pleading eye or look.

His gavel falls, the sentence gravely entered,
The law is served, the dossier is centered,
15 The boy droops towards the prison like a spaniel,
Clipped of his beaten life by modern Daniel.

[c1940s]

Man and Secretary
What an elaborate game that man engages in:
Trapped with his secretary on the train
He dictates letters, talks of policy
Or his projected visit to the west,
5 Indicts her choice of color, how she's dressed,
And plans still more humiliating jest.
She gladly wears for him the guillotine
Consigning self-love to the crowd that jeers,
Delicately, she with self-interest steers
10 Him to other victims in her attitude,
Thus all his problems are beheaded, roll
Into the large briefcase of their guarded life
Which pays with every journey higher toll.

[c1940s]

Some Notes on Our Time

Instead of epithets the street
Hurls dust and wind into my face;
Whores teeter in precarious grace
On their broken shabby feet.

5   Half of our world is now dead,
The other half deserves to be;
We are betrayed by casuistry
Of the rational human head.

And look at what has come about—
10   The poison brews in every heart.
The web and woof now fall apart
Before the scholar's genteel snout.

And look at what has come about—
You see it in the streets at night
15   The glowing of the red red light
Where beauty has been put to route.

The women walk on creaking shanks,
The men are soft and wrapped in wool.
Alas for what is wonderful.
20   The mediocre swell the ranks.

[c1940s]

Untitled

Black doves in my cherry tree
Who has laid this curse on me?

Black doves in the moaning rain
When will peace be mine again?

5   Peace will never now be found
Till they lay you underground.

The one who once had held you dear
Shall weep upon your pale bier.

O black doves in my cherry tree
10   Who has cried this curse on me?

The flowers bleed upon the ground
Tears upon my burial mound.

And black doves in my cherry tree
Fly and hover silently.

[c1940s]

He Calls
Set your dreams aside and come;
Long since faded is the sun;
We will go where waters hum,
Quiet one, wistful one.

5   Leave your raven thoughts an hour;
And of smiles have you none?
Look, I brought you this sweet flower,
Quiet one, wistful one.

But how cold the night is falling—
10   Surely now your dreams are done?
I am here, your lover calling,
Quiet one, wistful one.

[c1940s]

Doubles

My life is all revealed in twos
by sons who grow, plants which divide,
and loves which find me though I lose
the one where I'm identified.

5   There is the plain uncryptic two:
as well, the rocking secret one;
it is the second does undo
what the first is built upon,

And disregards the taming law
10 of order for the wild pair,
which pulls me tight beneath the claw
of my old chaos, new despair.

[c1950s]

Untitled

He who hobnobs
With ubiquitous Dobbs,
May come to share
The fame of Kildare

5 Don't toy with Toye
Don't lure McLure,
Because William is coy
And Millar is pure.

Pass Anne Wilkinson
10 A nursery bun
And to critic Weaver
Hand a meat cleaver;

To those advisors
And early risers,
15 Smith Scott & Frye—
Pie in The Sky.

That is The Text
For the smooth, the unvexed
Composers of words;
20 Free as the birds

Inoffensive as clams
Restrained will we fly
To the courtliest measure
Take sober pleasure;

25 And let the jack pine
Moan and whine
And the blue spruce
Ooze weepy juice

While deciduous trees
30   Complain to the breeze,
Well-a-day & alack
Laurels to *Tamarack.*

[c1956–1960s]

Untitled

the dandelion children
who live in the grasses
and talk all night—
the wind says *hush*
5   the sky says *sleep*
from deep in the grasses
they cry for their mothers
and for dandelion milk
in the stems of their mothers
10   but the mothers don't answer
their mothers are dead
scattered into seed in the grasses
buried in earth
deeper than grasses
15   and the dandelion children
are awake all night
calling and calling
the ghosts of the prairie
their voices ride on the wind
20   and fall from the sky

[c1960s]

Untitled

It's six o'clock
drive east on Finch
the road is broken
5   the city's dark,
but not as dark
as the dark places
in my heart.

It's six o'clock
10   I want to talk
about my heart
of valleys broken by
frames and lights
highrise ghost
15   brightgaze ships
that rise
in transepts above
the city's
bluffs and troughs.

20   High valleys ships
their galleons rock
a zillion rags
the homing pigeons
and speeds of light
25   now fall and rise
on seas of dark
yet do not touch
a dark as dark
as the dark places
30   in my heart.

[c1960s]

A Word

Someone said a word
Once in bitterness,
Nor ever dreamed I heard
The word in its excess.

5   And kept the memory
Like precious poison got
Till the word so given me
Grew into a thought.

The thought began to burn
10 Through my troubled sleep—
I could not unlearn
What I had learned so deep.

Now I am old and wise
But still I am not free,
15 Still is in my eyes
A strange intensity,

And in my mind is still
Something that I heard;
Not sharp enough to kill
20 Was that passing word—

But fixed enough to strain
A life's eternal tone,
And curl up in the brain
And break against the bone.

25 It seems he said a word
Once in bitterness.
He never dreamed I heard
The word in its excess.

[c1960s]

Untitled

I will build a mountain
of pure roses over the
chimney tops of London
garland the
5   chains of flats
with green vines and
standing on a mountain
of flowers I will aim
hoops at the stars
10   spirals of energy
will graze me
with brightness
and from the very mountaintop
of roses I will speak words
15   across the sea
and a stranger's luminous name.

[c1965–1975]

In Jerusalem
In Jerusalem everything
is irrevocable and
carries the same weight
the buying of
5   an eight-grush postage
stamp means no less
than the placement of a wreath
on the public altar or even
the giving of the firstborn to God.

10   In this place everything
resonates into a busy crowded eternity
where some are experts at copying old marriage contracts
others at carving ancient seals.

Here I rub shoulders with the
15   ghost of Amos
as easily as I cower
under the angry glances
of Arab shopkeepers
and all the while
20   downy blue-eyed angels
are smiling at me from greeting cards
printed by the Little Sisters of Mercy.

The thunderous dark forehead
of Moses glowers
25   from the hillsides and the quarries
and look there the original Miriam
and all the other Miriams that came after her
since the beginning of time
their ghosts are restless
30   as waves of sand scattered
over the desert.

Their cries split the rock into layers
they rise through it to the topmost hills
for the many Miriams are numerous
35 numerous as the grains of sand.

[c1970s]

Untitled

Lamenting the archaeology of home
it took me three days to make friends
with Paris
Paris the city where the man I loved
5   told me his love was over
the city whose gentle light was darkened
by his strident voice suddenly unfamiliar
black with anger
no matter innocent no matter guilty
10   no matter spring in the square, no matter summer
sun on the balcony milky coffee in white bowls
no matter the sleeping statues awakened—
no matter. My quarrel
with the mild city muddied
15   the waters of springtime
held back by the dam of forgetfulness
loss festered and grew
taller than any towers
imagined anywhere closer
20   closer to my warm home

[c1970s]

Swimming Away
wheeling through water
my hands are fins
             primordial
ferns spastic
5   rubber propellers

             machines
churning
             the green
speech of lace
10   here Neptune
opens his giant hand
laps me in his long
lukewarm sleeves

water whispers
15   a bubbling wall of lace
and my ghostly voice
             against the interface
of dead while tiles cry out
the woes "late too late"
20   all faceless age now gathers up and sings
there is no shining land
Milton's azure shores:
no ebony Egyptian cairn of kings

a waiting world
25   permanent winter:
dead poets here have sunk
their southern spears
deep into sea-sides
their golden axlewheels
30   tilt and speed
from walls
and a ghostly voice commands:

swimmer
       dissolve the grids
35   my open iron seas
escape
       the dread magician
and his empty membrane dolls
      sidetrack murderous
40   clown

     tread water upwards
through the mountains
folds
     of curling darkness
45   slip through his knots
     and ropes:
through swarms of fish
through showers of dead leaves
beat upwards
50   and emerge humble and homeless but alive
     a worm
on city pavements

wheeling still
    in water feel
55 how the touching sun
now turns the lens
of afternoon the tall
workman walking
    an upright swimmer
60 with his rolled-up sleeves: barearmed
and bareheaded; his eyes are
    naked
on my water shield they see
the old cemetery
65   recede in
drowning dreams and the
    razorsmooth
clipped calmness drops
    slowly in ravines
70 yet I wingless
    hang
from ceramic banks
a homeless angel
limply washed ashore
75 by the stiff arm of will
when all I meant was just to swim away
wheel through water
with hands alive fins or fine
primordial ferns

[c1970s]

For Oliver Girling
(with a woolen cap from Newfoundland)

I might Oliver
have brought you a pullover
but the St. John's shops
didn't have tops.

5   So I brought you instead
a thing for your head;
you can maintain
a temperate brain
if you just wrap
10   it up in this cap.

It's extremely plain
that a temperate brain
when the March winds rage
will make you a sage
15   on this wintry day
that you've come of age.

So Happy Birthday

[c1970s]

My Orphan Poems

My fainting (distant) voice
I beg you to wait for me
a week, a month, a year—
just till I've finished
5   this one book review,
just till I've edited
the poems of a great
dead poet, till I've taught the three
more classes I have to teach—
then I promise I will close
10   the door on some grey wintry day to this bare
cluttered room where
we live you and I
my orphan poems
and I will give myself
15   to you utterly
with all my self
all my love
Wait for me. I'm coming. I'll be there in a minute, even if it takes me a year.

[c1970–1983]

Departure from Kashima
(After a Painting by an Unknown Artist on a 14th-Century Scroll)

Departure is the same
everywhere whether it is
you or me leaving home
or a Japanese nobleman
5   sitting on a reindeer
leaving Kashima on an
evening in the fourteenth
century when the moon is high.
He carries his sword
10   at his side and his
household goods are packed
in a saddlebag or hidden
in his wide sleeves.

The painter shows him
15   dressed in travel clothes—
checkered pants, a red cloak,
and a black cap with a feather,
under it his face looks
disconsolate and his beard,
20   lately trimmed by his servant,
is drooping.

The painter also shows
two figures in the foreground,
they are seated beside the road
25   which stretches out
unknown before them,
the men are not friends
but simply townspeople or
beggars hoping for an alms
30   from the departing traveler.

Whoever they are
the painter shows them
small and gradually fading
in their ballooning sleeves;
35   even as we look at them
they grow smaller and smaller
until finally they vanish
in the wake of the nobleman's
departure.

40   Later
the moon will sink
and time will pass,
all traces
of the journey to Kashima
45   will disappear,
the traveler will age
in a distant city,
he will long for home,
he will lose heart
50   and he will learn
slow year by slow year
to be expert in the
melancholy practice
of exile.

[c1980s]

Happy New Year
In September I
send out Jewish
New Year cards
big and fat and
5   flowery as wedding
invitations,
they sing *leshona
tova*, a good year
to you!

10   The envelopes are
wide enough to hold
a whole world or at
least an orchestra,
and a hall full of
15   people crowding their
names into the big
golden book of
the New Year.

I send these fat
20   envelopes to my
old friends; may
their lives be
full of folded
blessings and may
25   the painted bluebirds
sing a dozen verses
of good news from their
biblic Hebrew trees.

And to the dead
30 I send greetings too:
may they tell each other
happy jokes and
enjoy long slow
conversations with God
35 under the daisied
garlands and the blue
canopies of a flawless
prairie heaven.

[c1980s]

Cycles

Every ten years
or so the monarch
butterflies return,
the toad wakes up from
5   his hundred-year sleep,
opens the sliding doors
of his eyes and guards
the garden again.

He pretends he's just
10   a dry wrinkled leaf but
his gesture fools no one,
the milkweed around him
grows riotously and the
dandelions have disappeared,
15   it is not their season.

But the fireflies!
For five years their
lights were out all over
the world and now
20   all of a sudden their
lamps are flaring again
on the shores of
Nova Scotia and the swampy
places on the Bay of Quinte.

25   They say everything
has its season but
sometimes it takes ten
years for the world
to turn full circle,
30   but it does turn and
will turn and summer is
not its only season.

Sometimes in winter
I can hear Beethoven
35 still humming to
himself somewhere above
the chimneys: the sound
of his voice warms me and makes
me feel less lonesome
40 here on earth.

[c1980–1985]

A Garland for Terry
Remember not the pain
It breaks the heart to hear

He was a runner a messenger on wings, brushed with the fragrance of
Early snow he ran with the fire of light.

5   Long before Canada was a
Place or a people, gods
Ruled the earth. One of them, Prometheus, pitied the helplessness and
    suffering of mortal men and women, so
He stole the fire from the gods and gave it to man. For this, Zeus, the
10   king of the gods, punished him by
Chaining him to a rock. There, Prometheus endured his agony for a
    thousand years, until Zeus fell
From power.

Terry Fox relived the myth of Prometheus. In his own
15   Body and spirit, he determined to do something that
Had never been done before—to run from one end of
Canada to the other, a distance of 5300 miles.

On April 12th 1980, Terry dipped his foot into the Atlantic Ocean in
St. John's. Consigning his disease to the sea, he drew energy from that
20   Ancient source and began his marathon.

Remember not the pain
It breaks the heart to hear

Remember how he ran through April's slanting rain: where we heard
    death whistling down the wind—
25   He heard songs.
Their tunes carried him along the line of tides, past marsh grasses and
    the half-open doors of little houses
Built to face the sun; coastal fishermen put down their nets
To smile.

30   From Glovertown to Gambo, from Gander to South Brook Junction, from
     Deer Lake to Cornerbrook, from there to the ferry at
     Port aux Basques. The place names read like a poem. Over the sea to
          Nova Scotia—to Sydney and to Sheet Harbour,
     To Dartmouth and to Springhill, then across to Prince Edward
35   Island, Borden and Charlottetown.

     Charlottetown—a lady of a city with a lace
     Cap and wooden white houses like buttons on
     Her black old bosom.

     But he was homesick. He remembered the
40   Blind Pacific, and his mind curved back
     To Port Coquitlam where the ocean
     Unrolls naked in sunshine.

     The long road to home was still ahead.

     In New Brunswick he ran into a summer of wild
45   Lupins and the drowsy note of bees.
     Past fields and fences he ran, past loneliness, into Quebec, where wheat
          plantings along the river rippled,
     And only the silent air waved flags of greeting.

     From Quebec and the Plains of Abraham he ran to Montreal,
50   To Ottawa, Hamilton and Toronto.
     In the city's offices typewriters froze to a static silence, and in the
          shipping rooms and warehouses that rise
     From Lake Ontario, work stopped. Ten thousand people poured into the
          streets to wait; an old woman crossed
55   Herself, two girls whispered—everywhere the crowds raised vaulted
          voices in celebration.

     They remembered not the pain
     It breaks the heart to hear

     Pain was his prison but he soared above
60   Its walls on strands of transparent air.

Running, he unharnessed birds, jumped over cows, picked plums from
    orchards, crushed strawberries underfoot—
And leaped high as the waters of
Niagara's Fall until he became the
65   Enchanted land of all ourselves.

Then heading north he ran past French River Trading Post through the
    small towns of Ontario
And its clouds of Black Flies,
Companioned always by his friends,
70   And each town's children.

Now came the sad times and the hard times,
The thin times and the crying times, but
Always still the heroic times as he ran
Through all the days of August to the last
75   Exhausted evening in Thunder Bay.

Remember not the pain
It breaks the heart to hear
And build no citadels
Of grief in those caves
80   Of green light where the self is the other,
And the mother is father, where sister is
Brother and single is double, and the
Double is neither.

He was a runner, a messenger on wings; brushed with the fragrance of
85   early snow
He ran with the fire of light.

Terry Fox died June 6, 1981.

1985

To Manitoba Margaret on Her Sixtieth Birthday July 19/86
(with a gift of French lace stockings)

I wish I could mime for you
I wish I could rhyme for you
all your deeds and your times;

It would take rivers of words
5   and skies full of birds
and musical notes
spilling from boats;

As a token instead
I take up this chance
10   to greet you and give
some frou frou from France.

Then all eyes will admire
the mercurial fire
not just of your hand
15   of your heart or your mind—

but of your elegant limbs;
to praise which we'll sing
our secular hymns.

1986

Untitled
(*For My Brother Alex*)

The secret of my brother
lies in his nature & his heart
& there is no other

By nature he was a rebel
5   to my father a very devil
he preferred hockey to school
and freedom to rule
to his brothers he was hero
& helped against their fear o
10   he beat up the big bullies
that chased them after schoolies
to his sister he was older
on a bicycle much bolder
with his friends he was much tougher
15   & like all boys much rougher

He had another side
he always like to hide
he had a lovely tenor
and sang O Sole Mio
20   as well as Away to Rio
& nobody was better
at fixing what was broken
strictly by the letter
but best of all & better
25   his heart would melt like butter
if a friend felt down & seedy
he was there to help the needy
he didn't have a bite
but had a bark so loud
30   you'd hear it in a crowd
best of all & foremost
his heart was like the sun
that shines on Ivory Coast
of this we will not boast
35   but proceed to make a toast
to praise my lovely brother
here's to Alex may he live
in good health another
80 years!

[c1995]

On a Homely Afternoon
Please sit by me
and rehearse tomorrow
what we will say
each to each
5   as time passes
we meet in sleep
a walk beside the beach.

Come in and
have some tea
10   a meal with me
the lines don't show
and if they do
I'm beautiful
within.

15   The trembling begins
and look at him
he wants to smile
I pretend I'm Japanese
and softly titter
20   because my gums
will show.

My hair is falling
out you know,
I think I'll buy a wig.
25   The tea is cold.
You had better go
His quiet feet,
on streets below,
reveal relief.

[c1990s]

Untitled

Sometimes I imagine us
in our old age
putting on a record
of Chopin looking at
5   the apple tree
outside our window
expecting our children
and children's children
for a meal

[c1990s]

Some of Them Wonder

I suppose
some of them wonder
what an old poet
like her can have
5   to say these days.

Not much:
but she knows about
sunbursts
those explosions
10   of wrinkles
fanning out from
under the nose
fanning up from
over the breasts
15   and a new discovery—
lines rocketing
across the vertical
of the cheeks.

She knows all about
20   sunbursts and how
life flows away
through those radiating
channels in slow
25   measure as it hurries her
down the long slope
the steep gradient
of death.

[c1990s]

Untitled
How bitter it is
in my old age
to have only the cares
of my children
5   to feel my long ago
lost girlhood
as alien to me
as a top spinning
on the cliff's edge
10   and toppling over; who cares?
to feel the carefully laid out
lawns of summer
are green corpses lying
in suburban coffins
15   everything now reminds me
of cemeteries
where though it is everywhere you never
actually see death

[c1990s]

Untitled

I am addressed to you
(like it or not) your
mother;
already
5   a part of me has been
dispatched by the slow
freight years
from now you'll find it
on your doorstep
10   ragged parcel of
legacies. It contains
a complete misunderstanding
of the world,
an empty
15   darkness, a noisemaker
full of grief to rattle at the feast
four weeks before Passover
when the winter's deep and fast
and has us gripped in soot
20   when it was your grandfather's
birthday
(but Haman is not
dead) rather the
comedian merely a bad actor
25   with no talent for deceit
what's the use just untie the
parcel put me on like
clothes from childhood
that still fit you smile my
30   smile

[c1990s]

Untitled
Instead of swallows nesting & flying
in the carport
I have my perilous journeys
across endless bridges
on narrow causeways
and at home
strange cats prowl
the patio

There are no songs
humming sunlight against
my windows
instead my wintry barren self
surrounded by beautiful cold things
erasing the history of my summers
& leaving layers
of piled up years
that slide down towards
endings and
nothingness

I try to be cheerful
to write bravely
about death and
about old age, nothingness
but it isn't poetic

[c1990s]

Undone Things

I will die fat and busy,
never having had time
to work out a diet
do exercise
5   or organize my papers

When I die
all my unfiled papers
will fly out of their baskets
and mourn me with inky tears

10   The books I promised to read and review
will grow arms and legs
rise up from my desk
and from the funeral procession
they will stand over my grave
15   sighing—but you promised

And I did promise,
I intended to keep my promises
I really wanted to read them all
and write about them all
20   but when you're dead
you certainly can't spend time
just reading even if you wanted to
it's too cold and dark.

I never baked the cakes or answered the letters
25   I wanted to, or tried out
the recipes my friends gave me
or visited all the mothers
of my friends
who were in old age homes

30   I never sewed all the beautiful silk
     I bought thinking that sometime I'd make a dress
     I know I'll never do it now
     I'll just die being fat and busy
35   I suppose I should be glad if it works out that way.

     [c1990s]

Ecology
September,
I look at the garden
hurben Yerushalyim!
All the leftovers
of summer—
5   the munched-up flowers
and bitten-off leaves
all mixed into a ragged
autumn casserole.

Well, I suppose
10   even slugs have to eat
something,
I'm just glad
they aren't eating me.

[c1990s]

Who Listens to Poets

Old people no longer listen to poets
they are glad if they can walk in warm sun,
middle-aged people have no time for it,
they are dedicated
5   to getting the most out of life,
only they have not decided what it is
that is most, or where to find it;
and young people never ever listened
to the poets.

10   Poets listen to themselves and other poets,
they listen to the trees who bend and lean
they hear the opening of earth's age-old wound,
and stand in the bare gardens covering their eyes,
they know, they know, death comes to everyone,
15   but why does it come decking its skeleton
in colored leaves, and wind the winey light?

How do people learn to grow old,
how do they learn to take each death's
visitation? how do they learn to find enough
20   in warm sunlight, and live on thinned out love?
how do they hear the northern tempered speech
of oldness, forgive the shameful gold
of these last leaves, or learn an outward peace
within their smaller reach?

25   They do not learn age, we make a treaty with it:
peace with this life, with years, with failing breath,
peace with the eternal loss of the beloved,
and peace with the slow oncomingness of death.

[c1990s]

The Collected Poems
of Miriam Waddington
TRANSLATIONS—SELECTED

YIDDISH TRANSLATIONS

Anonymous

Jewish Folk Song
For Dov Noy—Gatherer of Folk Songs

Note: This is probably a father speaking since only a father gives a dowry.
He also says bei mir—meaning chez nous, at my home. He uses the past tense
in addressing the girl.

I have a daughter of eighteen
a prettier girl you've never seen.

Don't convert my darling child
and I'll give you a dowry like Rothschild

5   Leather shoes at home you wore
with Stephan you will scrub the floor;

With me you studied books I gave
with Stephan you'll study in the grave;

I have a daughter of eighteen
10   a prettier girl you've never seen

alt. last couplet:
I have a daughter of eighteen
a darker beauty you've never seen.

(undated)

Jacob Glatstein (1896–1971)

Yizkor

Always new and forever present
are the cries of our dead cities,
and morning dew is fresh and blooming
while in the graveyards of our twilight exile,
5   the words of our prayers are always newly minted
and even our ancient funeral pleas
echo with the newness of today—
(how petty now seems the death of merely one person!)

The martyred death of our millions is legendary;
10 despite their death we live and are re-born
for they gave us life.
Although they died they forced the ghetto gates to open
and kept us proud and safe from slavery—
they gave us faith.

15 If not for their shining sacrifice
we would all have died a shameful death
without revenge or solace and bereft of hope;
it wasn't just to entertain their captors
that our blind Samsons broke their ranks;
20 they fought to punish crime.

And not just in secret guerrilla skirmishes
or out of hidden bunkers tense with fear,
not separately but united in a brave convoy
did our brothers signal their revolt;
25 even the timid became courageous—
and the enemy paid.

Brothers, let us now inscribe them
in a modern *machzor* and invent a new prayer book;
compared to theirs all the martyrdoms of history
30 are hereby cancelled and will count as nothing;
evil cannot hold the reins and rule the world
as long as we remember them and hear their cries
on every road.

In all our prayers let us remember them
35   in every memorial let us mourn them,
with every *yisgadal* let them be recognized,
and may they bless all our *hatikvahs* with their light.

(1990)

N. Y. (Noyekh Yitskhok) Gotlib (fl 1930s–1940s)

Singing

I shall go on singing until I die,
What more than song is left to me?
On the autumn strings of quivering grass
The hungry wind plays hauntingly.

5 October sun melts to copper
And pains the tree-tops metal-bright,
A leaf drops and nourishes
The barren famished earth.

Distance aflame with the setting sun,
10 My heart's red flag to you I send,
What more than song is left to me?
I shall sing to the end.

(undated)

Chaim Grade (1910–1982)

The Overcoat

A strange overcoat follows me, collar turned up,
sleeves empty—it tries to strangle me—
a coat with its owner missing, like those sarcophagii
dug up on rusty sites of ruins, or like
5   torsos without legs, shoulders without arms,
or the marble corner of some broken effigy:
this empty collar forever blocks my way,
a headstone, reminder from the graves.

The overcoat was mine, felt my mother's tears
the time she said goodbye to me for good;
10   and now it follows me, its glazed immobile eyes,
like the rain of eyes inside the ghetto walls,
stare from my bedclothes like frozen fish in ice,
and the dangling sleeves, once so stroked and loved
by quiet hands, now thrash about and wail:
15   "Why did you forsake us, give us to the dead?"

But the ghetto was dead; dead and waiting burial,
spread out and scattered over seven shabby streets,
I felt clouds of fog like chloroform engulf me
until my coat was soaked with rain from all dead eyes,
20   I was the only one left in all those ghetto alleys
and when I touched a cobblestone I touched the dead,
the cobbles were human skulls, not stones at all,
the faces earthen, the foreheads soft with weeds.

No rain that falls can wash away my dead ones:
25   the washing raindrops fell like surrealist eyes,
until stuff that was a pillow for my wandering
turned hard and bristly as a wildboar skin;
it may be rain can lighten marks of murder
those victims cried their wrong above the dark
30   until I told myself: "I'll just cover them up,
quiet them with my overcoat: and then I'll go."

Since then my overcoat keeps dogging me, reminding:
"I am the last witness of your murdered home,
you thought to put your memories behind you
35   to leave me rotting in those seven ghetto streets?
But can a tree stripped of its bark survive and grow?
Without me you are dead: embalmed: and do not know.
The ghetto lies there dead, and still is waiting burial;
and I your overcoat am waiting on my heap of rubble.

(undated)

Rokhl Korn (1898–1982)

The Beginning of a Poem
It is fear, it is threat not to speak of,
It is standing on the threshold of pain,
It is the figure that looms in the doorway,
Shadowy, funereal, and gray.

5   It is genesis of firstness, the always,
It is the torrent that sweeps you away,
And makes you forsake all your dear ones
To welcome an awesome new love.

And all because some eagle-flying notion
10   Has seized you in its cruel sharp claws,
And holds you captive and torments you
To the last boundary of your breath

Until your blood is ready for the sacrifice;
Now nothing can save you from the angel's sword,
15   And nothing prevent your final going under
Except a lucky rhyme or somersaulting word.

Then all grows silent in your deepest self,
You hear the sound of every falling star,
And you become a delicate earthen vessel
20   Filled with the transparent flow of tears.

And you imagine: suddenly the world has ripened,
And earth is mother to the lonely wanderer's step,
God himself, you think, would have to worship
This ultimate, ecstatic, perfect moment—

25   And this is only the beginning of a poem.

(1982)

An Evening in the Old People's Home

Under the pillars of the broad balcony,
on chairs set out in rows
as if upon an open stage
the old people sit with folded hands.
5   They are like wax figures all set to pose
for twilight, whenever it arrives,
with its brush and palette, ready to paint
each one's singular portrait.

Their white heads are framed with wild grief
10 are like those coins of snow that winter leaves behind
as casually as a tip for the fresh green of grass.

Words are as lean and dry and bare
as the days and nights of these old people;
they chew the cud of memory in the long hours
15 while everything they ever knew or were
recedes beyond the furthest reach of distance.

They yawn, they sigh, and throw a few brief glances
at the street once faithful and familiar,
once packed with laughter and the shouts of children—
20 that was before the street joined all the other streets
in search of new suburban districts—
that was long before it left them here
with the *Moshev Zkeynim*, the Old People's Home,
like so many unclaimed pawn tickets
25 among the patched-up crumbling houses.

Now spring floats towards the balcony
carrying the scent of lilac and of jasmine flowers,
the hands of the old people, cradled in their laps,
clasp and unclasp, while their thoughts
30 rock, and rock, and keep on rocking
the sleepless emptiness of night.

(1989)

The Housemaid

The orchards of her home
still blossom in her glances
and in her dreams great flocks
of geese are feathered;
5   she used to drive baby geese
to the pond every spring
and guard them from the
crows and owls but now
for days she walks around
10   bewildered and her whole
body greedily drinks in
the fragrance from the new-cut
wood piled up by the stove
ready for burning.

15   Her faraway home was so
beautiful but it was a small
farm poor and rocky and
there were seven mouths
to feed so she the oldest
20   came to the city and here
her two hands are now the oars
which row her life through
dark and steamy kitchens.

When she gets a letter
25   from the neighbor's son
she runs to strangers
hanging on their glances,
first she reads their faces
for goodwill then begs them
30   quietly to read her letter,
to tell her all they
must tell all   all that
he has written! Then she
sees their scornful smiles
35   at his loutish crudely formed
letters which for her contain
the alphabet of love,
and she blushes, hides her face
for shame.

40   All week long her heart
composes answers until
at last it's Sunday and
the words are put down
beside each other like
45   invalids on pink paper
decorated with doves
and wreaths of roses.
Her girl friend scribbles
the words in a hurry then
50   reads out whatever was
dictated ending with
kisses and respectfully
yours; she smiles fleetingly
and in the corners of her mouth
55   lurk the shy love words
she has nursed all week
and there they hover
captive and unspoken.

Sometimes in an hour of rest
60   she opens her old prayer book
with a gold cross embossed
on its black cover; with awkward
hands she caresses the strange
letters, words full of God
65   and love and mercy and her eyes
grow dreamy thinking about
the miraculous world of A B C.

The world she knows
is tied in a thousand knots,
70   even the world of her prayer book
with its circles and lassos
is like some Judas: treacherous:
ready to sell her in a minute
for thirty hard days
75   labor in every month.

(1969)

Nuns Who Saved Jewish Children

They are God's eternal brides,
These grass widows of the Holy Ghost,
Yet He seldom visits or brings news
Of their Mother Mary's grieving love.

5   They know Mary's downcast eyes
Only from the murals in their church,
Their own motherhood is parched and withered
And shrivels in their hands from drought.

But sometimes they escape on summer nights
10   Their fast of strictness and forget to pray,
Or hear the tapping of a child's hands
Against the locked doors of their cloistered hearts.

Then when morning comes and calls them all to penance
On convent floors laid out in brick and stone,
15   Their hair-shirts sting and stir the traces
Of all their dreams and hidden secret doubts.

And so in the hour when angels roam the world,
And mercy knocks at every gentle gate,
The nuns' hearts surely burst asunder
20   With the birth of a new kind of God,

And their billowing trailing robes—
Black waterfalls pouring through a wind—
Cool the shameful fires of Treblinka
And soothe a Jewish child's fevered head.

25   The homeless child's smile draws the sky
With all its light into their gloomy cells,
Their shy motherhood is fed and nourished
By the hunger of the child's starving hands.

When the nuns kneel down again to pray
30   Their words walk barefoot through the smoking ruins,
Their murmurous voices rise, grow luminous,
And light the darkness of a Jewish mother's grave.

(1967)

Mani Leib (pseudonym of Mani Leib Brahinsky, 1883–1953)

Seven Brothers
Of seven brothers
with gray eyes
and with blue eyes
three are tall as
5   palm trees sinewy
and proud and upward-
looking and three
stand low as sugar
canes sweet-rooted
10   firm upon the
earth and I the
singer of this
song hang like a
green willow
15   between winds.

And now the father
of us all is dead:
our woe, our woe!
he dwindled like
20   a thin oak in a
receding landscape
and on that
sad and rainy day
his seven sons
25   arose from fog
and with hands
filled with rain
we covered our
father's eyelids
30   with the black
shards of death:
then all of us
helped shovel the
red clay of Long
35   Island over his
coffin.

And afterwards
the seven of us
put up a wooden
40   marker on his grave
and then like a clump
of trees caught
suddenly in an alarm
of wind our forest-
45   voices shook with
one lament, the single
prayer we sent up
for the dead:
yisgadal!

50   On the rainy day
our father died we
seven brothers with
gray and blue and sorrowing
eyes said our last
55   good-byes: we parted
on the outskirts
of New York
and each one of seven
went his solitary way
60   on one of seven
solitary avenues.

(1969)

Itsik Manger (1901–1969)

Auld Lang Syne: New Year's Eve
We sing auld lang syne together
and warmly join hands
the wine in the glass burns crimson
. and the light from the mirror blinds.

5   I raise my voice for auld lang syne
though my eyes are swollen and red
I sing with you but my hands are joined
to the hands of six million dead.

(1987)

Ballad of the Dying Christopher Marlowe

Who is that frenzied creature
with the wild dishevelled hair?
Who brings to Marlowe's deathbed
the poet's secret fear?

5   Marlowe mutters darkly
it's that monster Jew alas,
I recognize his shuffling step,
what brings you Barabbas?

The silent figure flashes
10   a dagger bright as flame
he bends and whispers to him:
I've come to avenge my name!

Years ago you dreamed me
while fuzzy with women and wine,
15   and now I'm at your deathbed
to make your last night mine!

(The December wind is blowing
three ravens against the door,
three ravens against the window
20   tap out n e v e r m o r e)

The poet moans in fever
my dream has come to pass!
I dread your fiery beard your eyes
and your vengeance Barabbas!

25   The apparition trembles
his answer chokes with pain:
while I studied to serve God
you lied that I served Mammon!

To you I'm a road uncharted
30   a forest shrouded in night
to God I'm the gentle dove of prayer
who rejoices in his might.

The December night blows bitter,
black and icy and sharp,
35   it swells into a funeral dirge
on Marlowe's wild harp.

(The December wind is blowing
three ravens against the door,
three ravens against the window
40   tap out n e v e r m o r e)

(1987)

Evening
Evening's barefoot monk
descends from the church on the hill
his long shadow falls
across the empty market place.

5   The turtledoves in the dovecote
murmur to each other sleepily
and our house breathes the peace
and piousness
of ryebread and evensong.

(1980)

Fairy Tales
Beggars in the stories of old
wandered ragged up and down
from town to village, back to town,
from one house to another.

5   And the stories always ended
with the children being told
how the beggars were rewarded
with crowns of purest gold.

(1980)

Fate

Me was once a wild boy
long ago in Galilee,
threw burrs at old man Moses' beard,
snowballs at Jesus from a tree.

5   Now Moses temples in New York,
and Jesus is the Lord of they,
while me is still a wild boy
with head of woe and lackaday.

(1987)

Night
I stole the little cross
(your sister-in-law's gift)
and buried it in the garden
under the full moon's light.

5   Suddenly: listen, a skirt rustles
everything breathes: danger!
and beside me rises the night
like a young nun trembling with anger.

(1990)

Quiet Garden
For Mani Leib

The gravedigger says:
look how my garden grows
I weed it faithfully
day in day out
5   and lay a wreath
upon each burial mound.

But this that I sing to you
is no death song,
it's the real thing
10   like it's supposed to be:
a quiet cemetery
in plain moonlight
where the worm crawls its path
and the firefly knows his way;

15   Where fear the black bat
swollen with the night
flies through villages
calling at every house
and flaps his wings with
shuddering cries of grief;

20   Then fear enters my song,
this place of ordered quiet,
becomes a stillness
among the other stillnesses
and in this garden's quiet
25   all cries of grief are stilled.

(undated)

Under the Ruins of Poland

Under the ruins of Poland
lies my fair-haired love,
her dead face, my fallen city,
are more real to me than love.
5   *My fate, my sorrow.*

The squire's pretty wife
confessed her trifling sins,
she wakened the next morning
new, redeemed, and cleansed.
10   *My fate, my sorrow.*

Across the ruins of Poland
the snow lies thick and deep,
but the headache of my darling
will not mend with sleep.
15   *My fate, my sorrow.*

Her death sits down beside me
to write letters to the world,
but words to tell her suffering
are worn-out and cold.
20   *My fate, my sorrow.*

Above the ruins of Poland
a hawk flies high and stays,
that bird of giant darkness
shadows all my days.
25   *My fate, my sorrow.*

That bird of huge ill-omen
has seized my heart its prey,
to carry the sad tidings
of this song, eternally,
30   *My fate, my sorrow.*

(Under the ruins of Poland
lies my fair-haired love,
her dead face, my fallen city,
are more real to me than love.
35   *My fate, my sorrow.*)

(1979)

Perets Markish (1895–1952)

From An Elegy for Shlomo Mikhoels

Snow covers the wounds on your face;
Darkness cannot harm you now,
Even in death your anger lights your eyes,
And accusation bursts your broken heart.

5   "Immortality, I cross your dishonored threshold
With the mark of murder written on my face—
It's the badge of my people in one-sixth of the world—
The sign of hatred—remember it!"

"Read well these traces, inscribe them in your soul,
10   We all like to deny the suffering of the past—
Know that every mark on this battered face
Stands for a mother and child who resisted death!"

Mikhoels, the hand of hate was withered by your love,
Snow will never drift across to blind your eyes
15   That speak to us and cry aloud your anger,
Which rises mountainous, and shatters Russian skies.

***

Sleep peacefully, Mikhoels, the sleep beyond all sorrow
Even in death your sharp mind flashes fire,
The stars of justice, watchful, guard your sleep,
20   And Levi Yitshak's song is in our ears.

Must brightness die because the world is darkness?
How high must snowdrifts drift to bury woe?
Your hands are blessings like two holy candles,
And light the Jewish ark of long ago.

25   You used to close your eyes and ponder,
An act that made your clamorous thoughts be still,
Now you've closed your eyes against grief forever
To spare the ark the sacrilege of tears.

The empty mirror pulses, flows around you,
30   As if you stood there, making up for a play—
I see your lips unfold—and look, they're moving!
Your own words rise, and lift you to the sky!

(1972)

Melekh Ravitch (pseudonym of Zekharye-Khone Bergner, 1893–1976)

To a Poet Who Wrote about Jewish Persecution

The poet reads lines about slaughter,
we applaud him with might and with main,
then a thin autumn smile like sun after rain
spreads over his face concealing his pain.

5   As one to a man, the audience roars:
Encore, read us your piece about blood, Jewish Blood!
The poet obliges and thinks to himself
in the Creator's own words: *ki tov, all is good.*

But there's still a third party to this wretched affair—
10   the corpses themselves; with clanging applause   .
that sounds, in truth, like nothing on earth,
they come rattling their skulls and their claws.

As if this isn't enough, the corpse entourage
encircles our poet (sweet minstrel of slaughter),
15   they refuse to stop clapping and even their feet
pick up the rhythm and beat it out hotter.

The audience is startled; in a failure of nerve
people rush from the hall without taking their coats,
while running, the wives yell out to their men:
20   *Do you call this a reading, you stupid old goats!*

Haven't we suffered from Hitler enough,
Must we suffer from our own Jewish poets as well,
who drag into reciting their poems on slaughter
a fine bunch of corpses straight out of hell?

25   The poet is left alone on the stage,
and slowly recovers his breath,
he thanks all the powers of rhyme and of time
that he hasn't been crushed quite to death.

Those who know the poetic tradition,
30   know that death in a poem is sweet,
so we leave our hero, the poet,
to be trampled by his own metric feet.

(1988)

What More Do You Want

What more do you want, what's coming to you
That you whine and buzz like a bee?
You don't like it here—well you came from somewhere
So you can just go back where you came from.

5   See here, comrade, you've a mind I am sure,
You write poems for Jews, are an artist as well,
So you know what it means I suppose
To get into God's side-show on a free ticket.

They keep pointing out local miracles,
10 Wonders of the sun, of the moon, and of what not?
Summers, winters, and springtimes and autumns,
And crowds of gorgeous women made for love.

So what do you want, eternal life or forever theatre?
When given an inch why must you take a yard?
15 You're putting the whole writing profession to shame,
You'll soon have the whole world laughing at us.

After all, you aren't God's one and only son,
There's quite a line-up and the seats are few;
There are no non-stop shows in this world of ours,
And shortest of all is the one-act play called life.

20 The Lord has shown you his finest stage sets,
You'd be better off doing a quick about-face
Whirling yourself into the dizzy space
On the Saturnalian carrousel of the world;

Or are you in love with zero? Earth is God's theatre
25 He owns no better, this is the best He can do,
So shove off, brother, drop dead! For you
The play is over, be a gentleman

Show your manners and take a bow,
Say "thank you for the pleasure" and say it loud;
30   Then wait for the stone to be tied round your neck
And the final shove into the last abyss.

(undated)

J. I. (Yankev Yitskhok) Segal (1896–1954)

At My Wedding
At my wedding
a red-haired madman fiddled
on the smallest gentlest little fiddle;
he played his sweet lament
5   and fabled song
while other fiddlers watched in dumb amazement.

Where did he learn it,
this red-haired simpleton?
When you consider that he lived and worked
10   in backward villages,
and played only at drunken gentile brawls;
if you can picture it, he could hardly
scratch together a handful of holy words—
not even to save himself.
15   As for sleeping, he bedded on a wooden bench,
and if a servant
gave him radishes from the master's garden,
he was fed.

It was at my wedding this poor devil played,
20   no one could stand still, yet all were rooted
ears in the air like pointed spears
while the little fiddle tenderly caressed
and fiercely scored the people,
tore them to bits, flayed them and drew blood
25   to all their veins
until strung as taut as violin strings
the old folk, doddering, cried out for mercy.

(1962)

Aunt Dvorah

Our only aunt called Dvorah
Has gone and left us too,
And on her grave is carved a small Menorah
And on each side a slender stalk of wheat.

5   That is how the stonecutter Reb Nachem
Worked it out, and in between, her name;
We stand and gaze into religious silence
As from our lips there falls a last amen.

No member of her family survived her,
10   Her comely daughters, Esther and Hadassah,
Were lost in the great burning
Beyond the ghetto walls, in some side street.

And when they brought them home to her
Their bodies raped and spoiled, well do I recall
15   How Dvorah clamped her mouth in iron silence
And sat, held in its bitter vise for days.

Widening her sorrow by their narrow graves
Our auntie used to sit, and in the evenings take
Her children's clothes and thoughtfully caress
20   Their measure; then shivering and bleak

She'd close the trunk and draw over face
A darkness deeper than cavernous wastes
Of empty cupboards and more desolate
Than all those hangers peeled and bare.

(1960)

The Great Truth

A great truth is hidden in the world
which all of us would like to find,
one with swift and angry force,
another with his burning mind.

5   A third relies on hope and prayer,
on faith in God, regard for man,
and all his acts are touched with joy,
truth is his neighbor everywhere.

But I and all my brother poets
10   seek truth in syllables and words,
we hear it sound its golden bell
occasional in nouns and verbs.

Then there comes the scoundrel doubt
to scoff and ask, how long how long
15   will poets wait outside a door
that can not open to their song?

All of us grow blank with fear,
but most of all, that rascal, doubt;
he slinks away and hides himself,
20   where none of us can find him out.

(undated)

A Jew

My comrades are all such travellers
buzzing around in planes,
with one look they take the measure
of the wide bend of the sky.

5   If they have breakfast in Montreal
they drink coffee in New York,
of course that's all very grand,
even wonderful—but also queer.

Theirs are pleasures I renounce
10   especially on rainy days
when I can sit down beside the window
and think about an old wayside inn;

And how a cart full of Hasidim
drove up there late one night
15   and changed the simple little inn
to a beautiful palace;

And how the small band of faithful
sat around the wooden table
as radiant as if they were gathered
20   in the corridors of heaven.

Later I couldn't even remember
the Torahs and Haggadahs
but my heart is still full
of sweet worshipful longing.

25   It's no use my turning east
and it's no use my praying west,
I'm forever on the road, in transit,
dragging my baggage of exile.

That world is all gone now,
30   there's no monument to mark it,
and the only leaf left from the deluge
is a page in a Yiddish book.

So what is the leaf's green message
what stories does it bring?
35   only that a tree stood on the road
lighted by a single star.

The tree is still standing there
with the little star on its branch,
and it shines so strangely on the road
40   and the tree too has grown strange;

But it survives, my Jewish tree,
like a talisman of homecoming
and it longs to gather all us Jews
from our spaceless boundaries of loss.

(1969)

Late Autumn in Montreal

The worm goes back to the earth
the wind glitters and sharpens his sword;
where did all the colored leaves fly
to, anyway? The branches are all locked
5   in a vise of sleep; the skies aspire
to climb higher, their clear-blue
washes over the rooftops and stillness
assures us that all is well.

Our churchy city becomes even more pious
10   on Sundays, the golden crosses shine and gleam
while the big bells ring with loud
hallelujahs and the little bells answer
their low amens; the tidy peaceful streets
lie dreaming in broad daylight murmuring
15   endearments to me who am such a Yiddish Jew
that even in my footsteps they must hear
how the music of my Yiddish song sounds
through the rhythm of my Hebrew prayer.

(1960)

Late Summer in Montreal

Mount Royal, our mountain king,
our forest legend, our huge village
city, today grows soft and mild,
the streetcars run peacefully
on polished wire strings, relax
on quiet tracks; today is Sunday
and in all the houses the windows
shine new-washed, the grey half-
yellow balconies are settled
with colonies of summer life and
the sound of radios floats like
prayers above hundreds of little
pagodas, interpreting chapter and
verse, preaching devotion and
well-being: a distant organ
pretends Mendelssohn, but it's
really Tehilim, and there below
in the poorest section of St. Dominique
.street weariness and worry have been
tossed aside like old women who
lean against brick walls and doze
in endless light; even the stone
brewery is locked behind high gates
and only at the back entrance
in the dirty alley its light
still burns, yellow and sad;
day or night the light bulb never
sleeps, is always watching and
awake, always distilling
its Monday morning spirit.

(1967)

Old Montreal

There's an old back street in Montreal
That was once the center of town,
Now the stone walls are yellow and burnt out,
And there's a broken-down church which God forsook

5   When he moved away to a new cathedral;
Yet whenever I walk that way
I imagine I hear ghostly bells ringing
Behind those ash-grey walls.

A little way down is an oblong cemetery
10   With small headstones, and smack in the middle
Stands a tall stained marble column
Keeping its long watch.

Not far away is the harbor market
With high buildings, wooden and blind,
15   And you can see a dirty red flag
Hung out for no reason at all, teasing the wind.

Between these narrow streets and glimpsing walls
The chimney of a dockside ship pokes out,
And a midday thread of smoke goes curling up
20   As from some cosy little winter house.

(1960)

Rhymes

Two respectable rhymes
skipped out of their pages
like two proud roosters
from golden cages;

5   They walked many a mile
in search of a home,
but could find no space
for themselves in a poem.

They grew tired and sad
10   but wherever they went
nobody advertised
poems for rent.

People whispered and said:
haven't you heard
15   that a rhyming word
is considered absurd?

In modern times
who needs rhymes?
Those high-flying words
20   went out with the birds.

At last one night
all weary and worn
they came to a house
in a field of corn;

25   and there lived a man
who still wrote lines
according to rules
from olden times.

So he took them in
30   with doubles and pairs,
and set them to music,
and gave them new airs.

Now they ring again
their bells and chimes,
35   and the children all sing
those respectable rhymes,

with one rhyme inside
and another one out:
the rhymes were befriended
40   and my poem is ended.

(1968)

Scenario

The enemy returns
home to his German village,
and the white blossom on the tree
waves to him, bends to him,
5   smiles to him, "Welcome!"

His dog jumps up to meet him
and trembles with recognition,
and all around him lie his fields
as fresh and frank as summer.

10 In the doorway of his house
waits the housewife, pale and dear,
lost in the joyous pulse of dream
she stands rooted and still as a bird.

He runs towards her
15 and she falls into his arms;
all is husband and wife between them,
together they enter their warm house.

But I, who the German enemy destroyed
in seed and root, in branch and bud,
20 whose last living child he has killed,
and whose native city he has bent
from its ancient Polish pride—

I am the one who in my rags,
my ribbons, and my pure bright hate,
25 remain outside, and like a beaten cur
I must watch and see

How these German trees still celebrate
the summer's whiteness, and German fields
submit their earth to the sharpened plough,
30 while in the barn German horses

Bear German colts, silky and fair,
which German lads will mount and ride
possessing July and the burning sun
between fertile forests of wheat and rye.

35   And Jewish children? Sealed within winds
are their quenched ashes and desolate crumbs;
and only the emptiness of street
will remember and miss them, and only
the echoing cobblestones will weep.

40   I know they will not ever be transformed
to innocence, they will never be
angels astride on palominos
in a blossoming heaven; they will never be such
as tumble though fields and gamboling, shout,
45   "Welcome!" around the feet of God.

(1960)

Teaching Yiddish

The children from my neighborhood
all come to me to learn Yiddish:
I tell them not to open their books,
I want to look at them and read
5 their faces as if they were pages
in a book; I want to know and be known,
so this is how I talk to them
without ever saying a word.

Dear boys and girls, Yiddish sons
10 and daughters, I want to teach you
what you've come to study but first
I have to learn how to read you I
have to write you and describe you
as you are and I don't really want
15 to be your teacher but an older
brother; so what shall we do?

First I think I'll read a story
by Sholem Aleichem just to see how much
you know about Yiddish laughter.
20 If you can laugh with real Yiddish flavor
at one of Sholem Aleichem's stories
I won't need further proof;
you'll do well with chumish in Yiddish,
and even with gemorah in Yiddish,
25 and with literature naturally—
in what but Yiddish?

But you're laughing already
Even before we get to Sholem Aleichem's
Motl Paisie the Cantor's son:
30 so today we're having our first lesson
in Yiddish laughter and all around me
shine your open faces and your lively eyes;
so let's tackle Sholem Aleichem head on
and go into a huddle of laughter.

(1969)

Zusman Segalovich (1884–1948)

Fragment from Ash

We the descendants of ash felled by misfortune,
. my generation will never sleep in peace—
my generation who has been marked forever—
after so much death, how can we have faith?
5   How poor you are in power, oh my people,
and how rich in sorrow, sainted and mute . . .
So gather your sorrows and portion them out
from world to world to the furthest reaches,
inscribe them with blood in our record's pages,
10   assign them to all generations past and future,
assign them to all, for this burden of pain
is too heavy for a single generation to bear.

My generation doesn't even know the *yahrzeit* of its fathers,
or who was killed where, or when, and behind what bars,
15   or who was burned when, and who devoured by dogs;
I'm alive and I don't want to know anything different.
I only want to stretch out on the ground and listen
for the ashes to move or to stir or to rustle—
the ashes of millions; then maybe I'll hear
20   some far stifled sound; I'll go searching and tapping
until maybe I'll find, oh maybe I'll find
some leftover bone of a Yankel or Shaindl,
or some child's finger that never got burned;
I'll keep it and cherish it, enfolding it deep,
25   in the heart of my prayers forever and ever.

(1990)

Sholem Shtern (1907–1990)

Blood-stained Roses
Shadows creep
Through wailing dawns,
And the heavens weep;
The Jewish village, emptied of people,
5   Is a chaos and nothingness;
So what good is it to you, my Lord and Creator,
To have such an empty world?
How can anything holy be at peace
In such a desolate dead stillness?
10   I will ask you, in the words of Reb Meyer, the chassid,
"Lord of all the world, how now? Nu?
What are they waiting for, up there, in heaven,
Maybe until I, Reb Meyer, will become old and gray?"

(undated)

Moyshe Teyf (1904–966)

Spring Greetings
Hello
    hello!
Listen to me
    I'm telephoning you
5   good people all over the world!
Surely you can tell
    just from my voice
that I'm in a first-class
top-of-the-morning mood;
10 and it's all because he's coming
he's on his way at last—
the first unbelievable day
    of spring!

And with his hand he's lifting
15 a winebeaker full of sun
and with his voice he's chanting
    l'chaym brieder!
L'chaym chaverim!
Drink drink all you tired old
20   grandfathers
drink up, all you rascally young
    grandsons!
And everybody say after me
    as I recite
25 the writer's joyous blessing:
springtimes of the world, unite!

(undated)

GERMAN TRANSLATIONS

Otto Rank (1884–1939)

School for Preparing

I unharness the clumsy horses of my mind
From the plough of prose and in their place
I harness a pair of light poetic prancers,
And look at them, they are winged too!
5   Come on, let's fly to the sun!
My nervous racers neigh and seem to mock me,
They paw the ground with delicate distaste:
"Do you really think this clowning with Pegasus
Will bring you closer to the distant Muse?

10   No man commands the creatures of Pegasus,
Whoever dares it pays for the attempt,
And do you want us to call you Master?
Then take a second look; we are not real."
"Say nothing more: your threats do not unnerve me,
15   I'm using you to help me towards the real,
And when I mount you, flyers of Pegasus,
At least you carry me in the right direction."
And if I should ever mount the true Pegasus,
I would not hesitate nor be afraid,
20   I would have learned from my journeying
How to rein imaginary horses, and that to ride
What seems unreal is only to come closer
To the heart of everything where all is real.

(1966)

Weltschmerz: Lines before Breakfast
Dedicated to myself on my nineteenth birthday

This morning I walked through the city
Sick in my heart and my soul,
I longed to be blind to the world,
To all but the ground at my feet.

5   Then my eyes flew suddenly upward,
Pulled by a magical force,
And my glance was arrested and nailed
To a bleak little black sign.

As I stood there, intent and bewildered
10   The inscription slowly grew clear,
And I read—alas that I read it—
"Headquarters: cremation committee."

Poor heart, what are you listening to?
Can you hear death composing lullabies?
15   Or laden with sorrow, do you feel
The pangs of longing in those printed words?

(1966)

RUSSIAN TRANSLATIONS

Rimma Fyodorovna Kazakova (1932–2008)

Under the Roof in My House
Under my roof in my house
in the same green city street
a man killed in the war
lives out his years beside me.

5   This war ended long ago
the man was finished too,
he still gets up in the morning,
shaves, walks, eats, and drinks.

He chews his cutlet carefully,
10   he lives but has no life,
the doctors are ruthless, they say
they can do nothing.

His eyes are transparently empty
they light on his uniform
15   where the medals shine like ikons
the only things war left to me.

He was such a fine Cossack,
with native shrewdness in his eyes,
he had the firm grip of a soldier
20   and the soft cheek of a father.

Dear father, dear comrade,
you are not old yet—
we could have had good times together
played foolish games,
25   done all sorts of things.

But in that sad war in a
foreign land so faraway now,
in an anonymous battle
you died for your country.

30   What will comfort me? Nothing,
        let me do up your coat for you,
        let me help you downstairs, let me
        find you a bench in the park.

        My father takes leave of me,
35   he stares after me for a long time:
        I know
                what to do
                        how to live;

        I know
40   what to hate
                        what to love.

        (1975)

Robert Ivanovich Rozhdestvensky (1932–1994)

Springtime Girl

If I could just be
        on a boat with her
just go on a journey
        long and leisurely
5   if I could just take her arm
firmly and if we could
        just once
take an ordinary walk together.
But instead
10   here I sit
asking her questions and
putting on my most
        businesslike
cut-and-dried expression:
15   *have you tightened the operations and*
when was this decision
        arrived at?
Figures
        nothing but figures
20   they leap at us
        like acrobats in a circus
whatever you had in mind comrade
        forget it
just remember
25   you're at work now.

Outside
        on the other side of the window
the tree drips
        drips with melting snow
30   but the thaw cannot melt
        my inner turmoil and

She sits and sighs
my springtime Valya my
            springtime girl
35   and the spring
            doesn't give a damn
for her precious job;

            I suppose in spring
we should expect
40   stocktakings, annual reports
and besides
            there are all those orders
which keep rolling in
and piling up
45   like hail
from Omsk
            from Biysk
from Leningrad
            Krasnoyarsk, from
50   Varna from
            Karlsbad and from
where not?

And all for Valya:
        all these orders
55   for Valya,
with here a fancy signature
and there a crabbed handwriting
and of course
        the better you work
60 the more orders
        you get;
odd isn't it?
        not really:
just the same
65   these orders
don't make life
        any easier.
Will fame
        ever burden
70 Valya's shoulders?
such fame
        would burden
shoulders less fragile:
and what if suddenly
75 she became too famous?
Proud
        overworked
                and indispensable;
what if she started saying:

80 *you there*
        don't tell me what to do and
just leave me alone!
But I don't believe it
        it could never
85 happen I believe
        something
quite different.

With any and in whatever
                    rank
90   Valya will remain
      the same joyous
      springtime girl
      she will remain
                    Valya
95   whom people trusted
      in Tashkent
                in Varna
      in Kharkov
                and in Weimar

100   What we need friend
                is clear sky
      and a fresh wind
                that blows
      not from the north:
105   what we need comrade
      is a true wind
                honest
      like Valya
                warm and
110   like Valya
                springlike.

      (1975)

Abbreviations

CP	Collected Poems
CRL	Canada: Romancing the Land
CTC	Call Them Canadians
DH	Driving Home: Poems New and Selected
DT	Dream Telescope
GW	Green World
GT	The Glass Trumpet
LAC	Library and Archives Canada
LL	The Last Landscape
MN	Mister Never
PG	The Price of Gold
SL	The Season's Lovers
SS	The Second Silence
SY	Say Yes
TV	The Visitants

Textual Notes

PREVIOUSLY PUBLISHED POEMS

The Exiles: Spain. 1. *Varsity* [U of Toronto] 11 Dec. 1936: 1 (signed Miriam Dworkin). 2. CP, p. 349.*

The Returner. 1. *Undergraduate* [University College, U of Toronto] 7.1 (1937): 15 (signed Miriam Dworkin). 2. CP, p. 350.*

Spanish Lovers Seek Respite. 1. *Undergraduate* [University College, U of Toronto] 8.1 (Fall 1937): 51* (signed Miriam Dworkin).

The Old Sailor. 1. *Undergraduate* [University College, U of Toronto] 8.2 (Spring 1938): 34 (signed Miriam Dworkin). 2. CP, p. 353.*

Organization. 1. *Undergraduate* [University College, U of Toronto] 8.2 (Spring 1938): 10 (signed Miriam Dworkin). 2. CP, p. 354.*

The Parting. 1. *Undergraduate* [University College, U of Toronto] 8.2 (Spring 1938): 59 (signed Miriam Dworkin). 2. CP, p. 351.*

Of Dreams. 1. *Undergraduate* [University College, U of Toronto] 9.1 (Fall 1938): 37 (signed Miriam Dworkin). 2. CP, p. 352.*

Out of Season. 1. *Undergraduate* [University College, U of Toronto] 9.1 (Fall 1938): 36 (signed Miriam Dworkin). 2. CP, p. 352.*

Struggle to Free the Spirit. 1. *Undergraduate* [University College, U of Toronto] 9.1 (Fall 1938): 37 (signed Miriam Dworkin). 2. CP, p. 353.*

Unheard Melodies. 1. *Undergraduate* [University College, U of Toronto] 9.1 (Fall 1938): 45 (signed Miriam Dworkin). 2. CP, pp. 350–51.*

Early Snow. 1. *Varsity* [U of Toronto] 9 Dec. 1938: 10 (signed Miriam Dworkin). 2. CP, p. 353.*

Night Wanderer. 1. *Canadian Poetry Magazine* 3.3 (Dec. 1938): 40 (signed Miriam Dworkin). 2. CP, pp. 351–52.*

Alone. 1. *Undergraduate* [University College, U of Toronto] 9.2 (Spring 1939): 13 (signed Miriam Dworkin). 2. CP, p. 355.*

Experience in Loneliness. 1. *Undergraduate* [University College, U of Toronto] 9.2 (Spring 1939): 58 (signed Miriam Dworkin). 2. CP, p. 356.*

Song I. 1. *Undergraduate* [University College, U of Toronto] 9.2 (Spring 1939): 19 (originally titled "Song"; signed Miriam Dworkin). 2. CP, p. 355.*

Starch. 1. *Undergraduate* [University College, U of Toronto] 9.2 (Spring 1939): 12 (signed Miriam Dworkin). 2. CP, p. 354.*

Woman at Evening. 1. *Undergraduate* [University College, U of Toronto] 9.2 (Spring 1939): 31 (signed Miriam Dworkin). 2. CP, p. 356.*

The Zoo. 1. *Undergraduate* [University College, U of Toronto] 9.2 (Spring 1939): 49 (signed Miriam Dworkin). 2. CP, p. 354.*

Dream Not of Heroes. 1. *Canadian Forum* Sept. 1939: 188 (signed Miriam Dworkin). 2. CP, pp. 356–57.*

In Our Time. 1. *Canadian Forum* Apr. 1940: 9 (signed Miriam Dworkin Waddington). 2. CTC, p. 195. 3. CP, p. 357.*

Erosion. 1. *Canadian Forum* Mar. 1941: 385 (signed Miriam D. Waddington). 2. SS, p. 43. 3. CP, p. 41.*

The Bond. 1. *Contemporary Verse* 1.3 (Mar. 1942): 10–11 (signed Miriam D. Waddington). 2. GW, 16th poem. 3. DH, pp. 68–69. 4. Gerri Sinclair and Morris Wolfe, eds., *The Spice Box: An Anthology of Jewish Canadian Writing* (Toronto: Lester and Orpen Dennys, 1981) 112–13. 5. CP, pp. 9–10.*

Second Generation. 1. *Contemporary Verse* 1.3 (Mar. 1942): 12 (originally titled "Immigrant, Second Generation"; signed Miriam D. Waddington). 2. GT, p. 64. 3. CP, pp. 107–08.*

Ladies. 1. *Contemporary Verse* 1.3 (Mar. 1942): 12 (signed Miriam D. Waddington). 2. CP, p. 358.*

Ballet. 1. *Providence Journal* [Rhode Island] 13 Sept. 1942: Sec. 6, p. 4 (originally titled "Modern Movement in a Ballet"). 2. GW, 7th poem. 3. CP, p. 4.*

Investigator. 1. *Providence Journal* [Rhode Island] 13 Sept. 1942: Sec. 6, p. 4. 2. *First Statement* 1.17 (Apr. 1943): 5 (signed Miriam D. Waddington). 3. GW, 9th poem. 4. Bliss Carman, Lorne Pierce, and V. B. Rhodenizer, eds., *Canadian Poetry in English* (Toronto: Ryerson P, 1954) 427–28. 5. SS, pp. 28–29. 6. DH, pp. 86–87. 7. Carl F. Klinck and Reginald E. Watters, eds., *Canadian Anthology* (Toronto: Gage, 1974) 440. 8. CP, p. 5.*

Branching from Golder's Green. 1. *Contemporary Verse* 2.5 (Sept. 1942): 12–13 (originally titled "Shutters"; signed Miriam D. Waddington). 2. CP, p. 358.*

Contemporary. 1. *Contemporary Verse* 2.5 (Sept. 1942): 13 (signed Miriam D. Waddington). 2. CP, pp. 357–58.*

Sorrow. 1. *Contemporary Verse* 2.5 (Sept. 1942): 12 (signed Miriam D. Waddington). 2. SS, pp. 29–30. 3. DH, p. 90. 4. CP, pp. 31–32.*

Uncertainties. 1. *Preview* (Jan. 1943): 6 (signed Miriam D. Waddington). 2. GW, 6th poem. 3. SS, pp. 16–17. 4. CP, pp. 3–4.*

Folkways. 1. *First Statement* 1.13 (Feb. 1943): 10 (originally titled "Social Worker"). 2. SS, p. 30. 3. DH, p. 89. 4. CP, p. 32.*

Contrasts. 1. *Canadian Poetry Magazine* 6.4 (Mar. 1943): 29 (signed Miriam D. Waddington). 2. CP, p. 361.*

I Love My Love with an S. 1. *Contemporary Verse* 7 (Mar. 1943): 8 (signed Miriam D. Waddington). 2. CP, p. 359.*

Integration. 1. *Contemporary Verse* 7 (Mar. 1943): 8–9 (originally titled "Proposal for Integration Toward a Common End"; signed Miriam D. Waddington). 2. GW, 19th poem. 3. CTC, p. 34 (excerpt). 4. DH, p. 71. 5. CP, pp. 11–12.*

Now We Steer. 1. *First Statement* 1.14 (Mar. 1943): 9–10 (signed Miriam D. Waddington). 2. CP, pp. 359–60.*

Time I. 1. *Iconograph* [New Orleans] 8 (Mar. 1943): n. pag.* (signed Miriam D. Waddington).

Two Poems (1). 1. *First Statement* 19 (Mar. 1943): 8. 2. CP, p. 360.*

Two Poems (2). 1. *First Statement* 19 (Mar. 1943): 8. 2. CP, pp. 360–61.*

Portrait I. 1. *First Statement* 14 (May 1943): 2 (originally titled "Portrait"). 2. GW, 4th poem. 3. DH, p. 70. 4. CP, pp. 2–3.*

Gimli. 1. *Canadian Forum* July 1943: 82 (signed Miriam D. Waddington). 2. GW, 2nd poem. 3. DH, p. 72. 4. CP, pp. 1–2.*

Girls. 1. *Preview* 14 (July 1943): 3. 2. GW, 20th poem. 3. CP, p. 12. 4. Gary Geddes, ed., *15 Canadian Poets x 2* (Toronto: Oxford UP, 1990) 161. 5. Gary Geddes, ed., *15 Canadian Poets x 3* (Toronto: Oxford UP, 2001) 82.*

Into the Morning. 1. *Canadian Forum* July 1943: 82 (signed Miriam D. Waddington). 2. GW, 3rd poem. 3. Louis Dudek and Irving Layton, eds., *Canadian Poems: 1850–1952* (Toronto: Contact P, 1952) 137. 4. CP, p. 2.* 5. CRL, plate 17 (excerpt).

Green World. 1. *Preview* 15 (Aug. 1943): 4 (originally titled "The Crystal"; signed Miriam D. Waddington). 2. *Chicago Review* 16.2 (Summer 1963): 73. 3. GW, 1st poem. 4. CTC, p. 41. 5. DH, p. 57. 6. Douglas Daymond and Leslie Monkman, eds., *Literature in Canada, Volume II* (Toronto: Gage, 1978) 340. 7. CP, p. 1.* 8. CRL, plate 10 (excerpt).

Indoors. 1. *First Statement* Aug. 1943: 7. 2. CP, p. 361.*

Lovers I. 1. *Preview* 15 (Aug. 1943): 4 (originally titled "The Lovers"; signed Miriam D. Waddington). 2. GW, 12th poem. 3. PG, p. 21. 4. CP, p. 7.*

Poem. 1. *Canadian Forum* Sept. 1943: 139 (signed Miriam D. Waddington). 2. CP, p. 362.*

Rocky Mountain Train. 1. *Preview* 17 (Dec. 1943): 3. 2. CP, p. 362.*

People I. 1. *Canadian Forum* Feb. 1944: 257 (originally titled "People"). 2. CP, pp. 362–63.*

Sympathy. 1. *First Statement* Feb. 1944: 11. 2. GW, 10th poem. 3. John Sutherland, ed., *Other Canadians: An Anthology of the New Poetry in Canada 1940–1946* (Montreal: First Statement P, 1947) 108. 4. DH, p. 88. 5. CP, pp. 5–6.*

Festival. 1. *Canadian Poetry Magazine* 7.3 (Mar. 1944): 28. 2. *Direction* [Outremont, Quebec] 2 [early 1944]: 2. 3. CP, p. 363.* 4. CRL, plate 6 (excerpt).

Fragments from Autobiography. 1. *Contemporary Verse* 10 (Apr. 1944): 10. 2. CP, pp. 363–64.*

Prairie I. 1. *Contemporary Verse* 10 (Apr. 1944): 9–10 (originally titled "Prairie"). 2. CTC, p. 233. 3. CP, p. 148.*

The Sleepers. 1. *Canadian Forum* Apr. 1944: 11. 2. GW, 11th poem. 3. CTC, p. 184. 4. J. L. Granatstein and Peter Stevens, eds., *Forum: Canadian Life and Letters 1920–70. Selections from the Canadian Forum* (Toronto: U of Toronto P, 1972) 221. 5. CP, p. 6.* 6. CRL, plate 7, 11 (excerpts).

Lake Superior. 1. *Canadian Poetry Magazine* 7.4 (June 1944): 35. 2. *Chatelaine* Jan. 1977: 76. 3. CP, p. 364.*

Avenues. 1. *Direction* [Outremont, Quebec] 2 [early 1944]: 2. 2. CP, p. 367.*

The Hub. 1. *Direction* [Outremont, Quebec] 2 [early 1944]: 2. 2. CP, p. 367.* 3. CRL, plate 9 (excerpt).

Partisans I. 1. *Direction* [Outremont, Quebec] 2 [early 1944]: 3 (originally titled "People's Army"). 2. *Canadian Poetry Magazine* 8.2 (Dec. 1944): 25. 3. CP, p. 365.*

Snow-whorls. 1. *Direction* [Outremont, Quebec] 2 [early 1944]: 3. 2. CTC, p. 130 (excerpt). 3. CP, p. 366.*

Windfalls: Bastard County. 1. *Direction* [Outremont, Quebec] 2 [early 1944]: 3 (originally titled "Bastard County Prospect"). 2. CP, p. 368.*

Letter to Margaret. 1. *Canadian Forum* Nov. 1944: 187. 2. CP, p. 368.*

Strange Country. 1. *Direction* [Outremont, Quebec] 3 [early 1944]: 6. 2. CP, pp. 364–65.*

In the Big City. 1. *First Statement* 2.10 (Dec. 1944–Jan. 1945): 15–16. 2. GW, 14th poem. 3. CTC, p. 163. 4. DH, p. 64. 5. Carl F. Klinck and Reginald E. Watters, eds., *Canadian Anthology* (Toronto: Gage, 1974) 440–41. 6. Evelyne Voldeng, ed., *Femme Plurielle* ([Ottawa]: Département d'études françaises, Carleton U, 1980) 56 (trans. by Evelyne Voldeng as "Dans le grande cite," p. 57). 7. CP, pp. 7–8.*

Circles. 1. *Contemporary Verse* 12 (Jan. 1945): 13. 2. GW, 18th poem. 3. SS, p. 10. 4. Ralph Gustafson, ed., *The Penguin Book of Canadian Verse* (Harmondsworth, UK: Penguin, 1958) 210. 5. CP, p. 11.*

Problems. 1. *Contemporary Verse* 12 (Jan. 1945): 12. 2. *First Statement* 2.11 (Feb.–Mar. 1945): 21. 3. Louis Dudek and Irving Layton, eds., *Canadian Poems: 1850–1952* (Toronto: Contact P, 1952) 138. 4. SS, p. 6. 5. CP, p. 19.*

Where. 1. *Contemporary Verse* 12 (Jan. 1945): 12. 2. GW, 23rd poem. 3. CP, p. 14.*

Cadenza. 1. *Canadian Forum* Feb. 1945: 264. 2. GW, 22nd poem. 3. John Sutherland, ed., *Other Canadians: An Anthology of the New Poetry in Canada 1940–1946*

(Montreal: First Statement P, 1947) 107. 4. Bliss Carman, Lorne Pierce, and V. B. Rhodenizer, eds., *Canadian Poetry in English* (Toronto: Ryerson P, 1954) 427. 5. CP, p. 13.★

In Exile. 1. *Canadian Forum* Mar. 1945: 287. 2. CTC, p. 69. 3. PG, p. 70. 4. CP, p. 129.★

Lullaby. 1. *First Statement* 2.12 (Apr.–May 1945): 29–30. 2. *Contemporary Poetry* [Baltimore] 5.2 (Summer 1945): 10. 3. GW, 24th poem. 4. John Sutherland, ed., *Other Canadians: An Anthology of the New Poetry in Canada 1940–1946* (Montreal: First Statement P, 1947) 106–07. 5. Bliss Carman, Lorne Pierce, and V. B. Rhodenizer, eds., *Canadian Poetry in English* (Toronto: Ryerson P, 1954) 429–30. 6. SS, pp. 2–3. 7. DH, pp. 58–59. 8. CP, pp. 14–15.★

Oasis. 1. *Saturday Night* 5 May 1945: 2. 2. CP, p. 369.★

Changes. 1. *Saturday Night* 19 May 1945: 2. 2. CP, p. 369.

Morning until Night. 1. *Canadian Forum* May 1945: 45. 2. *Experiment: A Quarterly of New Poetry* 2.2 (Summer 1945): 37–38. 3. GW, 25th poem. 4. SS, pp. 49–50. 5. DH, pp. 60–61. 6. CP, pp. 15–16.★

Wonderful Country. 1. *Queen's Quarterly* 52 (May 1945): 214. 2. SS, p. 2. 3. A. J. M. Smith, ed., *The Book of Canadian Poetry: A Critical and Historical Anthology* (Toronto: Gage, 1957) 465. 4. Ralph Gustafson, ed., *The Penguin Book of Canadian Verse* (Harmondsworth, UK: Penguin, 1958) 210–11. 5. Thelma Reid Lower and Frederick William Cogswell, eds., *The Enchanted Land: Canadian Poetry for Young Readers* (Agincourt, ON: Gage, 1967) 73. 6. DH, p. 56. 7. Jack David and Robert Lecker, eds., *Canadian Poetry* (Toronto/Downsview, ON: General/ECW P, 1982) 259. 8. CP, pp. 26–27.★

Summer in the Street. 1. *Canadian Poetry Magazine* 8.4 (June 1945): 18 (originally titled "Canadian Summer"). 2. GW, 21st poem. 3. DH, p. 73. 4. CP, pp. 12–13.★

Thou Didst Say Me. 1. *Contemporary Poetry* [Baltimore] 5.2 (Summer 1945): 11. 2. SS, pp. 9–10. 3. A. J. M. Smith, ed., *The Book of Canadian Poetry: A Critical and Historical Anthology* (Toronto: Gage, 1957) 462. 4. A. J. M. Smith, ed., *The Oxford Book of Canadian Verse: In English and French* (Toronto: Oxford UP, 1960) 342–43. 5. Ralph Gustafson, ed., *The Penguin Book of Canadian Verse* (Harmondsworth, UK: Penguin, 1967) 219–20. 6. John Metcalf and Gordon Callaghan, eds., *Salutation* (Toronto: Ryerson P, 1970) 107. 7. DH, pp. 62–63. 8. Konrad Gross and Wolfgang Klooss, eds., *Voices from Distant Lands: Poetry in the Commonwealth* (Würzburg, Ger.: Königshausen and Neumann, 1983) 100–01. 9. CP, p. 21.★ 10. CRL, plate 22 (excerpt).

Dog Days. 1. *Canadian Forum* July 1945: 91. 2. GW, 17th poem. 3. CP, pp. 10–11.★

Adagio. 1. *Contemporary Verse* 15 (Oct. 1945): 14. 2. SS, p. 54. 3. CP, p. 46.★

The Heart Cast Out. 1. *Contemporary Verse* 15 (Oct. 1945): 13 (originally titled "Heart Cast Out"). 2. CP, pp. 370–71.★

Museum. 1. *Canadian Forum* Dec. 1945: 216. 2. CP, p. 369.*

Unquiet World. 1. GW, 5th poem. 2. CTC, p. 207. 3. *Jewish Dialogue* (Rosh Hashanah 1971): 14. 4. DH, p. 63. 5. CP, p. 3.*

Arabian. 1. GW, 8th poem. 2. CTC, p. 87. 3. CP, p. 4.*

Tapestry I. 1. GW, 13th poem (originally titled "Tapestry"). 2. CTC, p. 102. 3. CP, p. 7.* 4. CRL, plate 23 (excerpt).

Who Will Build Jerusalem. 1. GW, 15th poem. 2. CP, pp. 8–9.*

Stillness. 1. *Contemporary Verse* 17 (Apr. 1946): 7–8. 2. CP, pp. 372–73.

Three Poems for My Teacher (1). 1. *Contemporary Verse* 17 (Apr. 1946): 6. 2. SS, p. 11. 3. DH, p. 122. 4. CP, p. 22.*

Three Poems for My Teacher (2). 1. *Contemporary Verse* 17 (Apr. 1946): 6–7. 2. SS, pp. 11–12. 3. DH, pp. 122–23. 4. CP, p. 22.*

Three Poems for My Teacher (3). 1. *Contemporary Verse* 17 (Apr. 1946): 6–7. 2. SS, p. 12. 3. CTC, p. 199. 4. DH, p. 123. 5. CP, pp. 22–23.

Time's Large Ocean. 1. *Contemporary Verse* 17 (Apr. 1946): 8–9. 2. SS, p. 47. 3. CP, p. 43.*

Interval. 1. *Canadian Forum* May 1946: 39. 2. SS, pp. 1–2. 3. Irving Layton, ed., *Love Where the Nights Are Long: An Anthology of Canadian Love Poems* (Toronto: McClelland and Stewart, 1962) 23. 4. DH, p. 76. 5. CP, p. 17.*

Growing. 1. *Canadian Forum* July 1946: 87. 2. SS, pp. 42–43. 3. CP, p. 40.*

A Ballad for the Peace. 1. *Canadian Forum* Aug. 1946: 107. 2. CP, pp. 371–72.*

Lovers II. 1. *Canadian Poetry Magazine* 10.1 (Sept. 1946): 12 (originally titled "Lovers"). 2. Earle Birney, ed., *Twentieth Century Canadian Poetry: An Anthology* (Toronto: Ryerson P, 1953) 78–79. 3. SS, p. 8. 4. CTC, p. 185 (excerpt). 5. DH, p. 74. 6. CP, pp. 20–21.* 7. CRL, plate 2 (excerpt).

The Music Teachers. 1. *Canadian Poetry Magazine* 10.1 (Sept. 1946): 13–15. 2. SS, pp. 52–53. 3. DH, pp. 66–67. 4. CP, pp. 44–45.*

Noon Hour Downtown. 1. *Canadian Poetry Magazine* 10.1 (Sept. 1946): 15. 2. CP, p. 373.*

Night in October. 1. *Canadian Poetry Magazine* 10.4 (June 1947): 39–41. 2. SS, pp. 22–23. 3. A. J. M. Smith, ed., *The Book of Canadian Poetry: A Critical and Historical Anthology* (Toronto: Gage, 1957) 463–64. 4. DH, pp. 80–81. 5. Carl F. Klinck and Reginald E. Watters, eds., *Canadian Anthology* (Toronto: Gage, 1974) 441–42. 6. Janice LaDuke and Steve Luxton, eds., *Full Moon: Anthology of Canadian Women Poets* (Dunvegan, ON: Quadrant Editions, 1983) 155. 7. CP, pp. 28–29.*

The Bread We Eat. 1. *Canadian Forum* Dec. 1947: 210. 2. SS, pp. 38–39. 3. CP, pp. 37–38.*

Soft Midnight of Summer. 1. *Canadian Poetry Magazine* 11.4 (June 1948): 34–35. 2. CP, pp. 373–74.*

Foundling. 1. *Outposts* 10 (Summer 1948): 12–13. 2. *Canadian Forum* Apr. 1949: 17. 3. SS, pp. 31–32. 4. CP, p. 32.*

Three Poems to a Pupil (1). *Contemporary Verse* 26 (Fall 1948): 14 (originally titled "Three Poems about Relationship: 1. The Beginning"). 2. SS, p. 13. 3. CP, p. 23.*

Three Poems to a Pupil (2). 1. *Contemporary Verse* 26 (Fall 1948): 15–16 (originally titled "Three Poems about Relationship: 2. Progressions"). 2. SS, pp. 14–15. 3. CP, pp. 23–24.*

Three Poems to a Pupil (3). 1. *Contemporary Verse* 26 (Fall 1948): 16–17 (originally titled "Three Poems about Relationship: 3. Where We Are Now"). 2. SS, pp. 15–16. 3. DH, p. 124. 4. CP, p. 25.*

Charity. 1. *Canadian Forum* Apr. 1949: 17. 2. SS, p. 37. 3. DH, p. 105. 4. CP, pp. 36–37.*

Dahlias. 1. *Canadian Forum* Sept. 1949: 137. 2. CP, pp. 374–75.*

St. Antoine Street (1). 1. *Contemporary Verse* 31 (Spring 1950): 17–18. 2. SS, p. 44. 3. DH, p. 108. 4. CP, p. 41.*

St. Antoine Street (2). 1. *Contemporary Verse* 31 (Spring 1950): 18–19. 2. SS, pp. 44–45. 3. DH, pp. 108–09. 4. CP, p. 42.*

St. Antoine Street (3). 1. *Contemporary Verse* 31 (Spring 1950): 20. 2. SS, pp. 45–46. 3. CP, pp. 42–43.*

Worlds. 1. *Contemporary Verse* 31 (Spring 1950): 16–17. 2. SS, p. 21. 3. CP, pp. 27–28.*

Trip from the City. 1. *Canadian Forum* July 1950: 90. 2. SS, p. 36. 3. DH, p. 104. 4. CP, p. 36.*

Catalpa Tree. 1. *Contemporary Verse* 37 (Winter–Spring 1951–52): 9–10 (originally titled "Catalpa"). 2. SS, p. 19. 3. A. J. M. Smith, ed., *The Oxford Book of Canadian Verse: In English and French* (Toronto: Oxford UP, 1960) 343–44. 4. A. J. M. Smith, ed., *Modern Canadian Verse: In English and French* (Toronto: Oxford UP, 1967) 204–05. 5. DH, p. 77. 6. CP, p. 26.*

In the Park. 1. *Contemporary Verse* 37 (Winter–Spring 1951–52): 9. 2. SS, p. 18. 3. DH, p. 79. 4. Douglas Daymond and Leslie Monkman, eds., *Literature in Canada, Volume II* (Toronto: Gage, 1978) 341. 5. CP, pp. 25–26.*

Restricted. 1. *Contemporary Verse* 37 (Winter–Spring 1951–52): 10–11. 2. Louis Dudek and Irving Layton, eds., *Canadian Poems: 1850–1952* (Toronto: Contact P, 1952) 137–38. 3. Bliss Carman, Lorne Pierce, and V. B. Rhodenizer, eds., *Canadian Poetry in English* (Toronto: Ryerson P, 1954) 428–29. 4. CTC, p. 193. 5. CP, p. 136.

Poems about War. 1. *Canadian Forum* Jan. 1953: 233. 2. SS, pp. 40–41. 3. CP, pp. 38–40.*

Fables of Birth. 1. *CIV/n* 3 (1953): 1 (originally titled "Fables"). 2. SS, pp. 24–26. 3. CP, pp. 29–31.*

Poem for a Three-Year-Old. 1. *Saturday Night* 27 Feb. 1954: 14.*

New Year's Concert. 1. *Fiddlehead* 20 (Feb. 1954): 2. 2. ss, p. 38. 3. cp, p. 37.*

Seashell. 1. *Queen's Quarterly* 61 (Autumn 1954): 365 (originally titled "The Sea Shell"). 2. ctc, p. 133. 3. dh, p. 83. 4. cp, p. 143.*

Bird's Hill. 1. *Fiddlehead* 22 (Nov. 1954): 5–6. 2. ss, pp. 55–56. 3. cp, p. 47.*

You and Me. 1. ss, pp. 4–5. 2. cp, p. 18.*

At Midnight. 1. ss, p. 5. 2. dh, p. 75. 3. cp, pp. 18–19. 4. Gary Geddes, ed., *15 Canadian Poets x 2* (Toronto: Oxford UP, 1990) 161–62. 5. Gary Geddes, ed., *15 Canadian Poets x 3* (Toronto: Oxford UP, 2001) 83.*

Novella. 1. ss, p. 6. 2. cp, p. 19.*

These Times. 1. ss, p. 7. 2. cp, p. 20.*

Childless. 1. ss, pp. 26–27. 2. cp, p. 31.*

Journey to the Clinic. 1. ss, pp. 32–35. 2. ctc, p. 38, 211 (excerpts). 3. dh, pp. 92–95. 4. cp, pp. 33–35.*

Prayer. 1. ss, p. 48. 2. cp, pp. 43–44.*

Getting Older. 1. ss, p. 51. 2. dh, p. 87. 3. cp, p. 44.*

City Street. 1. ss, p. 55. 2. dh, p. 85. 3. cp, p. 46.*

Inward Look the Trees. 1. ss, p. 57. 2. cp, p. 48.*

Portrait II. 1. *Queen's Quarterly* 63 (Spring 1956): 103 (originally titled "Portrait"). 2. A. J. M. Smith, ed., *The Book of Canadian Poetry: A Critical and Historical Anthology* (Toronto: Gage, 1957) 461–62. 3. ctc, p. 147 (excerpt). 4. cp, p. 377.*

Did You Me Dream. 1. *Fiddlehead* 28 (May 1956): 2–3. 2. sl, p. 41. 3. cp, pp. 65–66.*

Faces. 1. *Fiddlehead* 28 (May 1956): 3 (originally titled "Card Faces"). 2. cp, p. 377* (index mistakenly cites original title "Card Faces").

The Follower. 1. *Fiddlehead* 28 (May 1956): 2. 2. gt, p. 56. 3. cp, p. 103.*

Quiet Go to Midnight. 1. *Fiddlehead* 28 (May 1956): 3–4. 2. cp, p. 375.*

Jonathan Travels. 1. *Fiddlehead* 29 (Aug. 1956): 8. 2. sl, pp. 39–40. 3. *Fiddlehead* 50 (Fall 1961): 61. 4. cp, p. 65.*

The Prison Worker. 1. *Canadian Forum* Oct. 1956: 157. 2. cp, pp. 375–77.*

Looking at Paintings II. 1. *Fiddlehead* 30 (Nov. 1956): 6 (originally titled "Looking at Paintings (Louis Muhlstock's)"). 2. gt, p. 52. 3. cp, p. 101.*

Studio on Ste. Famille Street. 1. *Fiddlehead* 30 (Nov. 1956): 6. 2. cp, p. 378.*

Departure. 1. *Dalhousie Review* 35 (Winter 1956): 339. 2. cp, p. 378.*

Going Away and Coming Back. 1. *Canadian Poetry Magazine* 20.2 (Winter 1956–57): 24. 2. cp, p. 379.*

Housing Development. 1. *Canadian Poetry Magazine* 20.2 (Winter 1956–57): 22–23. 2. cp, pp. 378–79.*

Winnipeg. 1. *Canadian Poetry Magazine* 20.2 (Winter 1956–57): 6–7. 2. sl, pp. 12–13. 3. cp, pp. 52–53.*

The Orator. 1. *Nation* 20 Apr. 1957: 350. 2. SL, p. 31. 3. CP, p. 62.*

The Women's Jail. 1. *Nation* 11 May 1957: 426. 2. SL, p. 29. 3. DH, pp. 98–99. 4. Margaret Atwood, ed., *The New Oxford Book of Canadian Verse in English* (Toronto: Oxford UP, 1983) 190. 5. CP, p. 61.*

No Earthly Lover. 1. *Fiddlehead* 32 (May 1957): 23 (originally titled "The Wound"). 2. SL, p. 38. 3. CP, p. 64.*

The Journeying. 1. *Tamarack Review* 4 (Summer 1957): 31. 2. GT, p. 49. 3. DH, p. 173. 4. CP, p. 99.*

Ordinary Death. 1. *Tamarack Review* 4 (Summer 1957): 31. 2. CP, pp. 380–81.*

Signature. 1. *Tamarack Review* 4 (Summer 1957): 32. 2. CP, p. 380.*

Sympathy for a Bad Painter. 1. *Tamarack Review* 4 (Summer 1957): 32. 2. CP, p. 380.*

You Are My Never. 1. *Tamarack Review* 4 (Summer 1957): 30 (originally titled "Never"). 2. SL, p. 42. 3. DH, p. 129. 4. CP, p. 66.*

Limited Perspectives. 1. *Fiddlehead* 33 (Aug. 1957): 18. 2. CP, p. 382.*

Myth Etcetera: For Academic Critics. 1. *Canadian Forum* Oct. 1957: 159 (originally titled "Myth Etcetera"). 2. CP, pp. 382–83.*

Three Prison Portraits: 1. The Alcoholic. 1. *Journal of Social Work Process* 8 (1957): 59 (originally titled "Three Prison Portraits: The Alcoholic"). 2. SL, p. 24. 3. DH, p. 100. 4. CP, p. 58.*

Three Prison Portraits: 2. The Drug Addict. 1. *Journal of Social Work Process* 8 (1957): 59 (originally titled "Three Prison Portraits: The Addict"). 2. SL, p. 25. 3. DH, p. 101. 4. Margaret J. O'Donnell, ed., *Anthology of Commonwealth Verse* (London, UK: Blackie, 1963) 190. 5. CP, pp. 58–59.*

Three Prison Portraits: 3. The Non Supporter. 1. *Journal of Social Work Process* 8 (1957): 60 (originally titled "Three Prison Portraits: The Non-Supporter"). 2. SL, p. 26. 3. CP, p. 59.*

The Season's Lovers. 1. *Week-end Review* [*New Statesman*] 8 Feb. 1958: 172. 2. SL, pp. 55–56. 3. A. J. M. Smith, ed., *The Oxford Book of Canadian Verse: In English and French* (Toronto: Oxford UP, 1960) 344–45. 4. Ralph Gustafson, ed., *The Penguin Book of Canadian Verse* (Harmondsworth, UK: Penguin, 1967) 218–19. 5. A. J. M. Smith, ed., *Modern Canadian Verse: In English and French* (Toronto: Oxford UP, 1967) 206–07. 6. DH, pp. 170–71. 7. Desmond Pacey, ed., *Selections from Major Canadian Writers* (Toronto: McGraw-Hill Ryerson, 1974) 108–09. 8. Jack David and Robert Lecker, eds., *Canadian Poetry* (Toronto/Downsview, ON: General/ECW P, 1982) 260–61. 9. Konrad Gross and Wolfgang Klooss, eds., *Voices from Distant Lands: Poetry in the Commonwealth* (Würzburg, Ger.: Königshausen and Neumann, 1983) 102–03. 10. CP, pp. 72–73.*

An Elegy for John Sutherland. 1. *Fiddlehead* 35 (Winter 1958): 4 (originally published as "Elegy for John Sutherland"). 2. SL, pp. 51–52. 3. Lionel Stevenson, et al., eds., *Best Poems of 1958: Borestone Mountain Poetry Awards, 1959* (Palo Alto, CA: Pacific, 1960) 95. 4. CP, pp. 70–71.*

Artist and Subject. 1. *Fiddlehead* 36 (Spring 1958): 12. 2. CP, p. 383.*

When World Was Wheelbarrow. 1. *Queen's Quarterly* 65 (Spring 1958): 76. 2. SL, pp. 7–8. 3. Clare MacCulloch, ed., *Lobsticks* (Guelph, ON: Alive, 1974) 172–73. 4. CP, p. 50.*

Exchange. 1. *Harper's Magazine* (May 1958): 58. 2. SL, p. 37. 3. DH, p. 125. 4. CP, p. 64.*

Endings. 1. *New Orleans Poetry Journal* 1 (1958): 30–31. 2. CTC, p. 161 (excerpt). 3. Clare MacCulloch, ed., *Lobsticks* (Guelph, ON: Alive, 1974) 173. 4. CP, p. 384.*

The Midsummer Garden. 1. Irving Layton, ed., *Pan-ic: A Selection of Contemporary Canadian Poems* [New York] 2 (1958): n. pag. 2. GT, pp. 60–61. 3. CP, pp. 105–06.*

My Lessons in the Jail. 1. SL, p. 271. 2. Irving Layton, ed., *Pan-ic: A Selection of Contemporary Canadian Poems* [New York] 2 (1958): n. pag. 3. A. J. M. Smith, ed., *Modern Canadian Verse: In English and French* (Toronto: Oxford UP, 1967) 205–06. 4. DH, p. 102. 5. Donna Bennett and Russell Brown, eds., *An Anthology of Canadian Literature in English, Volume II* (Toronto: Oxford UP, 1983) 24–25. 6. CP, pp. 59–60. 7. Gary Geddes, ed., *15 Canadian Poets x 2* (Toronto: Oxford UP, 1990) 162–63. 8. Gary Geddes, ed., *15 Canadian Poets x 3* (Toronto: Oxford UP, 2001) 83.*

Poets and Statues. 1. SL, pp. 3–4. 2. DH, pp. 112–13. 3. CP, p. 49.*

The City's Life. 1. SL, pp. 9–10. 2. DH, p. 114. 3. Desmond Pacey, ed., *Selections from Major Canadian Writers* (Toronto: McGraw-Hill Ryerson, 1974) 111. 4. CP, pp. 50–51.*

Old Women of Toronto. 1. SL, p. 11. 2. DH, p. 99. 3. Margaret Atwood, ed., *The New Oxford Book of Canadian Verse in English* (Toronto: Oxford UP, 1983) 190. 3. CP, p. 51. 4. Kate Braid and Sandy Shreve, eds., *In Fine Form: The Canadian Book of Form Poetry* (Vancouver: Raincoast Books, 2005) 222.*

What Is Hard. 1. SL, p. 14. 2. CP, p. 53.*

The Young Poet and Me. 1. SL, p. 15. 2. CP, pp. 53–54.*

People Who Watch the Trains. 1. SL, p. 16. 2. CP, p. 54.*

Traffic Lights at Passover. 1. SL, pp. 17–18. 2. CP, pp. 54–55.*

The Through Way. 1. SL, pp. 19–20. 2. CP, pp. 55–56.*

In a Corridor at Court. 1. SL, p. 23. 2. CP, p. 57.*

To Be a Healer. 1. SL, p. 28. 2. CP, pp. 60–61.*

The Thief. 1. SL, pp. 32–34. 2. DH, pp. 96–97. 3. Desmond Pacey, ed., *Selections from Major Canadian Writers* (Toronto: McGraw-Hill Ryerson, 1974) 109–10. 4. CP, pp. 62–63.*

The Honeymoon. 1. SL, p. 44. 2. CP, p. 67.*

The Exhibition: David Milne. 1. SL, p. 45. 2. CP, p. 68.*

The Artist I. 1. SL, p. 46. 2. CP, p. 68.*

Semblances. 1. SL, pp. 47–48. 2. CP, p. 69.*

In the Mountains. 1. SL, p. 49. 2. CP, p. 70.*

Islanded. 1. SL, p. 50. 2. CP, p. 70.*

In the Sun. 1. SL, pp. 53–54. 2. Thomas Martin, Dorothy Chamberlin, and Irmgard Wieler, eds., *Man's Search for Values* (Toronto: Gage, 1966) 17. 3. DH, p. 78. 4. CP, pp. 71–72.*

Absent Space. 1. *Dalhousie Review* 38 (Winter 1959): 509. 2. CP, p. 385.*

Carnival. 1. *Queen's Quarterly* 66 (Spring 1959): 1. 2. GT, p. 48. 3. CP, p. 99.*

The Survivors. 1. *Midstream* 5 (Spring 1959): 88. 2. GT, p. 65. 3. Howard Schwartz and Anthony Rudolf, eds., *Voices within the Ark: The Modern Jewish Poets* (New York: Pushcart P, 1980) 768. 4. CP, p. 108. 5. Gary Geddes, ed., *15 Canadian Poets x 2* (Toronto: Oxford UP, 1990) 167–68. 6. Gary Geddes, ed., *15 Canadian Poets x 3* (Toronto: Oxford UP, 2001) 88.*

The Snows of William Blake. 1. *Queen's Quarterly* 66 (Summer 1959): 280. 2. Milton Wilson, ed., *Recent Canadian Verse* (Kingston, ON: Jackson, [1959]) 13. 3. GT, p. 96. 4. DH, p. 127. 5. CP, p. 124.*

Ballad for a Broadsheet. 1. *Canadian Forum* July 1959: 95. 2. CP, pp. 381–82.*

Night on Skid Row. 1. *Dalhousie Review* 39 (Winter 1960): 526–28. 2. GT, pp. 62–63. 3. DH, pp. 110–11. 4. Alan Powell, ed., *The City: Attacking Modern Myths* (Toronto: McClelland and Stewart, 1972) 161. 5. CP, pp. 106–07.*

On My Birthday. 1. *Delta* 2 (Spring 1960): 23–34 (originally titled "Lament on My Fortieth Birthday"). 2. GT, pp. 50–51. 3. CP, pp. 100–01. 4. Gary Geddes, ed., *15 Canadian Poets x 2* (Toronto: Oxford UP, 1990) 163–64. 5. Gary Geddes, ed., *15 Canadian Poets x 3* (Toronto: Oxford UP, 2001) 84–85.*

Above the Seaway. 1. *Queen's Quarterly* 67 (Summer 1960): 239.*

A Balkan Cemetery. 1. *Waterloo Review* 5 (Summer 1960): 41 (originally titled "In a Balkan Cemetery"). 2. GT, p. 54. 3. CP, p. 102.*

Nightmare. 1. *Fiddlehead* 45 (Summer 1960): 19 (originally titled "At Night"). 2. CTC, p. 84. 3. CP, p. 131.*

Boughs of Snow. 1. *Fiddlehead* 45 (Summer 1960): 21 (originally titled "The Boughs of Snow"). 2. CTC, p. 200. 3. CP, p. 146.*

Christ in a Loincloth. 1. *Fiddlehead* 45 (Summer 1960): 12 (originally titled "The Crucifix in Prison"). 2. *Fiddlehead* 68 (Spring 1966): 21–22. 3. GT, p. 59. 4. DH, p. 103. 5. CP, pp. 104–05.*

Driving to Work. 1. *Fiddlehead* 45 (Summer 1960): 11. 2. CP, pp. 386–87.*

Homage to Apollinaire with Some Words by John Dowland. 1. *Fiddlehead* 45 (Summer 1960): 22 (originally titled "Homage to Apollinaire"). 2. GT, p. 58. 3. CP, p. 104.*

The Lawbreakers. 1. Fiddlehead 45 (Summer 1960): 13. 2. CTC, p. 239. 3. CP, p. 387.*

The Mile Runner. 1. *Tamarack Review* 16 (Summer 1960): 35 (originally titled "Prairie Images"). 2. GT, p. 57. 3. DH, p. 113. 4. CP, p. 103. 5. Gary Geddes, ed., *15 Canadian Poets x 2* (Toronto: Oxford UP, 1990) 165. 6. Gary Geddes, ed., *15 Canadian Poets x 3* (Toronto: Oxford UP, 2001) 86.*

Montreal Night. 1. Fiddlehead 45 (Summer 1960): 14. 2. CP, p. 388.*

Mourning for Lost Causes. 1. Fiddlehead 45 (Summer 1960): 20. 2. Fiddlehead 50 (Fall 1961): 60. 3. CP, p. 385.*

Penelope. 1. *Waterloo Review* 5 (Summer 1960): 40 (originally titled "Penelope in Toronto"). 2. CTC, p. 230. 3. CP, pp. 135–36.*

Pleasures from Children. 1. Fiddlehead 45 (Summer 1960): 15. 2. GT, p. 55. 3. DH, p. 106. 4. CP, pp. 102–03.*

Sea Bells. 1. *Tamarack Review* 16 (Summer 1960): 36. 2. GT, p. 17. 3. Howard Sergeant, ed., *Commonwealth Poems of Today* (London: Cox and Whyman, 1967) 139–40. 4. DH, p. 107. 5. Carl F. Klinck and Reginald E. Watters, eds., *Canadian Anthology* (Toronto: Gage, 1974) 442–43. 6. CP, pp. 79–80.*

The Shape of Buildings. 1. Fiddlehead 45 (Summer 1960): 10. 2. CP, p. 386.*

The Stepmother. 1. Fiddlehead 45 (Summer 1960): 16.*

Surcease. 1. Fiddlehead 45 (Summer 1960): 19. 2. CP, p. 389.*

Three Worlds. 1. Fiddlehead 45 (Summer 1960): 17–18. 2. CP, pp. 388–89.*

Returning to Toronto. 1. *Tamarack Review* 24 (Summer 1962): 46 (originally titled "Four Poems of Toronto: Returning to Toronto"). 2. GT, p. 18. 3. Jack Hodgins and William H. New, eds., *Voice and Vision* (Toronto: McClelland and Stewart, 1972) 143. 4. CP, p. 80.*

Saints and Others. 1. *Tamarack Review* 24 (Summer 1962): 49–50 (originally titled "Four Poems of Toronto: Saints and Others"). 2. GT, pp. 14–15. 3. C. V. Wedgwood, ed., *A P. E. N. Anthology of Contemporary Poetry* (London, UK: Hutchinson, 1966) 170–71. 4. DH, pp. 136–37. 5. CP, pp. 77–78.*

A Song of North York between Sheppard and Finch. 1. *Tamarack Review* 24 (Summer 1962): 47 (originally titled "Four Poems of Toronto: A Song of North York between Sheppard and Finch"). 2. GT, p. 19. 3. DH, p. 158. 4. CP, pp. 80–81.*

Toronto the Golden-vaulted City. 1. *Tamarack Review* 24 (Summer 1962): 48–49 (originally titled "Four Poems of Toronto: Toronto the Golden Vaulted City"). 2. *Earth and You* [Toronto] 3.17–18 (1971): 34–45. 3. GT, p. 16. 4. DH, pp. 90–91. 5. Ernest W. Winter, ed., *Recollections of the Works Department* (Don Mills, ON: Nelson, 1975) 179–80. 6. CP, pp. 78–79.*

Camping. 1. *Queen's Quarterly* 69 (Autumn 1962): 360. 2. GT, p. 74. 3. DH, p. 151. 4. CP, pp. 112–13.*

The Land Where He Dwells In. 1. *Chicago Review* 16.2 (Summer 1963): 71–72. 2. Lionel Stevenson, et al., eds., *Best Poems of 1963: Borestone Mountain Poetry Awards*, 1964 (Palo Alto, CA: Pacific, 1964) 134–35. 3. GT, pp. 10–11. 4. DH, pp. 130–31. 5. Desmond Pacey, ed., *Selections from Major Canadian Writers* (Toronto: McGraw-Hill Ryerson, 1974) 111–12. 6. CP, pp. 74–75.*

The Forsythia Bush. 1. *Evidence* 7 ([1963]): 91–92. 2. *English* 19.103 (Spring 1970): 12–13. 3. CP, pp. 394–95.*

Piano Phrases in January. 1. *Evidence* 7 ([1963]): 92–93.*

The Gardeners. 1. *Canadian Poetry Magazine* 27 (Feb. 1964): 27–28. 2. GT, p. 32. 3. DH, pp. 118–19. 4. CP, pp. 89–90.*

Brotherly Love on Sherbrooke Street. 1. *Tamarack Review* 32 (Summer 1964): 86. 2. GT, p. 23. 3. CP, p. 83.*

Green World Two. 1. *Tamarack Review* 32 (Summer 1964): 88. 2. GT, p. 72. 3. Ralph Gustafson, ed., *The Penguin Book of Canadian Verse* (Harmondsworth, UK: Penguin, 1967) 220. 4. DH, p. 165. 5. Tobie Steinhouse, *Green World: A Suite of Six Etchings* (Montreal: Guide Graphique, 1977) n. pag. 6. Douglas Daymond and Leslie Monkman, eds., *Literature in Canada, Volume II* (Toronto: Gage, 1978) 342. 7. CP, pp. 111–12.*

The Terrarium. 1. *Tamarack Review* 32 (Summer 1964): 84–85. 2. GT, pp. 20–21. 3. CP, pp. 81–82.*

Things of the World. 1. *Tamarack Review* 32 (Summer 1964): 87. 2. GT, p. 9. 3. DH, p. 115. 4. Laurence R. Ricou, ed., *Twelve Prairie Poets* (Ottawa: Oberon P, 1976) 171–72. 5. CP, p. 74.*

Displacements. 1. *Volume 63* [University of Waterloo] 2 (Oct. 1964): 9 (originally titled "Displacements: 2"). 2. CP, p. 390.*

The Field of Night. 1. *Canadian Forum* Oct. 1964: 152. 2. GT, pp. 70–71. 3. DH, pp. 116–17. 4. Howard Schwartz and Anthony Rudolf, eds., *Voices within the Ark: The Modern Jewish Poets* (New York: Pushcart P, 1980) 769–70. 5. CP, pp. 110–11.*

Pictures in a Window. 1. *Volume 63* [University of Waterloo] 2 (Oct. 1964): 10. 2. GT, p. 42. 3. CP, p. 95.*

Seasons. 1. *Volume 63* [University of Waterloo] 2 (Oct. 1964): 8 (originally titled "Displacements: 1"). 2. CTC, p. 97. 3. CP, pp. 133–34.*

City Lover. 1. *Envoi: A Quarterly Review of New Poetry* [Cheltenham, UK] 23 ([1964]): 6. 2. CP, p. 390.*

Selma. 1. *Canadian Forum* Apr. 1965: 10 (originally titled "Selma and the Rest of It"). 2. GT, p. 75. 3. CP, p. 113.*

The Far City. 1. *Literary Review* [Fairleigh Dickinson University, Teaneck, NJ] 8 (Summer 1965): 570–71. 2. GT, p. 35. 3. CP, pp. 91–92.*

The Bright Room. 1. *Quarry* 15.1 (Sept. 1965): 9. 2. GT, p. 13. 3. CP, pp. 76–77.*

Prairie Thoughts in a Museum: 1. The Picture. 1. *Quarry* 15.1 (Sept. 1965): 10 (originally titled "Prairie Thoughts in a Museum"). 2. GT, p. 38. 3. CP, p. 93.*

Prairie Thoughts in a Museum: 2. The People. 1. *Quarry* 15.1 (Sept. 1965): 10 (originally titled "Prairie Thoughts in a Museum"). 2. GT, p. 38. 3. CP, p. 93–94.*

Prairie Thoughts in a Museum: 3. The Picture. 1. *Quarry* 15.1 (Sept. 1965): 11 (originally titled "Prairie Thoughts in a Museum"). 2. GT, p. 40. 3. CP, p. 94.*

Prairie Thoughts in a Museum: 4. The People. 1. *Quarry* 15.1 (Sept. 1965): 11 (originally titled "Prairie Thoughts in a Museum"). 2. GT, p. 41. 3. CP, p. 94.*

Goodbye Song. 1. *Quarry* 15.2 (Nov. 1965): 16–17. 2. GT, pp. 36–37. 3. DH, pp. 134–35. 4. CP, pp. 92–93.*

Hart Crane. 1. *Quarry* 15.2 (Nov. 1965): 16. 2. GT, p. 43. 3. CP, pp. 95–96.*

Remembering You. 1. *Prism International* 5.3–4 (Winter–Spring 1966): 9. 2. GT, p. 53. 3. DH, p. 133. 4. CP, p. 101.*

Summer Letters. 1. *Canadian Forum* Mar. 1966: 271. 2. GT, pp. 26–28. 3. DH, pp. 142–44. 4. CP, pp. 84–86.*

All Those Who Run in Fields. 1. *Fiddlehead* 68 (Spring 1966): 18–19 (originally titled "To Those Who Run in Fields"). 2. *New: American and Canadian Poetry* 3 (Apr. 1967): 4–5. 3. SY, pp. 45–46. 4. CP, pp. 181–82.*

East on Dorchester Street. 1. *Fiddlehead* 68 (Spring 1966): 19. 2. CP, p. 392.*

From a Dead Poet's Book. 1. *Fiddlehead* 68 (Spring 1966): 20–21. 2. GT, p. 12. 3. DH, pp. 126–27. 4. Elizabeth McCullough, ed., *The Role of Women in Canadian Literature* (Toronto: Macmillan, 1975) 7–8. 5. CP, pp. 75–76.*

The Hook. 1. *Fiddlehead* 68 (Spring 1966): 17. 2. CP, pp. 391–92.*

Love Patterns. 1. *Fiddlehead* 68 (Spring 1966): 14–16 (originally titled "Miriam, You Must Cast the Scholar Off"). 2. CTC, p. 183. 3. CP, pp. 137–38.*

New Year's Day. 1. *Fiddlehead* 68 (Spring 1966): 14. 2. GT, p. 22. 3. DH, p. 159. 4. John Metcalf, ed., *The Speaking Earth: Canadian Poetry* (Toronto: Van Nostrand Reinhold, 1973) 63. 5. CP, p. 82.*

Seeing beyond Brick. 1. *Fiddlehead* 68 (Spring 1966): 12 (originally titled "Beyond Brick"). 2. GT, p. 73. 3. Thelma Reid Lower and Frederick William Cogswell, eds., *The Enchanted Land: Canadian Poetry for Young Readers* (Agincourt, ON: Gage, 1967) 137. 4. CP, p. 112.*

Winter Two. 1. *Fiddlehead* 68 (Spring 1966): 11 (originally titled "In Mirrors and Dawns"). 2. GT, p. 84. 3. CP, pp. 117–18.*

The Wintry Man. 1. *Fiddlehead* 68 (Spring 1966): 12–13. 2. CTC, p. 25 (excerpt). 3. CP, pp. 390–91.*

Incidents for the Undying World. 1. *Tamarack Review* 40 (Summer 1966): 30–32. 2. GT, pp. 66–68. 3. Clare MacCulloch, ed., *Lobsticks* (Guelph, ON: Alive, 1974) 185–87. 4. CP, pp. 108–10.*

Saints and Bibliographers. 1. *Tamarack Review* 40 (Summer 1966): 32–34. 2. GT, pp. 14–15. 3. CP, pp. 88–89.*

Fortunes. 1. GT, pp. 24–25. 2. William Plomer, Anthony Thwaite, and Hilary Corke, eds., *A P. E. N. Anthology of Contemporary Poetry* (London, UK: Hutchinson, 1961) 102. 3. DH, pp. 120–21. 4. CP, pp. 83–84.*

The Clearing. 1. GT, p. 29. 2. CP, p. 87.*

Children's Coloured Flags. 1. GT, p. 34. 2. DH, p. 128. 3. CP, pp. 90–91.*

The Glass Trumpet. 1. GT, pp. 44–46. 2. DH, pp. 152–55. 3. CP, pp. 96–98.*

Falling Figure. 1. GT, pp. 76–81. 2. CP, pp. 113–16.*

Winter One. 1. GT, pp. 82–83. 2. DH, pp. 132–33. 3. CP, pp. 116–17.*

Committee Work. 1. GT, p. 85. 2. CTC, p. 113. 3. CP, p. 118.*

Night of Voices. 1. GT, pp. 86–87. 2. Laurence R. Ricou, ed., *Twelve Prairie Poets* (Ottawa: Oberon P, 1976) 173–74. 3. CP, p. 119.*

Desert Stone. 1. GT, pp. 88–89. 2. *Jewish Dialogue* (1971): 12. 3. DH, pp. 138–39. 4. Sarah Jackson, illus., *Finding Herself: Revelations behind the Mirror/Révélations derrière le miroir* (N.p.: n.p., [1980?]) n. pag. 5. Howard Schwartz and Anthony Rudolf, eds., *Voices within the Ark: The Modern Jewish Poets* (New York: Pushcart P, 1980) 770–71. 6. CP, p. 120.*

Losing Merrygorounds. 1. GT, pp. 90–91. 2. CP, p. 121.*

A Man Is Walking. 1. GT, pp. 92–93. 2. Laurence R. Ricou, ed., *Twelve Prairie Poets* (Ottawa: Oberon P, 1976) 175–77. 3. CP, pp. 122–23.*

The Oracle. 1. GT, pp. 94–95. 2. CTC, p. 149. 3. CP, pp. 123–24.*

The Eight-sided White Barn. 1. *Excalibur* [York U] 17 Feb. 1967: 5 (originally titled "Putting On and Taking Off: The Eight-Sided White Barn"). 2. *Imperial Oil Review* 52.1 (Feb. 1968): 25. 3. *Journal of the Otto Rank Association* [Doylestown, PA] 3.1 (June 1968): 52. 4. SY, pp. 30–31. 5. DH, pp. 172–73. 6. CP, pp. 170–71.*

Leaf. 1. *Excalibur* [York U] 17 Feb. 1967: 5 (originally titled "Putting On and Taking Off: Leaf"). 2. *New Measure* [Northwood, Middlesex, UK] 9 (Summer 1968): 50. 3. SY, p. 51. 4. CP, p. 183.*

My Travels. 1. *Excalibur* [York U] 17 Feb. 1967: 4 (originally titled "Putting On and Taking Off: My Travels"). 2. *Viewpoints: A Canadian Jewish Quarterly* 2.3 (1967): 54. 3. SY, pp. 8–10. 4. DH, pp. 146–49. 5. CP, pp. 155–57.*

Pont Mirabeau in Montreal. 1. *Excalibur* [York U] 17 Feb. 1967: 5 (originally titled "Putting On and Taking Off: Pont Mirabeau in Montreal"). 2. *New Measure*

[Northwood, Middlesex, UK] 10 (Late Final Issue 1969): 63. 3. sy, p. 33. 4. DH, p. 169. 5. CP, p. 172–73.*

Putting on and Taking Off. 1. *Excalibur* [York U] 17 Feb. 1967: 5 (originally titled "Putting on and Taking Off: Putting on and Taking Off"). 2. PG, p. 64. 3. CP, p. 272–73.*

Runners. 1. *Excalibur* [York U] 17 Feb. 1967: 5 (originally titled "Putting On and Taking Off: Runners"). 2. Thelma Reid Lower and Frederick William Cogswell, eds., *The Enchanted Land: Canadian Poetry for Young Readers* (Agincourt, ON: Gage, 1967) 3. 3. DT, p. 17.* 4. CRL, plate 24 (excerpt).

The Wakened Wood (4). 1. *Excalibur* [York U] 17 Feb. 1967: 4 (originally titled "Putting On and Taking Off: You as the Baffled Glance"). 2. *Wascana Review* 2.1 (1967): 32. 3. sy, pp. 36–37. 4. MN, p. 15. 5. CP, p. 175.*

The Wakened Wood (5). 1. *Excalibur* [York U] 17 Feb. 1967: 4 (originally titled "Putting On and Taking Off: You as Flowering Logs on the Gatineau"). 2. *Wascana Review* 2.1 (1967): 32. 3. sy, p. 37. 4. MN, p. 17. 5. CP, p. 175.*

You as Real. 1. *Excalibur* [York U] 17 Feb. 1967: 4 (originally titled "Putting On and Taking Off: You As Real"). 2. sy, p. 37. 3. CP, p. 175.*

Waking. 1. *Saturday Night* Feb. 1967: 23 (originally titled "Landscape"). 2. *New Measure* [Northwood, Middlesex, UK] 5 (Spring 1967): 5–6. 3. CTC, p. 180. 4. sy, p. 7. 5. *Chatelaine* Oct. 1972: 104. 6. DH, p. 174. 7. CP, p. 139.* 8. CRL, plate 12 (excerpt).

The Hockey Players. 1. *Saturday Night* Mar. 1967: 49 (originally titled "Child Hockey Players"). 2. CTC, p. 110. 3. DH, p. 85. 4. Shirley Irene Paustian, ed., *Through the Open Window* (Toronto: Oxford UP, 1983) 233. 5. CP, p. 144.*

Disposing of Mister Never as a Good Man. 1. *New: American and Canadian Poetry* 3 (Apr. 1967): 5–6. 2. *Saturday Night* June 1978: 51. 3. *Canadian Women's Studies/ Les cahiers de la femmes* [Centennial College] 1.3 (Spring/printemps 1979): 109. 4. MN, pp. 24–25. 5. TV, pp. 36–37. 6. CP, pp. 303–04.*

When You Paint My Portrait. 1. *New: American and Canadian Poetry* 3 (Apr. 1967): 7. 2. CP, p. 393.*

Games. 1. *New Measure* [Northwood, Middlesex, UK] 5 (Spring 1967): 8. 2. CP, p. 394.*

Laughter. 1. *New Measure* [Northwood, Middlesex, UK] 5 (Spring 1967): 9. 2. CTC, p. 51. 3. Mary Alice Downie and Barbara Robertson, eds., *The Wind Has Wings: Poems from Canada* (Toronto: Oxford UP, 1968) 14. 4. sy, p. 53. 5. DH, p. 84. 6. CP, p. 127.* 7. CRL, plate 15 (excerpt).

Portrait: Old Woman. 1. *New Measure* [Northwood, Middlesex, UK] 5 (Spring 1967): 7 (originally titled "Autumn"). 2. CTC, p. 167. 3. PG, p. 68. 4. Jack David and Robert Lecker, eds., *Canadian Poetry* (Toronto/Downsview, ON: General/ ECW P, 1982) 266. 5. CP, p. 144.*

Sea Thoughts. 1. *New Measure* [Northwood, Middlesex, UK] 5 (Spring 1967): 8 (originally titled "Games (2)"). 2. CTC, p. 198. 3. CP, p. 147.*

Tattoo Man. 1. *New Measure* [Northwood, Middlesex, UK] 5 (Spring 1967): 6. 2. CTC, p. 176. 3. CP, p. 143.*

Trumpets. 1. *New Measure* [Northwood, Middlesex, UK] 5 (Spring 1967): 6 (originally titled "Design"). 2. CTC, p. 20. 3. PG, p. 71. 4. CP, p. 125.*

Women Who Live Alone. 1. *New Measure* [Northwood, Middlesex, UK] 5 (Spring 1967): 8. 2. SY, p. 42. 3. CP, p. 179.*

From a Train Window. 1. *Adam International Review* 313–315 (1967): 42. 2. SY, p. 41. 3. CP, pp. 178–79.*

The Wakened Wood (1). 1. *Wascana Review* 2.1 (1967): 31 (originally titled "Notations: [1]"). 2. SY, p. 36. 3. CP, p. 174.*

The Wakened Wood (2). 1. *Wascana Review* 2.1 (1967): 31 (originally titled "Notations: 2"). 2. SY, p. 36. 3. MN, p. 18. 4. CP, p. 174.*

The Wakened Wood (3). 1. *Wascana Review* 2.1 (1967): 31 (originally titled "Notations: 3"). 2. SY, p. 36. 3. CP, pp. 174–75.*

Apollo Tree. 1. *Canadian Literature* 35 (Winter 1968): 76 (originally titled "The Apollo Tree"). 2. *New Measure* [Northwood, Middlesex, UK] 9 (Summer 1968): 50. 3. SY, p. 35. 4. CP, p. 174.*

Dark. 1. *New Measure* [Northwood, Middlesex, UK] 9 (Summer 1968): 52. 2. *Far Point* 1 (Fall–Winter 1968): 40. 3. SY, p. 43. 4. CP, pp. 179–80.*

Canadians. 1. *Saturday Night* July 1968: 24. 2. CTC, p. 243. 3. DH, pp. 175–76. 4. Robert Weaver and William Toye, eds., *The Oxford Anthology of Canadian Literature* (Toronto: Oxford UP, 1973) 505–06. 5. CP, p. 149. 6. John Robert Colombo, ed., *The Penguin Treasury of Popular Canadian Poems and Songs* (Toronto: Penguin Canada, 2002) 289–90.*

Breaking with Tradition. 1. *Far Point* 1 (Fall–Winter 1968): 41–42. 2. SY, p. 59. 3. Miriam Waddington, *A. M. Klein* (Toronto: Copp Clark Publishing/ Montreal: McGill-Queen's UP, 1970) 4–5. 4. CP, p. 187.*

Ukrainian Church. 1. *Far Point* 1 (Fall–Winter 1968): 38–39. 2. CTC, p. 203. 3. SY, pp. 50–51. 4. DH, pp. 145–46. 5. Laurence R. Ricou, ed., *Twelve Prairie Poets* (Ottawa: Oberon P, 1976) 168. 6. CP, pp. 140–41. 7. Gary Geddes, ed., *15 Canadian Poets x 2* (Toronto: Oxford UP, 1990) 165. 8. Gary Geddes, ed., *15 Canadian Poets x 3* (Toronto: Oxford UP, 2001) 86.*

The Little Fringes. 1. *Journal of the Otto Rank Association* [Doylestown, PA] 3.1 (June 1968): 53. 2. *New Measure* [Northwood, Middlesex, UK] 9 (Summer 1968): 51. 3. *Malahat Review* 8 (Oct. 1968): 15. 4. SY, p. 5. 5. CP, pp. 153–54.*

A Morning like the Morning when Amos Awoke. 1. *Wascana Review* 3.1 (1968): 23–24. 2. sy, pp. 64–65. 3. Alvin A. Lee, Hope Arnott Lee, and W. T. Jewkes, eds., *The Temple and the Ruin* (New York: Harcourt Brace Jovanovich, 1973) 135–36. 4. cp, pp. 190–91. 5. Gary Geddes, ed., *15 Canadian Poets x 2* (Toronto: Oxford UP, 1990) 168–69.*

The Magician. 1. *Wascana Review* 3.1 (1968): 20–22. 2. sy, pp. 16–17. 3. cp, pp. 161–62.*

What Is a Canadian. 1. ctc, p. 15. 2. pg, p. 44. 3. cp, p. 125.*

Child's Poem. 1. ctc, p. 22. 2. cp, pp. 125–26.*

Before I Go. 1. ctc, p. 29. 2. pg, p. 22. 3. cp, p. 126.*

The Children's Everlasting Tree. 1. ctc, p. 30. 2. cp, pp. 126–27.*

Untitled [Time makes him old]. 1. ctc, p. 43.*

Autumn Rain. 1. ctc, p. 46. 2. cp, pp. 145–46.*

Spring I. 1. ctc, p. 54. 2. cp, p. 128.*

Spring II. 1. ctc, p. 54. 2. cp, p. 128.* 3. crl, plate 25 (excerpt).

Gossip. 1. ctc, p. 59. 2. cp, p. 128. 3. Gary Geddes, ed., *15 Canadian Poets x 2* (Toronto: Oxford UP, 1990) 166–67. 4. Gary Geddes, ed., *15 Canadian Poets x 3* (Toronto: Oxford UP, 2001) 87–88.*

Friends I. 1. ctc, p. 63. 2. cp, pp. 128–29.*

Crowds. 1. ctc, p. 65. 2. P. K. Page, ed., *To Say the Least: Canadian Poets from A to Z* (Toronto: Press Porcépic, 1979) 48. 3. cp, p. 129.*

Jazz. 1. ctc, p. 70. 2. cp, p. 130.* 3. crl, plate 3 (excerpt).

Spring on the Bay of Quinte. 1. ctc, p. 72. 2. pg, p. 74. 3. Fran Newman, ed., *Round Slice of the Moon and Other Poems for Canadian Kids* (Richmond Hill, ON: Scholastic-tab, 1980) 29. 4. cp, p. 131.*

Fragment. 1. ctc, p. 74. 2. cp, p. 130.*

Adolescents. 1. ctc, p. 78. 2. cp, pp. 130–31.*

Quiet. 1. ctc, p. 90. 2. pg, p. 31. 3. cp, p. 131.* 4. crl, plate 1 (excerpt).

Temple. 1. ctc, p. 100. 2. cp, p. 134.*

Spring Rain. 1. ctc, p. 93. 2. sy, pp. 46–48. 3. John Metcalf and Gordon Callaghan, eds., *Salutation* (Toronto: Ryerson P, 1970) 100–02. 4. John Metcalf, ed., *The Speaking Earth: Canadian Poetry* (Toronto: Van Nostrand Reinhold, 1973) 54–55. 5. cp, pp. 132–33.*

Being Young. 1. ctc, p. 106. 2. cp, p. 134.*

Summer in the City. 1. ctc, p. 135. 2. sy, p. 52. 3. cp, pp. 142–43.*

The Lonely Love of Middle Age. 1. ctc, p. 141. 2. dh, pp. 156–57. 3. Sarah Jackson, illus., *Finding Herself: Revelations behind the Mirror/Révélations derrière le miroir* (N.p.: n.p., [1980?]) n. pag. 4. cp, pp. 141–42. 5. Tom Wayman, ed.,

The Dominion of Love: An Anthology of Canadian Love Poems (Madeira Park, BC: Harbour Publishing, 2001) 93.*

The Nun. 1. CTC, p. 144. 2. CP, p. 141.*

Mother Life. 1. CTC, p. 157. 2. CP, p. 145.*

Will There Come a Time. 1. CTC, p. 165. 2. CP, p. 145.*

At the Races. 1. CTC, p. 169. 2. CP, p. 139.*

People II. 1. CTC, p. 173. 2. CP, p. 150.*

Art History. 1. CTC, p. 179. 2. CP, p. 148.*

The Artist II. 1. CTC, p. 186. 2. CP, p. 135.*

The Fortune Tellers. 1. CTC, p. 188. 2. CP, p. 147.*

Toronto Rain. 1. CTC, p. 191. 2. CP, p. 136.*

The Happiness of Birds. 1. CTC, p. 218. 2. CP, p. 147.*

The Wheel. 1. CTC, p. 220. 2. PG, p. 69. 3. CP, pp. 134–35.*

Pleasure. 1. CTC, p. 222. 2. CP, p. 135.*

Summer. 1. CTC, p. 225. 2. John Metcalf, ed., *The Speaking Earth: Canadian Poetry* (Toronto: Van Nostrand Reinhold, 1973) 15. 3. CP, p. 140.*

The Secret Life. 1. CTC, p. 229. 2. CP, p. 139.*

Love of Country. 1. CTC, p. 235. 2. CP, p. 147.*

Swallowing Darkness Is Swallowing Dead Elm Trees. 1. *West Coast Review* 3.3 (Winter 1969): 20. 2. SY, pp. 60–61. 3. CP, pp. 188–89.*

Transition. 1. *Journal of the Otto Rank Association* [Doylestown, PA] 4.1 (June 1969): 52. 2. SY, p. 78. 3. John Newlove, ed., *Canadian Poetry: The Modern Era* (Toronto: McClelland and Stewart, 1977) 250. 4. CP, p. 201.* 5. CRL, plate 21 (excerpt).

Waking in London (1). 1. *Journal of the Otto Rank Association* [Doylestown, PA] 4.1 (June 1969): 49. 2. SY, p. 80. 3. Clare MacCulloch, ed., *Lobsticks* (Guelph, ON: Alive, 1974) 176. 4. CP, p. 202.*

Waking in London (2). 1. *Journal of the Otto Rank Association* [Doylestown, PA] 4.1 (June 1969): 49–50. 2. *Canadian Forum* Apr.–May 1970: 21. 3. *Canadian Literature* 52 (Spring 1972): outside back cover. 4. SY, p. 80. 5. CP, p. 202.*

Waking in London (3). 1. *Journal of the Otto Rank Association* [Doylestown, PA] 4.1 (June 1969): 50. 2. SY, p. 81. 3. CP, p. 203.*

Waking in London (4). 1. *Journal of the Otto Rank Association* [Doylestown, PA] 4.1 (June 1969): 50–51. 2. SY, p. 82. 3. CP, pp. 203–04.*

A Landscape of John Sutherland. 1. *Canadian Literature* 41 (Summer 1969): 85–86. 2. George Woodcock, ed., *The Sixties: Writers and Writing of the Decade* (Vancouver: U of British Columbia P, 1969) 85–86. 3. DT, pp. 15–16. 4. DH, pp. 12–13. 5. Miriam Waddington, ed., *John Sutherland: Essays, Controversies and Poems* (Toronto: McClelland and Stewart, 1972) 6. 6. CP, pp. 211–12.*

About Free Rides. 1. *Tamarack Review* 50–51 (1969): 44–47. 2. sy, pp. 11–13. 3. cp, pp. 157–59.*

Circus Stuff. 1. *Wascana Review* 4.1 (1969): 37–39. 2. sy, pp. 73–74. 3. cp, pp. 197–98.*

Dancing. 1. *Black Moss* 1.1 (1969): 6. 2. *Journal of the Otto Rank Association* [Doylestown, PA] 4.1 (June 1969): 53. 3. sy, p. 76. 4. cp, p. 199.*

How Each One Becomes Another in the Early World. 1. *New Measure* [Northwood, Middlesex, UK] 10 (Late Final Issue 1969): 63–64. 2. sy, pp. 32–33. 3. John Newlove, ed., *Canadian Poetry: The Modern Era* (Toronto: McClelland and Stewart, 1977) 248–49. 4. cp, pp. 171–72.*

Icons. 1. *Tamarack Review* 50–51 (1969): 41–44. 2. sy, pp. 88–90. 3. dh, pp. 166–69. 4. Desmond Pacey, ed., *Selections from Major Canadian Writers* (Toronto: McGraw-Hill Ryerson, 1974) 113–15. 5. Jack David and Robert Lecker, eds., *Canadian Poetry* (Toronto/Downsview, ON: General/ECW P, 1982) 261–64. 6. Margaret Atwood, ed., *The New Oxford Book of Canadian Verse in English* (Toronto: Oxford UP, 1983) 188–89. 7. Donna Bennett and Russell Brown, eds., *An Anthology of Canadian Literature in English, Volume II* (Toronto: Oxford UP, 1983) 27–28. 8. cp, pp. 208–10. 9. Rosemary Sullivan, ed., *Poetry by Canadian Women* (Toronto: Oxford UP, 1989) 91–94.*

Looking for Strawberries in June. 1. *Tamarack Review* 50–51 (1969): 49–51. 2. *Canadian Dimension* 6.3–4 (Aug.–Sept. 1969): 47. 3. sy, pp. 28–29. 4. dh, pp. 140–41. 5. Douglas Daymond and Leslie Monkman, eds., *Literature in Canada, Volume II* (Toronto: Gage, 1978) 342–43. 6. Donna Bennett and Russell Brown, eds., *An Anthology of Canadian Literature in English, Volume II* (Toronto: Oxford UP, 1983) 26–27. 7. cp, pp. 169–70.*

Time II. 1. *Black Moss* 1.1 (1969): 7. 2. sy, pp. 86–87. 3. cp, pp. 206–07.

Waiting in Alberta. 1. *Tamarack Review* 50–51 (1969): 49. 2. sy, pp. 84–85. 3. Laurence R. Ricou, ed., *Twelve Prairie Poets* (Ottawa: Oberon P, 1976) 169–70. 4. cp, pp. 205–06.*

The Woman in the Blue Hat. 1. *Wascana Review* 4.1 (1969): 39–40. 2. *Journal of the Otto Rank Association* [Doylestown, PA] 4.1 (June 1969): 51–52. 3. sy, pp. 77–78. 4. cp, p. 200.*

Understanding Snow. 1. sy, p. 1. 2. cp, p. 151.*

Living Canadian: Words to Electronic Music. 1. sy, pp. 2–3. 2. cp, pp. 152–53.*

Flying with Milton. 1. sy, p. 4. 2. cp, p. 153.*

Cape Cod. 1. sy, p. 6. 2. cp, p. 154.*

Disguises. 1. sy, pp. 14–15. 2. cp, pp. 159–60.*

About How Hard It Is to Find New Words in an Outworn World when You Are Not a Magician. 1. sy, pp. 19–21. 2. cp, pp. 163–64.*

Dream Telescope. 1. SY, pp. 22–27 (originally titled "In My Dream Telescope").
2. John Robert Colombo, ed., *How Do I Love Thee: Sixty Poets of Canada (and Quebec) Select and Introduce Their Favourite Poems from Their Own Work* (Edmonton: Hurtig Publishers, 1970) 30–34. 3. DT, pp. 5–13. 4. CP, pp. 165–68.*

Memory Box. 1. SY, p. 34. 2. CP, p. 173.*

How We Are Immortal in Others. 1. SY, pp. 38–39. 2. CP, pp. 176–77.*

Sorrow Song. 1. SY, p. 40. 2. John Metcalf, ed., *The Speaking Earth: Canadian Poetry* (Toronto: Van Nostrand Reinhold, 1973) 17. 3. Laurence R. Ricou, ed., *Twelve Prairie Poets* (Ottawa: Oberon P, 1976) 167. 4. CP, pp. 177–78.*

Someone Who Used to Have Someone. 1. SY, p. 44. 2. Carl F. Klinck and Reginald E. Watters, eds., *Canadian Anthology* (Toronto: Gage, 1974) 442. 3. Jon Pearce, ed., *Mirrors: Recent Canadian Verse* (Toronto: Gage, 1975) 70. 4. PG, pp. 30–31. 5. Allen Andrews, Diane Thompson, and Douglas Cronk, eds., *Canadian Viewpoints: An Anthology of Canadian Writing* (Victoria: Province of British Columbia Ministry of Education, 1983) 384–85. 6. CP, pp. 180–81.*

Owning the World. 1. SY, p. 49. 2. CP, p. 182.*

Birch Tree. 1. SY, p. 54. 2. CP, p. 183.*

Cinderella Poems. 1. SY, pp. 55–58. 2. CP, pp. 183–86.*

Shakedown. 1. SY, p. 58. 2. CP, p. 186.*

A Drawing by Ronald Bloore. 1. SY, pp. 62–63. 2. CP, pp. 189–90.*

Driving Home. 1. SY, pp. 66–69. 2. DH, pp. 160–64. 3. CP, pp. 192–94.*

A Man in Chicago. 1. SY, pp. 70–72. 2. CP, pp. 195–97.*

A Picture of O. 1. SY, p. 75. 2. CP, pp. 198–99.*

In London. 1. SY, p. 79. 2. CP, pp. 201–02.*

Sunday Evening Letters. 1. SY, p. 87. 2. CP, pp. 207–08.*

Love Poem. 1. SY, p. 83. 2. DH, pp. 150–51. 3. Homer Hogan and Dorothy Hogan, eds., *Listen! Songs and Poems of Canada* (Toronto: Methuen, 1972) 76. 4. Robert Weaver and William Toye, eds., *The Oxford Anthology of Canadian Literature* (Toronto: Oxford UP, 1973) 507. 5. Jon Pearce, ed., *Mirrors: Recent Canadian Verse* (Toronto: Gage, 1975) 125–26. 6. John Newlove, ed., *Canadian Poetry: The Modern Era* (Toronto: McClelland and Stewart, 1977) 251. 7. Konrad Gross and Wolfgang Klooss, eds., *Voices from Distant Lands: Poetry in the Commonwealth* (Würzburg, Ger.: Königshausen and Neumann, 1983) 101–02. 8. CP, pp. 204–05.*

Don't Say Anything. 1. *Poetry Review* 61.1 (Spring 1970): 45. 2. PG, p. 24. 3. CP, p. 252.*

Song for Sleeping People. 1. *Poetry Review* 61.1 (Spring 1970): 44–45. 2. Raymond Souster and Douglas Lochhead, eds., *Made in Canada: New Poems of the Seventies* (Ottawa: Oberon P, 1970) 184. 3. DH, p. 35. 4. Kenneth J. Weber and

Homer Hogan, eds., *Truth and Fantasy* (Toronto: Methuen, 1972) 2. 5. CP, pp. 231–32.*

Eavesdropping. 1. *Canadian Forum* Apr.–May 1970: 56. 2. DT, pp. 22–24. 3. DH, pp. 18–20. 4. Desmond Pacey, ed., *Selections from Major Canadian Writers* (Toronto: McGraw-Hill Ryerson, 1974) 117–18. 5. CP, pp. 214–16.*

Language as I Used to Believe in It. 1. *Canadian Forum* Apr.–May 1970: 58. 2. DH, pp. 32–34. 3. CP, pp. 229–31.*

The Nineteen Thirties Are Over. 1. *Saturday Night* Sept. 1970: 50. 2. Dorothy Livesay and Seymour Mayne, eds., *40 Women Poets of Canada* (Montreal: Ingluvin P, 1971) 135–36. 3. DH, pp. 22–23. 4. John Newlove, ed., *Canadian Poetry: The Modern Era* (Toronto: McClelland and Stewart, 1977) 252–53. 5. Douglas Daymond and Leslie Monkman, eds., *Literature in Canada, Volume II* (Toronto: Gage, 1978) 343–44. 6. Gerri Sinclair and Morris Wolfe, eds., *The Spice Box: An Anthology of Jewish Canadian Writing* (Toronto: Lester and Orpen Dennys, 1981) 110–11. 7. Jack David and Robert Lecker, eds., *Canadian Poetry* (Toronto/Downsview, ON: General/ECW P, 1982) 264–65. 8. Donna Bennett and Russell Brown, eds., *An Anthology of Canadian Literature in English, Volume II* (Toronto: Oxford UP, 1983) 29–30. 9. Konrad Gross and Wolfgang Klooss, eds., *Voices from Distant Lands: Poetry in the Commonwealth* (Würzburg, Ger.: Königshausen and Neumann, 1983) 99–100. 10. CP, pp. 223–24.*

Anxious. 1. Raymond Souster and Douglas Lochhead, eds., *Made in Canada: New Poems of the Seventies* (Ottawa: Oberon P, 1970) 185. 2. DH, p. 37. 3. Robert Weaver and William Toye, eds., *The Oxford Anthology of Canadian Literature* (Toronto: Oxford UP, 1973) 506. 4. P. K. Page, ed., *To Say the Least: Canadian Poets from A to Z* (Toronto: Press Porcépic, 1979) 45. 5. CP, p. 233.*

The World on Easter Morning. 1. Raymond Souster and Douglas Lochhead, eds., *Made in Canada: New Poems of the Seventies* (Ottawa: Oberon P, 1970) 185 (originally titled "All on an Easter Morning). 2. DH, p. 15. 3. CP, p. 220.

The Land of Utmost. 1. *Excalibur* [York U] 18 Mar. 1971: 13 (originally titled "Utmost"). 2. *Journal of Canadian Studies* 6.4 (Nov. 1971): 52. 3. PG, p. 55. 4. CP, pp. 268–69.*

Polemics. 1. *Excalibur* [York U] 18 Mar. 1971: 13. 2. *Journal of Canadian Studies* 6.4 (Nov. 1971): 53. 3. DH, pp. 36–37. 4. Carl F. Klinck and Reginald E. Watters, eds., *Canadian Anthology* (Toronto: Gage, 1974) 444. 5. CP, pp. 232–33.*

Sad Winter in the Land of Can. Lit. 1. *Excalibur* [York U] 18 Mar. 1971: 13 (originally titled "Sad Winter in the Land of Can Lit"). 2. *Journal of Canadian Studies* 6.4 (Nov. 1971): 51–52. 3. DH, pp. 30–31. 4. Carl F. Klinck and Reginald E. Watters, eds., *Canadian Anthology* (Toronto: Gage, 1974) 443–44. 5. Desmond Pacey, ed., *Selections from Major Canadian Writers* (Toronto: McGraw-Hill Ryerson,

1974) 115–17. 6. John Robert Colombo, ed., *The Poets of Canada* (Edmonton: Hurtig Publishers, 1978) 150–52. 7. CP, pp. 228–29.*

Elijah. 1. *Midstream* Mar. 1971: 56 (originally titled "Song: Elijah"). 2. DT, p. 20. 3. DH, p. 27. 4. CP, p. 213.*

Lately I've Been Feeling Very Jewish. 1. *Viewpoints: A Canadian Jewish Quarterly* 6.1 (Spring 1971): 18. 2. CP, p. 395. 3. Gary Geddes, ed., *15 Canadian Poets x 2* (Toronto: Oxford UP, 1990) 175. 4. Gary Geddes, ed., *15 Canadian Poets x 3* (Toronto: Oxford UP, 2001) 91.*

Protocol. 1. *Viewpoints: A Canadian Jewish Quarterly* 6.1 (Spring 1971): 49. 2. CP, p. 395.*

Why Should I Care about the World. 1. *Viewpoints: A Canadian Jewish Quarterly* 6.2 (Summer 1971): 44. 2. Dorothy Livesay and Seymour Mayne, eds., *40 Women Poets of Canada* (Montreal: Ingluvin P, 1971) 138–39. 3. *New: American and Canadian Poetry* 17 (Dec.–Jan. 1971–72): 4–5. 4. DH, pp. 28–29. 5. Elizabeth McCullough, ed., *The Role of Women in Canadian Literature* (Toronto: Macmillan, 1975) 16. 6. Gerri Sinclair and Morris Wolfe, eds., *The Spice Box: An Anthology of Jewish Canadian Writing* (Toronto: Lester and Orpen Dennys, 1981) 114–15. 7. CP, pp. 226–27.*

I Wish My Life Was a Movie. 1. *Saturday Night* Aug. 1971: 38 (originally titled "Spring Song"). 2. DH, pp. 14–15. 3. CP, pp. 219–20.*

The Following. 1. *Midstream* Aug.–Sept. 1971: 58 (originally titled "Return"). 2. DH, pp. 50–51. 3. CP, pp. 241–42.*

Between Cities. 1. *Jewish Dialogue* (Rosh Hashanah 1971): 12. 2. *Canadian Forum* Sept. 1972: 20. 3. DH, pp. 16–17. 4. CP, pp. 221–22.*

Leaves. 1. *Jewish Dialogue* (Rosh Hashanah 1971): 13. 2. DT, p. 14. 3. PG, p. 23. 4. CP, p. 211.*

Origins. 1. *Jewish Dialogue* (Rosh Hashanah 1971): 14. 2. *Literary Half-Yearly* [U of Mysore, India] 13.2 (July 1972): 228. 3. DH, p. 13. 4. CP, p. 219.*

Provincial. 1. *Jewish Dialogue* (Rosh Hashanah 1971): 14. 2. *Canadian Forum* Sept. 1972: 23. 3. DH, pp. 42–43. 4. Laurence R. Ricou, ed., *Twelve Prairie Poets* (Ottawa: Oberon P, 1976) 179. 5. M. G. Hesse, ed., *Childhood and Youth in Canadian Literature* (Toronto: Macmillan, 1979) 116–17. 6. CP, pp. 236–37.*

Fence Post. 1. *New: American and Canadian Poetry* 16 (Sept.–Oct. 1971): 56–57. 2. *Queen's Quarterly* 79 (Spring 1972): 58–59. 3. DH, pp. 24–25. 4. CP, pp. 224–25.*

Lights. 1. *Malahat Review* 20 (Oct. 1971): 120–21. 2. DH, p. 21. 3. CP, p. 222.*

My Kind of Internationalism. 1. *Journal of Canadian Studies* 6.4 (Nov. 1971): 52–53.*

Testing Free Enterprise. 1. *Journal of Canadian Studies* 6.4 (Nov. 1971): 53–54.*

Transformations. 1. Dorothy Livesay and Seymour Mayne, eds., *40 Women Poets of Canada* (Montreal: Ingluvin P, 1971) 137. 2. Julian Naengle, ed., *Words*

Etcetera: A Miscellany of Literature Art and Criticism (Bramley, Surrey/Paris: Words/ Shakespeare, 1971) 84. 3. Queen's Quarterly 79 (Spring 1972): 58. 4. Desmond Pacey, ed., Selections from Major Canadian Writers (Toronto: McGraw-Hill Ryerson, 1974) 119. 5. DH, p. 9. 6. Douglas Daymond and Leslie Monkman, eds., Literature in Canada, Volume II (Toronto: Gage, 1978) 344. 7. Laurence R. Ricou, ed., Twelve Prairie Poets (Ottawa: Oberon P, 1976) 178. 8. Konrad Gross and Wolfgang Klooss, eds., Voices from Distant Lands: Poetry in the Commonwealth (Würzburg, Ger.: Königshausen and Neumann, 1983) 98. 9. CP, pp. 217–18.*

Signs. 1. Saturday Night Feb. 1972: 10. 2. DH, pp. 10–11. 3. CP, pp. 218–19.*

Back at York University. 1. Impulse 1.3 (Spring 1972): 7–8 (originally titled "Back at York"). 2. PG, pp. 62–63. 3. CP, pp. 271–72.*

Moscow Roses. 1. Impulse 1.3 (Spring 1972): 41. 2. DH, p. 25. 3. CP, p. 225. 4. Rosemary Sullivan, ed., Poetry by Canadian Women (Toronto: Oxford UP, 1989) 94.*

Advice to the Young. 1. Saturday Night July 1972: 6. 2. DH, pp. 26–27. 3. Robert Weaver and William Toye, eds., The Oxford Anthology of Canadian Literature (Toronto: Oxford UP, 1973) 504. 4. Herman Voaden, ed., Look Both Ways: Theatre Experiences (Toronto: Macmillan, 1975) 226–27. 5. David Kemp and Marian M. Wilson, eds., A Child Growing Up: A Journey Through the Bittersweet Joys of Childhood Experience (Toronto: Simon and Pierre, 1979) 89. 6. Margaret Atwood, ed., The New Oxford Book of Canadian Verse in English (Toronto: Oxford UP, 1983) 191–92. 7. Donna Bennett and Russell Brown, eds., An Anthology of Canadian Literature in English, Volume II (Toronto: Oxford UP, 1983) 28–29. 8. CP, pp. 225–26.*

Ending. 1. Literary Half-Yearly [U of Mysore, India] 13.2 (July 1972): 229. 2. PG, p. 104. 3. CP, p. 291.*

Gift: Venus 24 Degrees in Virgo. 1. Literary Half-Yearly [U of Mysore, India] 13.2 (July 1972): 229–30. 2. DH, pp. 43–44. 3. CP, pp. 237–38.*

In Small Towns. 1. Literary Half-Yearly [U of Mysore, India] 13.2 (July 1972): 227–28 (originally titled "In the Small Towns"). 2. DH, pp. 38–39. 3. CP, pp. 233–34.*

New Religions. 1. Literary Half-Yearly [U of Mysore, India] 13.2 (July 1972): 232. 2. DH, p. 45. 3. CP, p. 238.*

A Space of Love. 1. Literary Half-Yearly [U of Mysore, India] 13.2 (July 1972): 231. 2. Chatelaine Jan. 1973: 46. 3. PG, p. 26. 4. MN, p. 9. 5. CP, pp. 253–54.*

Dreaming of Mister Never. 1. Canadian Forum Sept. 1972: 22 (originally titled "In France I Dream More than in Other Countries"). 2. rune [St. Michael's College, U of Toronto] 3 (Spring 1976): 54–55. 3. MN, pp. 12–13. 4. CP, pp. 299–300.*

Finding Amos in Jerusalem. 1. Canadian Forum Sept. 1972: 21. 2. DH, pp. 52–53. 3. CP, pp. 243–44.*

Imitations. 1. *Canadian Forum* Sept. 1972: 23. 2. DH, p. 39. 3. CP, p. 234.*

Snowfences. 1. *Canadian Forum* Sept. 1972: 21 (originally titled "Letter to Jamaica"). 2. CP, pp. 212–13.*

Tapestry II. 1. *Canadian Forum* Sept. 1972: 22 (originally titled "Tapestry"). 2. DH, p. 51. 3. CP, pp. 242–43.*

Totems. 1. *Canadian Forum* Sept. 1972: 22 (originally titled "Whittling"). 2. DH, p. 48. 3. CP, p. 240.*

Little Prairie Pictures. 1. *Artscanada* 29.3 (Early Autumn 1972): 19. 2. *Midstream* Oct. 1972: 64. 3. PG, pp. 11–12. 4. CP, pp. 246–48.* 5. CRL, plate 14 (excerpt).

Dead Lakes. 1. *Impulse* 1.3 (Spring 1972): 6–7 (originally titled "The Dead Lakes of Sudbury"). 2. *Copperfield* [Edmonton] 4 (Oct. 1972): 10. 3. DH, pp. 40–41. 4. CP, pp. 234–35.*

October 1970. 1. *Globe and Mail* 7 Oct. 1972: 35. 2. Clare MacCulloch, ed., *Lobsticks* (Guelph, ON: Alive, 1974) 182–84. 3. PG, pp. 48–50. 4. CP, pp. 264–65.*

Rivers. 1. *Saturday Night* Oct. 1972: 44. 2. Clare MacCulloch, ed., *Lobsticks* (Guelph, ON: Alive, 1974) 188. 3. PG, p. 15. 4. CP, pp. 249–50.*

The Bower. 1. DT, p. 21. 2. PG, p. 102. 3. CP, p. 214.*

Voyagers. 1. DH, p. 8. 2. CP, p. 217.*

Lot's Wife. 1. DH, p. 41. 2. CP, pp. 235–36.*

Renunciations. 1. DH, pp. 46–47. 2. CP, pp. 239–40.*

Motions. 1. DH, p. 49. 2. CP, p. 241.*

Beau-Belle. 1. *Descant* 6 (Spring 1973): 6–7 (originally titled "Love: Canadian Style"). 2. PG, p. 32. 3. CP, p. 256.*

Divinations. 1. *Descant* 6 (Spring 1973): 5 (originally titled "Divination"). 2. *Tamarack Review* 62 (First Quarter 1974): 57. 3. Clare MacCulloch, ed., *Lobsticks* (Guelph, ON: Alive, 1974) 174. 4. PG, p. 17. 5. CP, p. 250.*

Forest Poem. 1. *Descant* 6 (Spring 1973): 6. 2. *Ariel* 4.3 (July 1973): 57. 3. Clare MacCulloch, ed., *Lobsticks* (Guelph, ON: Alive, 1974) 175. 4. PG, p. 16. 5. CP, p. 250.*

Legends. 1. *Queen's Quarterly* 80 (Spring 1973): 48. 2. PG, pp. 18–20. 3. CP, pp. 251–52.* 4. CRL, plate 18 (excerpt).

Lovers III. 1. *Queen's Quarterly* 80 (Spring 1973): 48 (originally titled "Loves"). 2. PG, p. 59. 3. CP, p. 270.*

Past the Ice Age. 1. *Descant* 6 (Spring 1973): 4. 2. TV, p. 53. 3. CP, p. 331.*

Charlottetown. 1. *Impulse* 3.1 (Fall 1973): 4. 2. PG, p. 79. 3. CP, p. 278.*

The Dark Lake. 1. *Impulse* 3.1 (Fall 1973): 5. 2. PG, p. 29. 3. CP, pp. 255–56.*

Downtown Streets. 1. *Porcepic* 1.2 (1973): 118–19. 2. Clare MacCulloch, ed., *Lobsticks* (Guelph, ON: Alive, 1974) 177–78. 3. PG, pp. 104–05. 4. CP, pp. 291–92. 5. Gary Geddes, ed., *15 Canadian Poets x 2* (Toronto: Oxford UP, 1990) 172–73.*

Spring III. 1. *Saturday Night* Feb. 1974: 8 (originally titled "Spring"). 2. PG, p. 95.
3. CP, p. 286.★

Absences. 1. *Tamarack Review* 62 (First Quarter 1974): 60. 2. PG, p. 101. 3. CP,
pp. 289–90. 4. Rosemary Sullivan, ed., *Poetry by Canadian Women* (Toronto:
Oxford UP, 1989) 94–95.★

Harvest. 1. *Tamarack Review* 62 (First Quarter 1974): 62. 2. PG, p. 37. 3. CP, p. 258.★

National Treasures in Havana. 1. *Tamarack Review* 62 (First Quarter 1974): 64–65.
2. *Modern Poetry Studies* 5.2 (Autumn 1974): 201–02. 3. Clare MacCulloch, ed.,
Lobsticks (Guelph, ON: Alive, 1974) 179–81. 4. PG, pp. 41–42. 5. CP, pp. 260–61.★

Ten Years and More. 1. *Tamarack Review* 62 (First Quarter 1974): 59–60. 2. Howard
Sergeant, et al., eds., *Best Poems of 1974: Borestone Mountain Poetry Awards, 1975*
(Palo Alto, CA: Pacific, 1975) 4–5. 3. PG, pp. 96–97. 4. Margaret Atwood, ed.,
The New Oxford Book of Canadian Verse in English (Toronto: Oxford UP, 1983) 193.
5. Donna Bennett and Russell Brown, eds., *An Anthology of Canadian Literature
in English, Volume II* (Toronto: Oxford UP, 1983) 31. 6. CP, p. 287. 7. Rosemary
Sullivan, ed., *Poetry by Canadian Women* (Toronto: Oxford UP, 1989) 94–95.
8. Gary Geddes, ed., *15 Canadian Poets x 2* (Toronto: Oxford UP, 1990)
171–72. 9. Gary Geddes, ed., *15 Canadian Poets x 3* (Toronto: Oxford UP, 2001)
90–91.★

This Year in Jerusalem. 1. *Tamarack Review* 62 (First Quarter 1974): 56–57. 2. PG,
p. 47. 3. CP, pp. 263–64.★

Tourists. 1. *Tamarack Review* 62 (First Quarter 1974): 63. 2. PG, p. 78. 3. CP, p. 277.★

Two Trees. 1. *Tamarack Review* 62 (First Quarter 1974): 61. 2. *Queen's Quarterly* 83
(Summer 1976): 233. 3. PG, pp. 92–93. 4. CP, pp. 284–85.★

Wives' Tales. 1. *Tamarack Review* 62 (First Quarter 1974): 58–59. 2. PG, pp. 100–01.
3. John Newlove, ed., *Canadian Poetry: The Modern Era* (Toronto: McClelland
and Stewart, 1977) 254. 4. CP, p. 289.★

A Monument for Mister Never. 1. *Waves* 3.3 (Spring 1975): 27 (originally titled
"Utopia"). 2. MN, p. 21. 3. CP, p. 302.★

Poets Are Still Writing Poems about Spring and Here Is Mine: Spring. 1. *Waves* 3.3
(Spring 1975): 26–27. 2. PG, pp. 72–73. 3. CP, pp. 274–75.★

Friends II. 1. *Saturday Night* May 1975: 15 (originally titled "The Morning Mail").
2. PG, pp. 60–61. 3. CP, pp. 270–71.★

By the Sea: For A. M. Klein. 1. *Canadian Literature* 65 (Summer 1975): 53–54. 2. PG,
pp. 9–10. 3. CP, pp. 245–46.★

Husbands. 1. *Canadian Forum* Sept. 1975: 11. 2. PG, pp. 57–58. 3. CP, p. 269.★

London Night. 1. *Canadian Forum* Sept. 1975: 11 (originally titled "A London
Night"). 2. PG, pp. 27–28. 3. CP, pp. 254–55.★

Artists and Old Chairs. 1. *Canadian Literature* 71 (Winter 1976): 79–81. 2. PG, pp. 82–84. 3. CP, pp. 279–80.*

The Dead. 1. *Saturday Night* Mar. 1976: 16. 2. PG, pp. 98–99. 3. CP, p. 288.*

Tallness and Darkness. 1. *rune* [St. Michael's College, U of Toronto] 3 (Spring 1976): 53–54 (originally titled "Home"). 2. PG, pp. 39–40. 3. CP, pp. 259–60.*

Notes of Summer. 1. *University of Windsor Review* 2.2 (Spring–Summer 1976): 84. 2. PG, p. 36. 3. CP, pp. 257–58.*

Old Chair Song. 1. *University of Windsor Review* 2.2 (Spring–Summer 1976): 85. 2. PG, pp. 84–85. 3. CP, p. 281.*

Naive Geography. 1. *Queen's Quarterly* 83 (Summer 1976): 232. 2. *English Quarterly* 10.2 (Summer 1977): 76. 3. PG, p. 75. 4. CP, pp. 275–76. 5. *Queen's Quarterly* 100.1 (Spring 1993): 149.*

Winnipeg and Leningrad. 1. *Queen's Quarterly* 83 (Summer 1976): 231. 2. PG, pp. 51–52. 3. CP, p. 266. 4. *Queen's Quarterly* 100.1 (Spring 1993): 148.*

Old Wood. 1. *Chatelaine* Dec. 1976: 57. 2. CP, p. 399.*

Real Estate: Poem for Voices. 1. *cv/n* 2.4 (Dec. 1976): 16 (originally titled "Real Estate (Poem for Voices)"). 2. TV, pp. 50–52. 3. CP, pp. 328–30.*

What the Angel Said. 1. PG, p. 8. 2. CP, p. 245.*

Grand Manan Sketches. 1. PG, pp. 13–14. 2. Douglas Daymond and Leslie Monkman, eds., *Literature in Canada, Volume II* (Toronto: Gage, 1978) 344–45. 3. CP, pp. 248–49.*

Ecstasy. 1. PG, p. 21.*

An Unliberated Woman Seen from a Distance. 1. PG, p. 24. 2. CP, p. 253.*

Profile of an Unliberated Woman. 1. PG, p. 25. 2. CP, p. 253.*

The Things We Talked About. 1. PG, p. 34. 2. CP, p. 257.*

The Secret of Old Trees. 1. PG, p. 38. 2. CP, pp. 258–59.*

Snow Stories. 1. PG, pp. 45–46. 2. CP, pp. 262–63.*

How I Spent the Year Listening to the Ten O'Clock News. 1. PG, pp. 53–54. 2. CP, pp. 267–68. 3. Gary Geddes, ed., *15 Canadian Poets x 2* (Toronto: Oxford UP, 1990) 170–71. 4. Gary Geddes, ed., *15 Canadian Poets x 3* (Toronto: Oxford UP, 2001) 89–90.*

Morning on Cooper Street. 1. PG, p. 66. 2. CP, pp. 273–74.*

The Wind in Charlottetown. 1. PG, pp. 76–77. 2. CP, pp. 276–77.*

I Take My Seat in the Theatre. 1. PG, pp. 86–88. 2. CP, pp. 281–83.*

Afternoon on Grand Manan. 1. PG, p. 89–90. 2. CP, pp. 283–84.*

The Price of Gold. 1. PG, pp. 93–94. 2. CP, pp. 285–86.*

A Lover Who Knows. 1. PG, p. 103. 2. CP, p. 290.*

The Days Are Short. 1. PG, p. 106. 2. CP, p. 292.*

Where the North Winds Live. 1. PG, pp. 107–08. 2. CP, pp. 292–93.*

The Cave. 1. PG, pp. 109–12. 2. CP, pp. 294–96.*

Prairie II. 1. *NeWest Review* 2.8 (Apr. 1977): 7 (originally titled "Prairie"). 2. TV, p. 27. 3. CP, p. 317.*

Horoscopes. 1. *Toronto Life* Oct. 1977: 69 (originally titled "A Few Lyrics for the Season—Horoscopes"). 2. TV, p. 40. 3. CP, p. 323.*

Warnings. 1. *Toronto Life* Oct. 1977: 69 (originally titled "A Few Lyrics for the Season—Warnings from Captain Arctic"). 2. TV, p. 34. 3. CP, pp. 322–23.*

Mister Never Playing. 1. *Canadian Forum* Nov. 1977: 38 (originally titled "Playing"). 2. MN, p. 22. 3. TV, p. 9. 4. CP, pp. 302–03.* 5. CRL, plate 4 (excerpt).

Running up and down Mountains at Changing Speeds. 1. *Room of One's Own* 3.1 (1977): 8–9. 2. TV, pp. 54–55. 3. CP, pp. 331–33.*

When the Shoe Is on the Other Foot for a Change. 1. *Room of One's Own* 3.1 (1977): 10. 2. TV, p. 49. 3. CP, p. 328.*

Certain Winter Meditations on Mister Never. 1. *Tamarack Review* 74 (Spring 1978): 49–50 (originally titled "Certain Winter"). 2. MN, pp. 34–35. 3. TV, pp. 38–39. 4. CP, pp. 304–05.* 5. CRL, plate 13 (excerpt).

Feasts. 1. *Tamarack Review* 74 (Spring 1978): 54. 2. TV, p. 17. 3. CP, p. 311.*

Holiday Postcards. 1. *Queen's Quarterly* 85 (Spring 1978): 57. 2. TV, pp. 28–29. 3. CP, pp. 318–19.*

Lady in Blue: Homage to Montreal. 1. *Tamarack Review* 74 (Spring 1978): 47–48. 2. Morris Wolfe, ed., *Aurora: New Canadian Writing 1978* (Toronto: Doubleday, 1978) 58–59. 3. TV, pp. 56–57. 4. CP, pp. 333–34.*

Letter from Egypt. 1. *Headless Angel* [New College, U of Toronto] (Spring 1978): 5. 2. *Tamarack Review* 74 (Spring 1978): 51–52. 3. TV, pp. 32–33. 4. CP, pp. 320–21.*

Mister Never in a Dream of the Gatineau. 1. *Queen's Quarterly* 85 (Spring 1978): 58. 2. MN, pp. 10–11. 3. CP, pp. 298–99.*

Postcard from Underground. 1. *Tamarack Review* 74 (Spring 1978): 53. 2. *Canadian Author and Bookman* 57.2 (Winter 1982): 18. 3. *Canadian Dimension* May 1982: 35. 4. CP, pp. 399–400.*

Unemployment Town. 1. *This Magazine* Dec. 1978: 12. 2. TV, p. 30. 3. CP, p. 319.*

Prologue. 1. MN, p. 8. 2. CP, p. 297.*

Mister Never in the Gardens of France. 1. MN, p. 14. 2. CP, pp. 300–01.*

Mister Never on the Toronto Subway. 1. MN, p. 19. 2. CP, p. 301.*

Mister Never Shows Me How to Fall off the World. 1. MN, p. 20. 2. CP, pp. 301–02.*

The Big Tree. 1. *Waves* 7.2 (Winter 1979): 31. 2. *Canadian Dimension* May 1982: 35. 3. TV, pp. 12–13. 4. CP, pp. 307–08.*

Managing Death. 1. *Saturday Night* Nov. 1980: 92. 2. Morris Wolfe, ed., *Aurora: New Canadian Writing 1980* (Toronto: Doubleday, 1980) 217–18. 3. TV, p. 64. 4. CP, pp. 337–38.*

Crazy Times. 1. Morris Wolfe, ed., *Aurora: New Canadian Writing 1980* (Toronto: Doubleday, 1980) 220. 2. TV, p. 42. 3. CP, pp. 323–24.*

The Green Cabin. 1. Morris Wolfe, ed., *Aurora: New Canadian Writing 1980* (Toronto: Doubleday, 1980) 218–19. 2. TV, pp. 70–71. 3. CP, pp. 341–42.*

Honouring Heroes. 1. *Waves* 10.1–2 (Summer–Fall 1981): 96–97. 2. TV, pp. 16–17. 3. CP, p. 310.*

Conserving. 1. TV, pp. 10–11. 2. CP, pp. 306–07.*

The Milk of Mothers. 1. TV, pp. 14–15. 2. CP, pp. 308–09.*

South American Nights. 1. TV, p. 18. 2. CP, pp. 311–12.*

Primary Colours. 1. TV, pp. 19–22. 2. CP, pp. 312–15.*

Selves. 1. TV, pp. 23–26. 2. CP, pp. 315–17.*

History: In Jordan. 1. TV, p. 31. 2. CP, p. 320.*

How Old Women Should Live. 1. TV, pp. 43–44. 2. Konrad Gross and Wolfgang Klooss, eds., *Voices from Distant Lands: Poetry in the Commonwealth* (Würzburg, Ger.: Königshausen and Neumann, 1983) 103–04. 3. CP, pp. 324–25.*

Old Age Blues. 1. TV, pp. 45–46. 2. CP, pp. 325–26.* 3. CRL, plate 5 (excerpt).

Portrait of the Owner of a Small Garbage Can. 1. TV, pp. 47–48. 2. CP, pp. 326–27.*

Committees. 1. TV, p. 53. 2. *Toronto Life* Jan. 1982: 12. 3. CP, p. 331.*

Old Woman in a Garden. 1. TV, pp. 58–59. 2. CP, pp. 334–35.*

Celebrating Mavericks. 1. TV, p. 60. 2. CP, pp. 335–36.*

The Transplanted: Second Generation. 1. TV, pp. 62–63. 2. *Canadian Ethnic Studies/ Études Ethniques au Canada* 14.1 (1982): 23–24. 3. Konrad Gross and Wolfgang Klooss, eds., *Voices from Distant Lands: Poetry in the Commonwealth* (Würzburg, Ger.: Königshausen and Neumann, 1983) 104–06. 4. CP, pp. 336–37.*

The Visitants. 1. TV, p. 65. 2. Konrad Gross and Wolfgang Klooss, eds., *Voices from Distant Lands: Poetry in the Commonwealth* (Würzburg, Ger.: Königshausen and Neumann, 1983) 106–07. 3. George Amabile and Kim Dales, eds., *No Feather, No Ink: After Riel* (Saskatoon, SK: Thistledown P, 1985) 142. 4. CP, p. 338.*

The Secret-keeper. 1. TV, pp. 66–68. 2. CP, pp. 339–40.*

When We Met. 1. TV, p. 69. 2. *Canadian Ethnic Studies/Études Ethniques au Canada* 14.1 (1982): 49. 3. CP, p. 341.*

In a Summer Garden. 1. TV, p. 72. 2. CP, pp. 342–43.*

Elegies for a Composer. 1. TV, pp. 73–74. 2. CP, pp. 343–44. 3. Gary Geddes, ed., *15 Canadian Poets x 2* (Toronto: Oxford UP, 1990) 173–75.* 4. CRL, plate 26 (excerpt).

Bulgarian Suite. 1. TV, pp. 75–79. 2. CP, pp. 345–48.* 3. CRL, plate 8, 28 (excerpts).

Wake-up Song. 1. TV, p. 80. 2. CP, p. 348.*

Winter Storm. 1. *Queen's Quarterly* 89 (Spring 1982): 112. 2. CP, pp. 400–01.*

Questions. 1. *Poetry Toronto* Sept. 1982: n. pag. (originally titled "Problems"). 2. LL, p. 32.*

The Visitor I. 1. *Poetry Toronto* Sept. 1982: n. pag.* (originally titled "The Visitor"). Song II. 1. CP, pp. 66–67.*

Women. 1. CP, pp. 278–79.* 2. CRL, plate 19 (excerpt).

Magic. 1. CP, pp. 349–50.*

Partisans II. 1. CP, pp. 365–66.*

Three Prose Poems: Little Allegories of Canada. 1. CP, pp. 396–99.*

The Gift. 1. CP, pp. 401–02.*

Aspects of Owls I. 1. CP, pp. 402–03. 2. LL, pp. 58–59.*

Aspects of Owls II. 1. CP, pp. 403–04. 2. LL, pp. 60–61.*

The New Seasons: Light and Dark. 1. CP, pp. 404–05.*

The Angels Who Sweep I. 1. CP, pp. 405–08. 2. LL, pp. 13–16.*

The Angels Who Sweep II. 1. CP, pp. 408–09. 2. LL, pp. 17–19.* 3. CRL, plate 16 (excerpt).

Languages. 1. *Canadian Forum* Oct. 1987: 21. 2. LL, p. 33.*

The Last Landscape. 1. *Canadian Forum* Oct. 1987: 20. 2. LL, pp. 21–22.*

Mysteries. 1. *Canadian Forum* Oct. 1987: 20. 2. LL, pp. 81–82.* 3. CRL, plate 27 (excerpt).

Spring Night at Home. 1. *Canadian Forum* Oct. 1987: 21. 2. LL, pp. 72–73.*

Jacques Cartier in Toronto. 1. *Toronto Life* Dec. 1988: 67. 2. LL, p. 74.*

Living with Rumours of War. 1. *Quarry* 40.1–2 (Spring 1991): 183. 2. LL, p. 20.

Places. 1. *Quarry* 40.1–2 (Spring 1991): 181–82. 2. LL, pp. 55–56.*

The Archivist. 1. *Canadian Forum* Mar. 1992: 23. 2. LL, pp. 85–89.*

The Woman in the Hall. 1. *Canadian Forum* Mar. 1992: 22. 2. LL, pp. 3–5.*

Futures. 1. *Toronto Life* Apr. 1992: 26. 2. LL, p. 9.*

The Snow Tramp. 1. *Toronto Life* July 1992: 69. 2. LL, pp. 1–2.*

Instead of Lovers. 1. LL, pp. 6–8.*

Reflections. 1. LL, p. 10.*

The Life of a Woman. 1. LL, p. 11.*

Knives and Ploughshares. 1. LL, p. 12.*

The New Jasons. 1. LL, pp. 23–24.*

Amos. 1. LL, p. 25.

Ulysses Embroidered. 1. LL, pp. 26–27. 2. J. Paul Hunter, Alison Booth, and Kelly Mays, eds., *The Norton Introduction to Poetry* (New York: W. W. Norton, 2002) 363–64.*

Gardens and Us. 1. LL, pp. 28–30.*

Paper Boats. 1. LL, p. 31.*

Mechanics for Women. 1. LL, pp. 34–35.*

The Summer Girls. 1. LL, pp. 36–37.*
In the Hurly Burly Arcade. 1. LL, pp. 38–40.*
Mountain Interval I: Studio. 1. LL, pp. 50–51.*
Mountain Interval II: Pow Wow at Bragg Creek. 1. LL, pp. 52–54.*
A Few Things. 1. LL, p. 57.*
Freedom Games. 1. LL, pp. 62–63.*
A Man and His Flute. 1. LL, pp. 64–65.*
Orchestra. 1. LL, p. 66.*
Autumn. 1. LL, p. 67.*
Science and Literature. 1. LL, pp. 68–69.*
Jacques Cartier in Winnipeg. 1. LL, p. 75.*
Remembering Winnipeg. 1. LL, pp. 78–80.*
The Visitor II. 1. LL, pp. 83–84* (originally titled "The Visitor").
Peace Notes. 1. LL, p. 90.*
Untitled [The landscape sways]. 1. CRL, plate 29.*
Noises. 1. Canadian Jewish Studies 11 (2003): 6.*
Songs of Old Age. 1. Canadian Jewish Studies 11 (2003): 3–5.*
Spring Onions. 1. Canadian Jewish Studies 11 (2003): 7–10.*

PREVIOUSLY UNPUBLISHED AND UNCOLLECTED POEMS

Reveille. 1. MG31-D54, box 2, file 16, LAC.*
Romance. 1. MG31-D54, box 2, file 10, LAC.*
Politics. 1. MG31-D54, box 3, file 2, LAC* (signed Jane Herbert, a pseudonym).
Biology Room. 1. MG31-D54, box 2, file 9, LAC.*
The Pool. 1. MG31-D54, box 2, file 39, LAC.*
Tea Leaves. 1. MG31-D54, box 2, file 8, LAC.*
What Is This Life. 1. MG31-D54, box 3, file 2, LAC* (signed Jane Herbert, a
    pseudonym).
The Peasant's Revolt. 1. MG31-D54, box 2, file 10, LAC.*
The Flying Weather. 1. MG31-D54, LAC.*
Envoi. 1. MG31-D54, box 2, file 17, LAC.*
To a Three Year Old. 1. MG31-D54, box 3, file 2, LAC.*
Medea. 1. MG31-D54, box 3, file 3, LAC.*
At the Gate. 1. MG31-D54, box 3, file 3, LAC.*
The Pattern. 1. MG31-D54, box 3, file 3, LAC.*
Our Journey Was a Failure. 1. MG31-D54, box 3, file 3, LAC.*
Pleasures. 1. MG31-D54, box 3, file 3, LAC.*
Journey to Winnipeg: 1940. 1. MG31-D54, box 48, file 39, LAC.*

Love. 1. MG31-D54, box 2, file 30, LAC.*

Who in Their Love. 1. MG31-D54, box 2, file 37, LAC.*

At Court. 1. MG31-D54, box 49, file 3, LAC.*

Man and Secretary. 1. MG31-D54, box 2, file 33, LAC.*

Some Notes on Our Time. 1. MG31-D54, box 2, file12, LAC.*

Untitled [Black doves in my cherry tree]. 1. MG31-D54, box 2, file 16, LAC.*

He Calls. 1. MG31-D54, box 2, file 16, LAC.*

Doubles. 1. MG31-D54, box 2, file 31, LAC.*

Untitled [He who hobnobs]. 1. MG31-D54, box 3, file 6, LAC.*

Untitled [the dandelion children]. 1. MG31-D54, box 78, file 9, LAC.*

Untitled [It's six o'clock]. 1. MG31-D54, box 78, file 42, LAC.*

A Word. 1. MG31-D54, LAC.*

Untitled [I will build a mountain]. 1. MG31-D54, LAC.*

In Jerusalem. 1. MG31-D54, box 78, file 41, LAC.*

Untitled [Lamenting the archaeology of home]. 1. MG31-D54, LAC.*

Swimming Away. 1. MG31-D54, LAC.*

For Oliver Girling. 1. MG31-D54, box 49, file 11, LAC.*

My Orphan Poems. 1. MG31-D54, box 79, file 5, LAC.*

Departure from Kashima. 1. MG31-D54, box 78, file 10, LAC.*

Happy New Year. 1. MG31-D54, box 17, file 63, LAC.*

Cycles. 1. MG31-D54, box 78, file 7, LAC.*

A Garland for Terry. 1. MG31-D54, box 91, file 5, LAC* (words by Miriam Waddington; music by Harry Freedman; commissioned by the Victoria Symphony Orchestra).

To Manitoba Margaret on Her Sixtieth Birthday July 19/86. 1. MG31-D54, box 49, file 10, LAC.*

Untitled [(For My Brother Alex)]. 1. MG31-D54, box 79, file 19, LAC.*

On a Homely Afternoon. 1. MG31-D54, box 17, file 69, LAC.*

Untitled [Sometimes I imagine us]. 1. MG31-D54, LAC.*

Some of Them Wonder. 1. MG31-D54, box 49, file 4, LAC.*

Untitled [How bitter it is]. 1. MG31-D54, LAC.*

Untitled [I am addressed to you]. 1. MG31-D54, LAC.*

Untitled [Instead of swallows nesting & flying]. 1. MG31-D54, LAC.*

Undone Things. 1. MG31-D54, LAC.*

Ecology. 1. MG31-D54, box 78, file 12, LAC.*

Who Listens to Poets 1. MG31-D54, box 3, file 18, LAC.*

TRANSLATIONS—YIDDISH

Jewish Folk Song (Anonymous). 1. MG31-D54, box 75, file 6, LAC.★

Yizkor (Jacob Glatstein). 1. MG31-D54, box 75, file 8, LAC.★

Singing (N. Y. Gotlib). 1. MG31-D54, box 3, file 6, LAC.★

The Overcoat (Chaim Grade). 1. MG31-D54, box 75, file 7, LAC.★

The Beginning of a Poem (Rokhl Korn). 1. Rachel Korn, *Generations: Selected Poems* (Oakville, ON: Mosaic P, 1982) 13.★

An Evening in the Old People's Home (Rokhl Korn). 1. *Canadian Literature* 120 (Spring 1989): 20.★

The Housemaid (Rokhl Korn). 1. Irving Howe and Eliezer Greenberg, eds., *A Treasury of Yiddish Poetry* (New York: Holt, Rinehart and Winston, 1969) 302–04. 2. J. Michael Yates, Charles Lillard, and Ann J. West, eds., *Volvox: Poetry from the Unofficial Languages of Canada ... in English Translation* (Port Clements, BC: Sono Nis P, 1971) 117–19. 3. Rachel Korn, *Generations: Selected Poems* (Oakville, ON: Mosaic P, 1982) 16–17.★

Nuns Who Saved Jewish Children (Rokhl Korn). 1. *Viewpoints: A Canadian Jewish Quarterly* 2.3 (1967): 55. 2. Rachel Korn, *Generations: Selected Poems* (Oakville, ON: Mosaic P, 1982) 42.★

Seven Brothers (Mani Leib). 1. Irving Howe and Eliezer Greenberg, eds., *A Treasury of Yiddish Poetry* (New York: Holt, Rinehart and Winston, 1969) 90–92.★

Auld Lang Syne: New Year's Eve (Itsik Manger). 1. MG31-D54, box 75, file 20, LAC.★

Ballad of the Dying Christopher Marlowe (Itsik Manger). 1. MG31-D54, box 75, file 21, LAC.★

Evening (Itsik Manger). 1. Howard Schwartz and Anthony Rudolf, eds., *Voices within the Ark: The Modern Jewish Poets* (New York: Pushcart P, 1980) 310.★

Fairy Tales (Itsik Manger). 1. Howard Schwartz and Anthony Rudolf, eds., *Voices within the Ark: The Modern Jewish Poets* (New York: Pushcart P, 1980) 310.★

Fate (Itsik Manger). 1. MG31-D54, box 75, file 20, LAC.★

Night (Itsik Manger). 1. MG31-D54, box 49, file 11, LAC.★

Quiet Garden (Itsik Manger). 1. MG31-D54, box 75, file 21, LAC.★

Under the Ruins of Poland (Itsik Manger). 1. Howard Schwartz and Anthony Rudolf, eds., *Voices within the Ark: The Modern Jewish Poets* (New York: Pushcart P, 1980) 310–11.★

From An Elegy for Shlomo Mikhoels (Perets Markish). 1. MG31-D54, box 75, file 23, LAC.★

To a Poet Who Wrote about Jewish Persecution (Melekh Ravitch). 1. MG31-D54, box 75, file 27, LAC.★

What More Do You Want (Melekh Ravitch). 1. MG31-D54, box 3, file 6, LAC.*

At My Wedding (J. I. Segal). 1. Robert Weaver, ed., *The First Five Years: A Selection from the Tamarack Review* (Toronto: Oxford UP, 1962) 284. 2. K. Phyllis Dover, ed., *Poetry: An Anthology for High Schools* (Toronto: Holt, Rinehart and Winston, 1964) 149. 3. Irving Howe and Eliezer Greenberg, eds., *A Treasury of Yiddish Poetry* (New York: Holt, Rinehart and Winston, 1969) 151–52. 4. J. Michael Yates, Charles Lillard, and Ann J. West, eds., *Volvox: Poetry from the Unofficial Languages of Canada . . . in English Translation* (Port Clements, BC: Sono Nis P, 1971) 155.*

Aunt Dvorah (J. I. Segal). 1. *Tamarack Review* 17 (Autumn 1960): 39. 2. Robert Weaver, ed., *The First Five Years: A Selection from the Tamarack Review* (Toronto: Oxford UP, 1962) 285. 3. Irving Howe and Eliezer Greenberg, eds., *A Treasury of Yiddish Poetry* (New York: Holt, Rinehart and Winston, 1969) 157–58. 3. J. Michael Yates, Charles Lillard, and Ann J. West, eds., *Volvox: Poetry from the Unofficial Languages of Canada . . . in English Translation* (Port Clements, BC: Sono Nis P, 1971) 162.*

The Great Truth (J. I. Segal). 1. MG31-D54, box 75, file 29, LAC.*

A Jew (J. I. Segal). 1. Irving Howe and Eliezer Greenberg, eds., *A Treasury of Yiddish Poetry* (New York: Holt, Rinehart and Winston, 1969) 156–57. 2. J. Michael Yates, Charles Lillard, and Ann J. West, eds., *Volvox: Poetry from the Unofficial Languages of Canada . . . in English Translation* (Port Clements, BC: Sono Nis P, 1971) 160–61.*

Late Autumn in Montreal (J. I. Segal). 1. *Tamarack Review* 17 (Autumn 1960): 36. 2. *Canadian Literature* 42 (Autumn 1969): 41. 3. Irving Howe and Eliezer Greenberg, eds., *A Treasury of Yiddish Poetry* (New York: Holt, Rinehart and Winston, 1969) 153. 4. J. Michael Yates, Charles Lillard, and Ann J. West, eds., *Volvox: Poetry from the Unofficial Languages of Canada . . . in English Translation* (Port Clements, BC: Sono Nis P, 1971) 157.*

Late Summer in Montreal (J. I. Segal). 1. *Viewpoints: A Canadian Jewish Quarterly* 2.3 (1967): 56.*

Old Montreal (J. I. Segal). 1. *Tamarack Review* 17 (Autumn 1960): 37. 2. Robert Weaver, ed., *The First Five Years: A Selection from the Tamarack Review* (Toronto: Oxford UP, 1962) 283–84. 3. Irving Howe and Eliezer Greenberg, eds., *A Treasury of Yiddish Poetry* (New York: Holt, Rinehart and Winston, 1969) 152. 4. John McInnes and Emily Hearn, eds., *Hockey Cards and Hopscotch* (Toronto: Nelson, 1971) 11. 5. J. Michael Yates, Charles Lillard, and Ann J. West, eds., *Volvox: Poetry from the Unofficial Languages of Canada . . . in English Translation* (Port Clements, BC: Sono Nis P, 1971) 156.*

Rhymes (J. I. Segal). 1. Mary Alice Downie and Barbara Robertson, eds., *The Wind Has Wings: Poems from Canada* (Toronto: Oxford UP, 1968) 6. 2. Irving Howe and Eliezer Greenberg, eds., *A Treasury of Yiddish Poetry* (New York: Holt, Rinehart and Winston, 1969) 153–54.*

Scenario (J. I. Segal). 1. *Tamarack Review* 17 (Autumn 1960): 41–42. 2. Robert Weaver, ed., *The First Five Years: A Selection from the Tamarack Review* (Toronto: Oxford UP, 1962) 286–87. 3. Irving Howe and Eliezer Greenberg, eds., *A Treasury of Yiddish Poetry* (New York: Holt, Rinehart and Winston, 1969) 158–59. 4. J. Michael Yates, Charles Lillard, and Ann J. West, eds., *Volvox: Poetry from the Unofficial Languages of Canada . . . in English Translation* (Port Clements, BC: Sono Nis P, 1971) 163–64.*

Teaching Yiddish (J. I. Segal). 1. Irving Howe and Eliezer Greenberg, eds., *A Treasury of Yiddish Poetry* (New York: Holt, Rinehart and Winston, 1969) 155. 2. J. Michael Yates, Charles Lillard, and Ann J. West, eds., *Volvox: Poetry from the Unofficial Languages of Canada . . . in English Translation* (Port Clements, BC: Sono Nis P, 1971) 158–59.*

Fragment from Ash (Zusman Segalovich). 1. MG31-D54, box 49, file 22, LAC.*

Blood-stained Roses (Sholem Shtern). 1. MG31-D54, box 3, file 6, LAC.*

Spring Greetings (Moyshe Teyf). 1. MG31-D54, box 75, file 31, LAC.*

TRANSLATIONS—GERMAN

School for Preparing (Otto Rank). 1. *Journal of the Otto Rank Association* (Doylestown, PA) 1.1 (Fall 1966): 29.* Adapted by Miriam Waddington from the literal English translation of Annemarie Neumann of the original German poem by Otto Rank.

Weltschmerz: Lines before Breakfast (Otto Rank). 1. *Journal of the Otto Rank Association* (Doylestown, PA) 1.1 (Fall 1966): 27.* Adapted by Miriam Waddington from the literal English translation of Annemarie Neumann of the original German poem by Otto Rank.

TRANSLATIONS—RUSSIAN

Under the Roof in My House (Rimma Fyodorovna Kazakova). 1. *Waves* 3.3 (Spring 1975): 22.* Translated by Yvonne Grabowski and Miriam Waddington.

Springtime Girl (Robert Ivanovich Rozhdestvensky). 1. *Waves* 3.3 (Spring 1975): 23–25.* Translated by Yvonne Grabowski and Miriam Waddington.

Explanatory Notes

The Old Sailor
5 I am old, very old: This poem was first published when Waddington was a twenty-year-old undergraduate student.

Unheard Melodies
8 The smiles meeting smiles: an allusion to T. S. Eliot's "The Love Song of J. Alfred Prufrock," especially lines 26–27, "There will be time, there will be time / To prepare a face to meet the faces that you meet"

The Bond
1 Jarvis street: a street in downtown Toronto, the locus for prostitution

18 Adelaide: Adelaide Street, a one-way street in downtown Toronto

Investigator
18 Niagara: Niagara Falls, the world famous waterfall on the Niagara River

Branching from Golder's Green
title Golder's Green: an area in north London which has had a significant Jewish population since the early twentieth century

2 one-way street called The Park: The London Jewish Cultural Centre is located on The Park, near Golder's Hill Park.

8 Walmer Road: a street in the Annex neighbourhood of Toronto

Contemporary
7 Finuycane: World War II Irish fighter pilot Brendan Éamon Fergus "Paddy" Finucane (1920–1942) died near Le Touquet in northeastern France. His Spitfire was hit by a ground shot and sank into the sea.

Folkways
10 the Don: The Don River traverses Toronto.

14 Castlefrank: Castle Frank Road, a street in the Rosedale neighbourhood of Toronto

I Love My Love with an S
13 Kildonan: former rural municipality in Manitoba. Today, Old Kildonan, East Kildonan, and West Kildonan are suburban residential neighbourhoods of Winnipeg.

Integration
13 Shuswap: a region in British Columbia that encompasses six primary areas, including Chase, South Shuswap, North Shuswap, Salmon Arm, Sicamous and Eagle Valley, and Falkland

Now We Steer
32 Auden: British-born poet W. H. Auden (1907–1973), noted for "In Memory of W. B. Yeats" (1939) and "September 1, 1939" (1940)

32 Spender: British-born writer Stephen Spender (1909–1995), lived in Germany and anticipated the rise of Nazism in his novel *The Temple* (1988)

32 Thomas Wolfe: American writer Thomas Wolfe (1900–1938), best known for his autobiographical novel *Look Homeward, Angel* (1929). Controversy surrounding the novel prompted Wolfe to leave his hometown of Asheville, North Carolina for eight years.

Portrait I
1 Lady by Renoir: French Impressionist Pierre-Auguste Renoir (1841–1919) often painted women in bourgeois settings. Fellow painter Suzanne Valadon (1865–1938) frequently modelled for Renoir.

1 au bord de la Seine: *Au bord de la Seine à Argenteuil* (1878), by French Impressionist Pierre-Auguste Renoir

Gimli
title Gimli: rural municipality in south-central Manitoba on the western shore of Lake Winnipeg. Gimli is a cottage and resort town whose population swells each summer as 100,000 tourists visit annually to swim, fish, and boat on Lake Winnipeg. The large number of Icelandic settlers in and around the area gave Gimli its name: home of the Norse Gods, Gimli is usually translated as "heaven."

Indoors

13–14 gothic vista of the arch / Framing old Saint Mary's: St. Mary's Church, Roman Catholic church located at 130 Bathurst Street, Toronto. The Gothic Revival church was designed by Joseph Connolly and completed in 1889; the tower was finished in 1905.

Fragments from Autobiography

11 John Kirby: American jazz musician John Kirby (1908–1952) was active during the 1930s with the Onyx Club Boys, named after the New York City club in which they played.

19 Jericho: the Battle of Jericho, chronicled in the Book of Joshua in which the Israelites sought to conquer Canaan. Joshua commanded the Israelites to march around Jericho for six days. On the seventh day, after the priests sounded the rams' horns, they gave out the war cry, the city walls fell, and the Israelites destroyed Jericho and its inhabitants.

Letter to Margaret

title Margaret Avison: Canadian poet Margaret Avison (1918–2007) who twice received the Governor General's Literary Award for *Winter Sun* (1960) and *No Time* (1989)

In Exile

6 daisies of Michaelmas: E. F. Benson's novel *Paul* (1906) refers to "daisies of Michaelmas."

11 Oz: L. Frank Baum's *The Wonderful Wizard of Oz* (1900)

Adagio

15 valkyriewise: In Norse mythology, the valkyrie is a female figure who decides who dies in battle. She selects half of the fallen and brings them to the afterlife hall of the slain.

Museum

1 Rodin Museum: Rodin Museum in Philadelphia, where Waddington lived as a graduate student in 1944–1945

Who Will Build Jerusalem

4 tilts at windmills: an allusion to Miguel de Cervantes's *Don Quixote* (part 1, chapter 8, 1605) when Quixote fights windmills he imagines to be giants. The expression has come to mean facing futile battles.

Stillness
21 Joan of Arc: A patron saint of France, Joan of Arc (c1412–1431) is considered a national heroine for her role in rallying French troops during the Hundred Years' War (1337–1453), notably during the siege of Orléans (1429).

Three Poems for My Teacher (1)
title Jessie Taft: Jessie Taft (1882–1960) taught at the University of Pennsylvania's School of Social Work where she pioneered functional processes in the theory and practice of casework. Waddington studied under Taft and they developed a close connection.

A Ballad for the Peace
28 Leningrad: Saint Petersburg, the Imperial capital of Russia (1713–1728; 1732–1918), was known as Leningrad from 1924 to 1991.

The Music Teachers
1 gargoyle: an architectural detail added to large churches and other public buildings, often designed to function as rainspouts. Particularly prominent in Gothic architecture (but also visible in temples of the ancient Greek and ancient Egyptian periods), gargoyles traditionally appear as grotesques or fantastical animals so that the rain run-off would seem to be flowing from the figures' mouths.

12 Schubert: Franz Schubert (1797–1828), prolific Austrian composer in the Romantic style

13 Verdi: Giuseppe Fortunino Francesco Verdi (1813–1901), influential Italian composer, mainly of opera

15 Scheherazade: legendary Persian queen and storyteller of *One Thousand and One Nights*

25 Atlantis: legendary island thought to have sunk in the Atlantic Ocean around 9600 BCE

27 Rialto: commercial centre of Venice, Italy, distinguished by the Rialto Bridge over the Grand Canal

28 Abe Lincoln: Abraham Lincoln (1809–1865), renowned for his honesty and moral integrity, was president of the United States from 1861 to 1865.

The Bread We Eat
6–7 blood / Of . . . Christ: the Eucharist, a Christian sacrament commemorating Christ's Last Supper by consuming consecrated bread and wine

St. Antoine Street (1)
title **St. Antoine Street:** Saint Antoine Street, Montreal

In the Park
7 **haunted oedipus:** an allusion to Sophocles's tragedy *Oedipus the King* (c429 BCE)

Fables of Birth
5 **David:** Biblical figure and second king of Israel, traditionally thought to have reigned during the tenth century BCE. According to the prophet Samuel, David was anointed to succeed Saul and proved his heroism by slaying the Philistine giant Goliath.

20 **Matisse:** French painter Henri Matisse (1869–1954), best known for his use of intense colours in works such as *Madras Rouge* (1907) and *The Yellow Curtain* (1915)

Bird's Hill
title **Bird's Hill:** Birds Hill Provincial Park is located near the town of Birds Hill northeast of Winnipeg, Manitoba. Named for James Curtis Bird (c1773–1856), a Hudson's Bay Company fur trader who owned the land, the town's high elevation provided refuge during flooding.

You and Me
3 **Navajo:** The Navajo of the southwestern United States are the largest federally recognized tribe in the United States. The Navajo Nation is an independent governmental body.

16 **David's star:** The six-pointed Star of David is the universal symbol of Judaism and also appears on the Israeli flag.

Journey to the Clinic
56 **Guy-Gee:** bilingual pronunciation of Guy Street/rue Guy, located in downtown Montreal

60 **Saint Antoine:** Saint Antoine Street, Montreal

Prayer
title **Virginia Robinson:** Virginia Robinson (1883–1977) taught at the University of Pennsylvania's School of Social Work and published several books, including *Jessie Taft: Therapist and Social Work Educator* (1962), a biography of her colleague and lifelong companion, and *The Development of a Professional Self* (1978).

Jonathan Travels
title Jonathan: Jonathan Waddington, the poet's younger son, born 1951

5 Coleman burners: portable compact stoves used by field troops during World War II. In the postwar era, Coleman burners were popularized as portable camping stoves.

Studio on Ste. Famille Street
title Ste. Famille Street: Sainte-Famille Street in downtown Montreal

title Louis Muhlstock: Austrian-born painter Louis Muhlstock (1904–2001), especially active during the 1930s in Montreal

Housing Development
7 great Elizabeth: Elizabeth I (1533–1603), queen of England from 1558 to 1603, a period of religious and political upheaval. Her reign became renowned for its drama and poetry and the acceleration of seafaring exploration.

8 Herbert: British poet George Herbert (1593–1633). An Anglican priest, Herbert published The Temple, sacred verse in subject and style.

8 Wyatt: British poet Thomas Wyatt (1503–1542) is credited with writing the first-known sonnets in English.

14 Phaeton's golden cars: an allusion to the Greek myth of Phaeton who sought proof that his father was Helios, the sun god. To signal his love, Helios allowed Phaeton to drive the chariot of the sun for one day.

31–32 Jason oceans spanned / To find the golden fleece: In the Greek myth of Jason and the golden fleece, the Argonauts pursued the golden fleece to reclaim the throne seized by Jason's uncle.

Winnipeg
10 Selkirk's ghost: Thomas Douglas, Fifth Earl of Selkirk (1771–1820), established the Red River Colony in Manitoba. Moved by the plight of Scottish crofters displaced by their landlords, Selkirk purchased land in Canada for Scottish settlers and became part owner of the Hudson's Bay Company to control the area's fur trade. As a result of conflict with the emerging Metis community, Selkirk was charged with unlawful occupation and spent his remaining years in court. The city of Selkirk, the village of East Selkirk, Winnipeg's Selkirk Avenue and neighbourhood of Point Douglas are all named in his honour.

26 Red: The Red River originates in North Dakota and Minnesota and flows north towards Lake Winnipeg. Once a key trade route for the Hudson's Bay

Company, used by fur traders and the Metis community, it has also been the site of major floods in 1950, 1997, and 2009.

26 Assiniboine: A tributary of the Red River, the Assiniboine River is 1,070 kilometres long and runs through Saskatchewan and Manitoba. The name comes from the Assiniboine First Nation: "assine" (stone) and "bwan" (Sioux). Some believe the name reflects the practice of heating stones to cook food.

27 Merlin drew the wrong Excalibur: The wizard Merlin is associated with Arthurian legend. Chronicled in Geoffrey of Monmouth's *Historia Regum Britanniae* (c1136), Merlin is usually depicted as half-mortal and half-supernatural. Excalibur is King Arthur's sword. The name derives from the Welsh word "Caledfwlch" meaning "caled" (battle, hard) and "bwlch" (breach, gap, notch). Geoffrey of Monmouth (c1100–1155) latinized the name to "Caliburnus" which associated it with "calibs" or "chalybs" (steel).

30 Kildonan: former rural municipality in Manitoba. Today, Old Kildonan, East Kildonan, and West Kildonan are suburban residential neighbourhoods of Winnipeg.

Signature

4 Pope: British poet Alexander Pope (1688–1744), most famous for his use of the heroic couplet, especially in his verse essay *An Essay on Criticism* (1711). Written in iambic pentameter, the poem reflects the dominant literary ideals of the eighteenth century, particularly the importance of criticism and emulating classical authors such as Virgil, Homer, Horace, and Longinus. Pope's other poems include the mock-heroic epic *The Rape of the Lock* (1712), *The Dunciad* (1728), and translations of Homer's *Iliad* and *Odyssey*.

An Elegy for John Sutherland

title John Sutherland: Canadian poet, literary critic, and editor John Sutherland (1919–1956) founded the literary magazines *First Statement* and *Northern Review* and established First Statement Press. He issued the anthology *Other Canadians: An Anthology of the New Poetry in Canada, 1940–46* and was the first publisher of the verse of Irving Layton.

Exchange

3 Byron dark and Shelley fair: major British poets of the Romantic period. George Gordon Byron (1788–1824), later known as Lord Byron, lived much of his life outside England, partly because he acquired a reputation for scandalous behaviour. In 1816 he lived at the Villa Diodati near Lake Geneva, Switzerland with fellow writers Percy Bysshe Shelley (1792–1822) and his wife Mary Godwin Shelley (1797–1851). The Shelleys' relationship with Byron was most productive, particularly in 1816 when Mary Shelley wrote *Frankenstein* (1818) and Shelley wrote "Hymn to Intellectual Beauty" and "Mont Blanc," which helped establish his importance among the second generation of Romantic poets. Shelley's most famous poems include *Queen Mab* (1813), "Ozymanadias" (1818), and "Ode to the West Wind" (1819).

Endings

17 Atlases: In Greek mythology, the god Atlas sided with the Titans against the Olympians led by Zeus. After his defeat, Atlas was condemned to hold the earth up on his shoulders.

Poets and Statues

1 Craig Street: a street in Montreal

8 song of Solomon: The Song of Songs of Solomon, commonly referred to as The Song of Songs or Song of Solomon, is the twenty-second book of the Hebrew Scriptures. Also known as Canticle of Canticles, it consists of 117 verses on the subject of human love.

9 Solomon is nowhere: Shebaless: The Biblical Solomon—renowned as wise and just—succeeded his father, King David, and ruled Israel for forty years. The Hebrew Scriptures suggest the Queen of Sheba, ruler of what is now Ethiopia and Eritrea, wanted to meet Solomon. One Ethiopian account describes the intimate relationship between Sheba and Solomon and claims that their son founded a dynasty that was believed to have ruled for nearly three thousand years.

The Young Poet and Me

15 St Augustine: St. Augustine (354–430), also known as Augustine of Hippo since he was Bishop of Hippo Regius (present-day Annaba, Algeria), wrote *On Christian Doctrine*, *Confessions*, and *City of God*. His writings influenced Western Christianity, particularly its ideas of original sin, just war, salvation, and divine grace. Augustine converted to Christianity after a life of hedonism. Influenced by Virgil and Cicero, Augustine's ideas on human will and ethics in turn influenced Schopenhauer and Nietzsche.

16 St Theresa: St. Theresa (1515–1582), also known as Teresa of Avila, was a Spanish mystic and Catholic theologian. Fascinated from childhood by accounts of the lives of the saints, Teresa claimed religious ecstasy. One vision of a seraph driving a fiery golden lance through her heart inspired Renaissance sculptor Giovanni Lorenzo Bernini's *Ecstasy of St. Teresa*.

Traffic Lights at Passover

title Passover: Jewish holiday that commemorates the story of Exodus, in which the ancient Israelites were freed from slavery in Egypt. According to the Book of Exodus, the Israelites were aided by ten plagues, the last of which killed the firstborn son of each Egyptian family. The Israelites were commanded to mark their doorposts with lamb's blood so God would know to "pass over" their homes.

5 Côte des Neiges: Côte-des-Neiges Road in Montreal

21 bitter herbs: At the Seder, a ritual feast that marks the beginning of the Jewish holiday of Passover and includes a retelling of the story of the liberation of the Israelites from slavery in ancient Egypt, bitter herbs are eaten in keeping with the Biblical commandment "with bitter herbs they shall eat it" (Exodus 12:8).

28 Elijah: Hebrew prophet in the ninth century BCE. Elijah was believed to defend the worship of Yahweh, the god of Israel, over the more popular Baal, and to have raised the dead. According to the Book of Kings, Elijah ascended to heaven before his death. His expected return was interpreted as a harbinger of the Messiah. Elijah appears in the Babylonian Talmud, is compared to Jesus and John the Baptist in the Christian Scriptures, and is regarded as a righteous prophet in Islam. The Cup of Elijah—a cup of wine poured for the prophet—is part of the Seder, a ritual feast that marks the beginning of the Jewish holiday of Passover and includes a retelling of the story of the liberation of the Israelites from slavery in ancient Egypt.

32 hayom yom shaini: (Hebrew) Today is the second day [of the week], i.e., Monday

The Through Way

title Montreal's Dorchester Street: Dorchester Street, the former name of Boulevard René-Lévesque, is a major east-west street in downtown Montreal, dominated by high-rise office towers. The street was named in 1844 in honour of Guy Carleton, First Baron Dorchester (1724–1808), former governor of Quebec and Governor General of Canada. Although it was renamed in 1987 for the former premier of Quebec, portions of the street retain the name Dorchester.

4 from Peel to Demontigny: Peel Street is a major north-south street in downtown Montreal. Rue de Montigny, renamed Boulevard de Maisonneuve in 1966, is a major east-west street in downtown Montreal.

27 Ralentir, arrête ici: (French) Slow down, stop here.

The Thief
5 Cote des Neiges: Côte-des-Neiges Road in Montreal

14 Maisonneuve: a former town that is now part of Montreal. Maisonneuve was named for Paul Chomedey de Maisonneuve (1612–1676), a French military officer hired to lead French colonists to build the settlement of Ville-Marie on the island of Montreal. From 1642 to 1669, Maisonneuve was the first governor of Montreal.

The Exhibition: David Milne
title David Milne: During World War I, Canadian artist David Milne (1882–1953) drew and painted British soldiers and the battlefields of Belgium and France. After the war, his work focused primarily on landscapes and watercolours.

Absent Space
6 El Greco: (Spanish) El Greco (The Greek) was the nickname of Doménikos Theotokópoulos (1541–1614), an artist of the Spanish Renaissance. Born in Crete, then part of the Republic of Venice, El Greco moved first to Venice and then Rome in the tradition of Greek artists before him. In 1577, he moved to Toledo, Spain, where he developed his distinctive style considered a precursor to and inspiration for twentieth century Cubism and Expressionism.

12 Rouault: Georges Henry Rouault (1871–1958), French artist of the Fauvist and Expressionist period, known especially for heavy black contouring similar in appearance to leaded glass

Carnival
title Ghitta Caiserman: Canadian artist Ghitta Caiserman-Roth (1923–2005) was born in Montreal. In her figurative work, she drew on her experience in Montreal factories during World War II and her knowledge of working class neighbourhoods in Halifax to address religious and social concerns and themes of family life.

The Snows of William Blake
title William Blake: British artist William Blake (1757–1827), seminal figure in the early Romantic period whose philosophical and mystical views were not always appreciated in his lifetime. Although deeply familiar with the Bible, Blake opposed all forms of organized religion and developed his own mythical iconography featured in his life's work that combined poetry and engraving. He is best known for writing and illustrating *Songs of Innocence* (1789) and *Songs of Experience* (1794), and *The Marriage of Heaven and Hell* (1790).

Ballad for a Broadsheet

16 Eastertide: also called the Easter Season or Paschal Time, the fifty-day period from Easter Sunday to Pentecost Sunday

37 RAPUNZEL: German fairy tale popularized by the Brothers Grimm in the nineteenth century, adapted from the French tale *Persinette* by Charlotte-Rose de Caumont de La Force originally published in 1698. Rapunzel is a beautiful maiden with long golden hair.

46 Adam's time: According to the creation narrative in the Book of Genesis, Adam was the first human being.

47 CAIN KILLED ABEL: In the Hebrew Scriptures, Cain and Abel were two sons of Adam and Eve. Cain committed the first murder when he killed Abel out of jealousy.

Night on Skid Row

15 billet-doux: (French) love letter

22 ave: hail

22 evoe: Bacchanalian exclamation

34 strasse: (German) street

On My Birthday

24 Hans Andersen: Danish writer Hans Christian Andersen (1805–1875) was noted for his fairy tales, particularly "The Emperor's New Clothes" (1837), "The Little Mermaid" (1837), and "The Ugly Duckling" (1843), which depict themes of beauty, goodness, and honesty.

Above the Seaway

4–6 It was July, the Juliet of months / . . . / before Romeo's voice: William Shakespeare's tragedy *Romeo and Juliet* is believed to have been written between 1591 and 1595. Juliet was born in the month of July, as her Nurse says, "Come Lammas-eve at night shall she be fourteen" (I.iii.18). On Lammas Day (loaf-mass day), observed on 1 August in England and Scotland, tenants and churchgoers would prepare a loaf of freshly harvested wheat.

5 Orwell: Influential British novelist George Orwell (born Eric Blair, 1903–1950), best known for *Animal Farm* (1945) and *Nineteen Eighty-Four* (1949)

Boughs of Snow

3 motherless Poe: American author Edgar Allan Poe (1809–1849), best known for such Gothic tales as "The Fall of the House of Usher" (1839) and "The Tell-Tale Heart" (1843), and his poem "The Raven" (1845). Poe's mother died of pulmonary tuberculosis (known as consumption in the nineteenth century) when he was a toddler, not long after his father had abandoned the family.

4 preacher Donne: British poet and clergyman John Donne (1572–1631), best known for his sonnets, elegies, erotic and liturgical verse, such as *Holy Sonnets*. Born into a Catholic family in which several relatives were executed for their beliefs, Donne renounced Catholicism and was ordained into the Church of England. As Dean of St. Paul's Cathedral, he was celebrated for his sermons.

5 William Blake: British artist William Blake (1757–1827), seminal figure in the early Romantic period whose philosophical and mystical views were not always appreciated in his lifetime. Although deeply familiar with the Bible, Blake opposed all forms of organized religion and developed his own mythical iconography featured in his life's work that combined poetry and engraving. He is best known for writing and illustrating *Songs of Innocence* (1789) and *Songs of Experience* (1794), and *The Marriage of Heaven and Hell* (1790).

28 the blind eye of father Milton: British poet John Milton (1608–1674) served as Secretary for Foreign Tongues under Oliver Cromwell during the period England was under Republican rule. After the monarchy was restored in 1660, Milton, then totally blind, required protection from his political enemies. He continued to write, began dictating the epic poem *Paradise Lost* to his daughters and others in 1658 and completed the work in 1664. *Paradise Regained* and *Samson Agonistes* followed in 1671.

Homage to Apollinaire with Some Words by John Dowland

title John Dowland: John Dowland (1563–1626), Renaissance composer for the British ambassador to the French court during the reign of Elizabeth I, in the Danish court of Christian IV, and as a lutenist in the British court of James I

1 Guillaume: Guillaume Apollinaire (born Wilhelm Albert Włodzimierz Apolinary Kostrowicki, 1880–1919), Italian-born French poet of Polish descent best known for coining the term "Surrealism" to describe the iconoclastic cultural movement that followed World War I

Montreal Night

2 wedgwood: pottery made by Josiah Wedgwood and Sons since 1759. Wedgwood has remained a popular brand name of luxury decorative porcelainware into the twenty-first century.

7 Côte des Neiges: Côte-des-Neiges, a neighbourhood in Montreal

Penelope

title Penelope: in Homer's *Odyssey*, the faithful wife of Odysseus, King of Ithaca. Penelope waited for her husband's return from the decade long Trojan War and a further ten years as he wandered the Mediterranean. As other Trojan warriors returned home, Odysseus was presumed dead by many. Consequently, Penelope was pursued by suitors who wished to replace Odysseus as king and prevent the succession to the throne of their son Telemachus. She avoided choosing a suitor and then challenged them to a contest that she knew only Odysseus (who had returned to Ithaca in disguise) could win. After participating in and winning the contest, Odysseus, along with his son Telemachus, killed all the suitors and, after one more test, reunited with Penelope.

Pleasures from Children

1 Er ist gewesen: (German) He has been

5 Das ist eine Maedchen?: (German) This is a girl?

Sea Bells

1–4 Five fathoms deep / . . . / paced my grave: The first stanza and other lines in the poem allude to Ariel's Song (I.ii.399–403) in William Shakespeare's *The Tempest*. Ariel, an invisible airy spirit, sings this song to Ferdinand who is encouraged to believe his father is dead.

The Stepmother

7 jaune: (French) yellow

Saints and Others

3 tall Toronto: In 1962, when this poem was first published, the tallest buildings in Toronto were the twenty-eight storey Royal York Hotel (built in 1929; now the Fairmont Royal York) and the thirty-four storey Canadian Bank of Commerce (built in 1930; now Commerce Court North).

17 Lucifer: (Latin) light-bearer. Lucifer has become the popularized name for Satan since Milton wrote of "God's most beautiful and rebellious angel" in *Paradise Lost*.

43 Titanic: The passenger steamship RMS *Titanic* sank in the north Atlantic Ocean on her maiden voyage on 15 April 1912.

A Song of North York between Sheppard and Finch
title North York between Sheppard and Finch: In 1998, the city of North York amalgamated with other cities and municipalities to form the Greater Toronto Area. In 1962, when this poem was first published, North York was not yet a borough, but the area was becoming increasingly suburbanized, as nearby Highway 401, which traverses Toronto and parallels Sheppard Avenue and Finch Avenue, afforded increased accessibility to the city's outlying areas.

20 Yonge street: Yonge Street is the main arterial road running through Toronto, including North York.

Toronto the Golden-vaulted City
title Toronto: In 1962, when this poem was first published, Toronto was Canada's second largest city after Montreal. Toronto was inhabited by Huron tribes when the first French traders arrived. By 1759, the French had largely abandoned the area and were replaced by British settlers. This community increased during the American Revolutionary War with the influx of United Empire Loyalists.

11 Alas poor York: This line alludes to William Shakespeare's *Hamlet*, in which Hamlet addresses Yorick's skull (V.i.182). Until 1834, the city of Toronto was named York.

17 Caligari: *The Cabinet of Dr. Caligari* (1920), a silent film directed by Robert Wiene, is representative of German Expressionist art that followed World War I.

Piano Phrases in January
18 Waldstein sonata: Ludwig van Beethoven's *Waldstein* sonata (1804), formally known as the Piano Sonata No. 21 in C major, Op. 53, composed during his "heroic" decade (1803–1812). Beethoven dedicated the sonata to Count Ferdinand Ernst Gabriel von Waldstein of Vienna, a patron and close personal friend. .

33 celastrus scandens: Also known as bittersweet, celastrus scandens is native to central and eastern North America. Its fruit is poisonous to humans (but favoured by birds), and its seeds were used by Native Americans and pioneers to induce vomiting and to treat tuberculosis and venereal disease.

The Gardeners

26 Abishag: in the Hebrew Scriptures, the young woman chosen to be an aid to the ageing King David and to keep him warm at night

Brotherly Love on Sherbrooke Street

title Sherbrooke Street: a major east-west artery in Montreal

1 Philadelphia: nicknamed "The City of Brotherly Love" since its name, translated from the modern Greek, means love ("philos") of brother ("adelphos")

The Terrarium

3 mona lisa: Leonardo da Vinci's *Mona Lisa*, a portrait of Lisa Gherardini, painted between 1503 and 1519 and considered the most famous painting in the world. Viewers have long been intrigued by the enigmatic smile on the subject's face.

The Field of Night

title Philip Surrey: Canadian figurative painter Philip Surrey (1910–1990)

5 the golden fleece of song: an allusion to the Greek myth of Jason and the golden fleece. The Argonauts pursued the golden fleece to reclaim the throne seized by Jason's uncle.

Pictures in a Window

10 Childe Roland: a character in Robert Browning's poem "Childe Roland to the Dark Tower Came" (1855), likely suggested by Edgar's speech in William Shakespeare's *King Lear* (III.iv.181–183). The medieval term "childe" refers to an untested knight (not a child), and "Roland" evokes *La Chanson de Roland*, an epic poem of the eleventh century and the oldest surviving work of French literature.

17 Hansel and Gretel: well known fairy tale chronicled by the Brothers Grimm and published in 1812

Selma

title Selma: Occurring in 1965, when this poem was first published, the riots in Selma, Alabama were a turning point in the American civil rights movement.

Prairie Thoughts in a Museum: 3. The Picture

10 Hart Crane: American poet Hart Crane (1899–1932). Crane's published works include *White Buildings* (1926) and *The Bridge* (1930). A modernist writer, Crane was particularly interested in crafting a poetic response to T. S. Eliot's *The Waste Land* (1922).

11 Edgar Poe: Between 1837 and 1844, American author Edgar Allan Poe (1809–1849) lived in several rented houses in Philadelphia. The sole surviving house at 432 North Seventh Street in the city's Spring Garden neighbourhood is now the Edgar Allan Poe National Historic Site. During this prolific period, Poe published thirty-one stories, including "Murders in the Rue Morgue" (1841) and "The Tell-Tale Heart" (1843), as well as literary criticism and book reviews.

Prairie Thoughts in a Museum: 4. The People

13 Robinson Crusoe: Daniel Defoe's *Robinson Crusoe* (1719) is a fictional autobiography of a castaway who spends twenty-eight years on a remote tropical island near Trinidad. Likely influenced by the experiences of Alexander Selkirk (1676–1721), Defoe's novel became immensely popular and still is widely read.

13 Henry Hudson: British explorer Henry Hudson (c1560/70s–1611?) searched for a western passage to Asia around present-day New York City and north of Quebec. In June 1611, Hudson, his son, and a handful of loyal crew members were set adrift in a small boat by mutineers and never were seen again. The mutineers returned to England, were charged with and then acquitted of murder. Hudson's Bay later was named for the explorer.

Hart Crane

title Hart Crane: American poet Hart Crane (1899–1932) suffered from depression and committed suicide by jumping from a ship into the Gulf of Mexico.

Summer Letters

22–23 king Ead- / mund's head: Edmund, King of East Anglia, who died in 869 or 870. Accounts of his death vary. The reference here is to Edmund's Christian commitment even as his enemies proceeded to behead him. His body was taken to Beadoriceworth, present-day Bury St. Edmunds.

23–24 Ael- / fric's homilies: Aelfric of Eynsham (c955–1010), British abbot who wrote Old English homilies and hagiographies

29–30 king Ael- / fred: Alfred the Great (c848/849–899), King of Wessex from 871 to 899

43–44 Paul / Klee: German-Swiss artist Paul Klee (1879–1940) whose works are notable for colour and tonality

63–64 ealdor- / man Byrhtnoth: At the Battle of Maldon, Anglo-Saxon leader Byrhtnoth (d 991) refused peace in exchange for a tribute and so was killed. Although the British side lost the battle and King Aethelred eventually paid off the Vikings, Byrhtnoth was regarded as a hero.

65 king Lear: William Shakespeare's tragedy *King Lear* (1603–1606) is based on a medieval legend. In Shakespeare's play, Lear suffers from the hard-heartedness of two of his three daughters, Goneril and Regan.

76 Mutual street: a street in downtown Toronto

All Those Who Run in Fields

14–15 Did Christ believe in giants? / He died at age thirty-four: According to conventional belief, Jesus Christ died at age thirty-three. The reference here to Christ's death at age thirty-four reflects the instability of historical religious details.

39 Othello: tragic hero of William Shakespeare's *Othello* (1601–1604). A successful military general who is also a Moor, Othello is vulnerable to rumours that his Venetian wife Desdemona is unfaithful.

East on Dorchester Street

title Dorchester Street: Dorchester Street, the former name of Boulevard René-Lévesque, is a major east-west street in downtown Montreal, dominated by high-rise office towers. The street was named in 1844 in honour of Guy Carleton, First Baron Dorchester (1724–1808), former governor of Quebec and Governor General of Canada. Although it was renamed in 1987 for the former premier of Quebec, portions of the street retain the name Dorchester.

Incidents for the Undying World

19 St John's: capital city of Newfoundland and Labrador and the most easterly city in North America, settled before 1620

26 T. S. Eliot: American-born poet, playwright, and literary critic T. S. (Thomas Stearns) Eliot (1888–1965) whose work and ideas dominated twentieth-century English literature

29 Prufrock: "The Love Song of J. Alfred Prufrock" (1915) was T. S. Eliot's first published work. A dramatic monologue written in stream of consciousness, the poem has come to exemplify modernist style.

35–36 mermaids singing, / and unlikely Lazarus: images from T. S. Eliot's "The Love Song of J. Alfred Prufrock"

48 Glastonbury: the ruins of Glastonbury Abbey in Somerset, England. Medieval Christian legends claimed that the Abbey was founded by Joseph of Arimathea and linked the Abbey to the story of the Holy Grail and to King Arthur.

53 Hart House tower: University of Toronto's Hart House (a student centre) was financed by Vincent Massey (1887–1967), the first Canadian-born Governor General and an alumnus of the university, and was named for Massey's grandfather, Hart Massey (1823–1896). Hart House's bell and clock tower—named Soldiers' Tower—commemorates members of the university who served in the two World Wars.

72–74 lapis lazuli / . . . / like Yeats did his three Chinamen: Anglo-Irish poet and playwright W. B. Yeats (1865–1939). "Lapis lazuli" and "three Chinamen" are allusions to Yeats's poem "Lapis Lazuli" (1938).

Saints and Bibliographers

17–18 Lan- / celot: According to Arthurian legend, Lancelot was believed to have been raised by the Lady of the Lake after his parents were driven into exile. King Arthur considered him the most trusted knight, but Lancelot fell in love with Queen Guinevere and their affair undermined Camelot, which prevented him from securing the Holy Grail.

22 Apollinaire: Italian-born French poet of Polish descent Guillaume Apollinaire (born Wilhelm Albert Włodzimierz Apolinary Kostrowicki, 1880–1919), known for his iconoclastic gestures, such as calling for the Louvre to be burnt down, which briefly made him a suspect in 1911 when the *Mona Lisa* disappeared

24 sonne l'heure: (French) the hour chimes, from "Chanson d'Automne" (1866) by Paul Verlaine

24–25 je / demeure: (French) I remain, likely from Guillaume Apollinaire's "Le Pont Mirabeau" (1913)

25 temps passé: (French) time past

26 Allan Gardens: one of Toronto's oldest parks, founded in 1858 and named for George William Allan (1822–1901), one-time mayor of Toronto and senator who donated the property to the Toronto Horticultural Society

28 kennst du das land: (German) Do you know the land?; likely from Goethe's novel *Wilhelm Meisters Lehrjahre* (*Wilhelm Meister's Apprenticeship*, 1795–1796)

Fortunes

20 Punch and Judy: traditional puppet show that can be traced to sixteenth century Italian *commedia dell'arte*, with the character of Pulcinella as the precursor to the combative and exuberant Punch. Originally intended for adults, the content became more family oriented from the late Victorian period onward.

32 shloime-kapoir: (Yiddish) expression meaning mixed-up or confused

40–41 the laidly worm of Spindlestone, / no longer the bewitched princess: *The Laidly Worm of Spindleston Heugh*, also known as *The Laidly Worm of Bamborough*, Northumbrian ballad about a kind king who marries a beautiful but cruel witch who turns his granddaughter, Princess Margaret, into a dragon

The Clearing

13–15 Moses who hears / the flares of burning / cactus: According to the Book of Exodus, Moses observed a bush that burned but was not consumed by fire while he was a shepherd on Mount Horeb. From this bush Moses heard the voice of God who instructed him to liberate his fellow Hebrews from bondage in Egypt.

Children's Coloured Flags

10 jamais je ne t'oublierai: (French) I will never forget you, from the traditional song, "A La Claire Fontaine," considered the anthem of New France and Quebec before "O Canada" became the official national anthem

The Glass Trumpet

33 gimli: rural municipality in south-central Manitoba on the western shore of Lake Winnipeg. Gimli is a cottage and resort town whose population swells each the summer as 100,000 tourists visit annually to swim, fish, and boat on Lake Winnipeg. The large number of Icelandic settlers in and around the area gave Gimli its name: home of the Norse Gods, Gimli is usually translated as "heaven."

Falling Figure

97–99 die luft ist / kuhl and ich / so traurig bin: (German) the air is / cool and I / am so sad, from the folk song "Die Lorelei" (1827) by Heinrich Heine

102–03 rock / maid lorelei: rock on the eastern bank of the river Rhine in Germany. The name Lorelei translates from the Rhine dialect to "murmuring rock." The heavy river current and area echo once created a murmuring sound that is no longer easily audible due to increasing urbanization. The legend of a young enchantress who bewitches men to fall to their deaths from the high cliff-side of the rock is chronicled by Clemens Brentano in his ballad "Zu Bacharach am Rheine" (1802), which tells of Lore Lay who was ordered to a nunnery but asked for one last view of the Rhine and then fell to her death.

115–17 die luft / ist kuhl und es / dunkelt: (German) the air / is cool and it / darkens, from the folk song "Die Lorelei" (1827) by Heinrich Heine

118 ruhig: (German) quiet, calm

Winter One

15 Aramaic: Semitic language dating back over three thousand years. Originally from what is present-day central Syria, the language spread across Europe and North America with the Assyrian disapora. Biblical Aramaic and the Aramaic of Jesus was spoken during the period of Old Aramaic (1100 BCE to 200 CE).

Committee Work

10 Don Mills: an area in northeastern Toronto, conceived originally as a planned community separate from the city. When this poem was first published, the rural character of Don Mills was disappearing as residential, commercial, and industrial development grew rapidly.

12–13 joseph-coloured / hudson bay blankets: wool blankets traded by the Hudson's Bay Company. The Biblical story of the fraternal betrayal of Joseph (Genesis 37) is suggestive of the Hudson's Bay Company's treatment of aboriginal fur traders.

Desert Stone

31–32 blind Moses younger / brother: In the Hebrew Scriptures, Miriam is elder sister to Moses.

A Man Is Walking

26 lythrum fireweed: Commonly known as loosestrife, lythrum is visually similar to fireweed (Epilobium angustifolium) but distinctly different. Once thought to be sterile, purple loosestrife is now known to dominate and displace native vegetation after planting.

29 Gimli: rural municipality in south-central Manitoba on the western shore of Lake Winnipeg. Gimli is a cottage and resort town whose population swells each the summer as 100,000 tourists visit annually to swim, fish, and boat on Lake Winnipeg. The large number of Icelandic settlers in and around the area gave Gimli its name: home of the Norse Gods, Gimli is usually translated as "heaven."

The Eight-sided White Barn

title White Barn: a structure located on the campus of York University in Toronto where Waddington taught English from 1962 to 1983

4–5 Dufferin and / Steeles Avenue: Dufferin Street and Steeles Avenue are major streets in Toronto, intersecting in the northwestern part of the city.

My Travels

24–25 Bar / Kochba: Simon Bar Kochba (or Shimon bar Kokhba, Simon ben Kosiba), leader of a Jewish rebellion against the Romans (132 CE). For three years, Bar Kochba led an independent Jewish state, but success was short lived as the Romans attacked the Betar fortress, killing all defenders, including Bar Kochba.

28 Jaffa: ancient port city, also known as Joppa, now part of modern day Tel Aviv. Located on the Mediterranean Sea, Jaffa has been critical in military operations for thousands of years. The city is mentioned in the Bible and has been the site of ancient Egyptian and Roman incursions.

31–32 Ramses / the Second: Ramses II (c1303 BCE–1213 BCE), one of the most powerful and longest reigning Egyptian pharaohs, also known as Ozymandias (the inspiration for Percy Bysshe Shelley's 1818 sonnet "Ozymandias")

50 ghetto: the Warsaw Ghetto (1940–1943), constructed by the Nazis to contain the Jewish population of the city before the inhabitants were sent to extermination camps of World War II. In early 1943, residents organized an uprising that briefly enabled their control of the ghetto, but the Nazis responded by burning or bombing the buildings, including the synagogue. Over fifty thousand people were killed or deported, and the ghetto effectively levelled.

54 Vistula: The Vistula River, the longest river in Poland, flows through many cities, including the complex of concentration camps collectively known as Auschwitz.

59 Lazienki Park: Baths Park or Royal Baths, the largest park in Warsaw, is on the site of a bathing pavilion. Significantly damaged during the Warsaw Uprising of 1944, the park was restored after World War II.

60 Chopin: Polish-born composer and piano virtuoso Frédéric Chopin (1810–1849). In 1926, a statue of Chopin was erected in Lazienki Park. It was destroyed by occupying Germans in 1940, restored in 1958, and now is a site for summer piano concerts.

64–65 Square / of the Three Crosses: square in central Warsaw. The three crosses include one cross atop St. Alexander's Church and two crosses atop nearby columns facing the church. Much of the Square of the Three Crosses, including St. Alexander's Church, was severely damaged during the Warsaw Uprising of 1944 and was restored after World War II.

Pont Mirabeau in Montreal
title Pont Mirabeau: a bridge over the Seine in Paris and the subject of Guillaume Apollinaire's poem "Pont Mirabeau" (1913)

4 sonne l'heure: (French) the hour chimes, from Guillaume Apollinaire's "Pont Mirabeau" (1913), as well as Paul Verlaine's "Chanson d'Automne" (1866)

5 je demeure: (French) I remain, from Guillaume Apollinaire's "Pont Mirabeau" (1913)

7–8 Montreal's Lafontaine / Park: Lafontaine Park in Montreal's Plateau Mont-Royal neighbourhood

Putting on and Taking Off
29–30 Lawren / Harris mountain: Canadian painter Lawren Harris (1885–1970), a member of the Group of Seven, who often demonstrated a stark abstract style in his landscapes

The Wakened Wood (4)
2–9 Chekhov / ... Olga Marie and brother / Michael: Russian author Anton Chekhov (1860–1904) married stage actress Olga Knipper—they met during the production of Chekhov's play *The Seagull* (1896)—although they rarely lived together. Chekhov's villa in Yalta housed his brother Mikhail and, after Chekhov's death, his sister Maria, who oversaw her brother's literary legacy.

The Wakened Wood (5)
6 Chaudiere: (French) cauldron or kettle. The Chaudière Falls on the Ottawa River west of Parliament Hill. The falls are sixty metres wide and drop fifteen metres and were described in 1613 by French explorer Samuel de Champlain as creating a basin or kettle in the rocks below.

Women Who Live Alone
8 Ali Baba: character in *Ali Baba and the Forty Thieves*. The story was thought to have been translated from Arabic into French by Antoine Galland, but Arabic manuscripts of the text pre-dating Galland's translation are not extant.

The Wakened Wood (3)
4–6 Levitan ... / his night on the / Volga: Isaac Levitan (1860–1900), Russian painter of *Evening on the Volga* (1888), whose work is notable for its melancholic mood. Levitan suffered from terminal cardiac disease and spent the final year of his life at the Crimean home of writer Anton Chekhov, his closest friend.

6 Volga: The Volga River, the longest and largest river in Europe, flows through central Russia.

Canadians

3 eskimo: a former term for indigenous peoples living in northern Canada. Today, "Eskimo" is considered pejorative in Canada and has been replaced by the term "Inuit."

23–24 Henry / Hudson: British explorer Henry Hudson (c1560/70s–1611?) searched for a western passage to Asia around present-day New York City and north of Quebec. In June 1611, Hudson, his son, and a handful of loyal crew members were set adrift in a small boat by mutineers and never were seen again. The mutineers returned to England, were charged with and then acquitted of murder. Hudson's Bay later was named for the explorer.

24 Etienne Brûlé: French explorer Etienne Brûlé (c1592–1633) was the first European to travel along the St. Lawrence River as far as Sault Ste. Marie, possibly Lake Superior and Lake Michigan. Brûlé lived among the Huron tribe and was a guide and interpreter for Samuel de Champlain (c1567–1635), but later was killed on suspicion of being an enemy.

34–35 Fathers / of Confederation: delegates who represented the British North American colonies at conferences in Charlottetown (1864), Quebec (1864), and London to discuss the union of British North America

37 Charles Tupper: Father of Confederation Charles Tupper (1821–1915), premier of Nova Scotia (1864–1967) and prime minister of Canada (1896)

37–38 Alexander / Galt: British-born Father of Confederation Alexander Galt (1817–1893), first minister of finance

38 D'Arcy McGee: Irish-born Father of Confederation Thomas D'Arcy McGee (1825–1868) was assassinated by Patrick J. Whelan, a suspected Fenian sympathizer, after D'Arcy McGee denounced the Fenian Brotherhood.

38–39 George / Cartier: Father of Confederation George-Étienne Cartier (1814–1873) served as minister of militia and defence. The Macdonald-Cartier Freeway, the official name of Highway 401 in Ontario, is named for Sir John A. Macdonald (Canada's first prime minister) and Sir George-Étienne Cartier.

39 Ambrose Shea: Father of Confederation Ambrose Shea (1815–1905). After he attended the Quebec conference in 1864, Shea encountered opposition to confederation in Newfoundland and left Canadian politics.

40 Henry Crout: British settler and historian of Newfoundland Henry Crout (c1612–1617)

40–41 Father / Raguneau: Father Paul Ragueneau (1608–1680), French-born Jesuit superior at the Huron mission when Jean de Brébeuf and Jérôme Lalemant were killed by the Iroquois. Ragueneau chronicled their deaths, the destruction of the mission, and the survivors' escape and resettlement in Quebec.

41 Lord Selkirk: Thomas Douglas, Fifth Earl of Selkirk (1771–1820), established the Red River Colony in Manitoba. Moved by the plight of Scottish crofters displaced by their landlords, Selkirk purchased land in Canada for Scottish settlers and became part owner of the Hudson's Bay Company to control the area's fur trade. As a result of conflict with the emerging Metis community, Selkirk was charged with unlawful occupation and spent his remaining years in court. The city of Selkirk, the village of East Selkirk, Winnipeg's Selkirk Avenue and neighbourhood of Point Douglas are all named in his honour.

42 John A.: Father of Confederation John Alexander Macdonald (1815–1891), first prime minister of Canada (1867–1873; 1878–1891)

Ukrainian Church

10 onion domes: Ukrainian churches with onion domes are familiar sights in Manitoba and Waddington would have grown up within easy sight of two of the most famous in Winnipeg: St. Ivan Suchavsky Sobor at 939 Main Street and St. Michael's Ukrainian Orthodox Church at 110 Disraeli Street.

A Morning like the Morning when Amos Awoke

title Amos: farmer and Hebrew prophet in the eighth century BCE who preached that the day of judgment was imminent to encourage the people of Israel to renew their religious faith

18–20 Hart / Crane's Indian / maiden: American poet Hart Crane (1899–1932). The second section of Crane's long poem *The Bridge* (1930) is titled "Powhatan's Daughter," also known as Pocahontas.

23 Hudson: the Hudson River, named for British explorer Henry Hudson, who explored the river in 1609. The Hudson River is 315 miles long, flows from north to south through eastern New York, and forms the border between New York City and New Jersey.

24 Whitman's lilacs: American poet Walt Whitman (1819–1892). His collection *Leaves of Grass* (1855) includes "When Lilacs Last in the Dooryard Bloom'd" (1865), an elegy written shortly after the assassination of American president Abraham Lincoln on 14 April 1865.

45–52 take / ... / down like waters: from Amos 5:23. Part of the passage, "let justice roll down," used by Martin Luther King, Jr. as the title of his annual essay in The Nation (which appeared from 1961 to 1966) on the state of civil rights and race relations in America

Spring on the Bay of Quinte

title Bay of Quinte: on the northeastern edge of Lake Ontario

Adolescents

5 lord byron: major British poet of the Romantic period, George Gordon Byron (1788–1824), later known as Lord Byron, who had a reputation for sexually scandalous behaviour and famous in his lifetime as a fashion plate

8 little fauntleroy: Little Lord Fauntleroy (1886), children's novel by Frances Hodgson Burnett

Art History

1 Lampman: Archibald Lampman (1861–1899), one of Canada's Confederation Poets, along with Charles G. D. Roberts (1860–1943), Bliss Carman (1861–1929), and Duncan Campbell Scott (1862–1947)

2 Varley: Canadian painter Frederick Varley (1881–1969), a member of the Group of Seven. An official war artist during World War I, Varley accompanied Canadian troops in France and Belgium. After the war, his paintings focused on the Canadian landscape and portraits.

6 Riel: Canadian activist Louis Riel (1844–1885). On behalf of Metis rights, Riel led the Red River Rebellion of 1869. In 1885, he participated in the Northwest Rebellion, was arrested and later tried. Convicted of treason, Riel was executed and his death intensified the antagonism between the Canadian government, the Metis community, and Quebec supporters that endured until well into the twentieth century.

7 Mackenzie: Alexander Mackenzie (1822–1892), second prime minister of Canada (1873–1878)

9 Tom Thomson: Canadian painter Tom Thomson (1877–1917) influenced the group of artists now known as the Group of Seven. Thomson disappeared and died under mysterious circumstances on Canoe Lake in Algonquin Park, Ontario.

Swallowing Darkness Is Swallowing Dead Elm Trees

23 Cleópatra: Cleopatra VII (c69 BCE–30 BCE), the last pharaoh of ancient Egypt before it became a Roman province in 30 BCE, forged both political alliances and personal relationships with Julius Caesar and then Mark Antony.

26 Antony: Marcus Antonius (Mark Antony, c83 BCE–30 BCE), Roman politician and general under Julius Caesar before joining forces with Cleopatra. As Roman forces prepared to invade Egypt, both Antony and Cleopatra committed suicide.

28 Lord / Selkirk: Thomas Douglas, Fifth Earl of Selkirk (1771–1820), established the Red River Colony in Manitoba. Moved by the plight of Scottish crofters displaced by their landlords, Selkirk purchased land in Canada for Scottish settlers and became part owner of the Hudson's Bay Company to control the area's fur trade. As a result of conflict with the emerging Metis community, Selkirk was charged with unlawful occupation and spent his remaining years in court. The city of Selkirk, the village of East Selkirk, Winnipeg's Selkirk Avenue and neighbourhood of Point Douglas are all named in his honour.

Waking in London (2)

3–4 the islands of / the Hebrides: a group of islands off the west coast of Scotland whose diverse culture reflects the successive influences of Celtic, Norse, and English-speaking peoples

13 Pierre Trudeau: Pierre Elliott Trudeau (1919–2000), fifteenth prime minister of Canada (1968–1979; 1980–1984). When this poem was first published, Trudeau was in his first year of office, after having served as justice minister under Prime Minister Lester B. Pearson.

Waking in London (4)

4 song of all songs: an allusion to The Song of Songs of Solomon, commonly referred to as The Song of Songs or Song of Solomon, the twenty-second book of the Hebrew Scriptures. Also known as Canticle of Canticles, it consists of 117 verses on the subject of human love.

17 Solomon: The Biblical Solomon—renowned as wise and just—succeeded his father, King David, and ruled Israel for forty years. Much of the Book of Proverbs is attributed to Solomon.

18 Trafalgar Square: Built in 1845, London's Trafalgar Square commemorates the Battle of Trafalgar (21 October 1805) during the Napoleonic Wars (1803–1815). The British naval victory was led by Admiral Lord Horatio Nelson (1758–1805), who defeated French and Spanish ships near Cape Trafalgar in southwest Spain.

Nelson's Column, topped by a statue of Horatio Nelson, stands in the centre of Trafalgar Square.

26 empty-cloaked Hamlet: In the Shakespearean play, Hamlet refers to his "inky cloak" (I.ii.77), which contrasts the festive garments worn by Claudius, Gertrude, and their wedding guests.

A Landscape of John Sutherland

title John Sutherland: Canadian poet, literary critic, and editor John Sutherland (1919–1956) founded the literary magazines *First Statement* and *Northern Review* and established First Statement Press. He issued the anthology *Other Canadians: An Anthology of the New Poetry in Canada, 1940–46* and was the first publisher of the verse of Irving Layton.

About Free Rides

2–3 Moscow's / Gorky Park: Moscow park named for social realist author Maxim Gorky (born Alexei Maximovich Peshkov, 1868–1936)

17–19 what / fountains did I hear what / icy speeches: the penultimate line of "Passage" (1925) by American poet Hart Crane

19–20 Kennst du / das land: (German) Do you know the land?; likely from Goethe's novel *Wilhelm Meisters Lehrjahre* (*Wilhelm Meister's Apprenticeship*, 1795–1796)

21–23 the snow is seeking / everywhere we cannot hear / our voices for the wind: from "Farewell to Dostoevsky" (1926) by Scottish poet Hugh MacDiarmid (born Christopher Murray Grieve), but Waddington reverses the original lines

24 je suis comme le roi: (French) I am like the king. From *Le Spleen de Paris* by French poet Charles Baudelaire, published posthumously in 1869

25–26 death has reared / himself a throne: from the opening line of "The City in the Sea" (1831), a poem by American writer Edgar Allan Poe

26–27 blue- / brooched Troilus: The classical notion of a beautiful, youthful Troilus as symbolic victim was revised by medieval authors who focused instead on his experience as a Trojan warrior and introduced the brooch that Troilus gives Cressida. Geoffrey Chaucer depicts Troilus as laughing from heaven.

37 Faustus: or Faust, a figure from German legend who, in a deal with the devil, exchanges his soul for unlimited knowledge and worldly pleasures, depicted in Christopher Marlowe's *Dr. Faustus* (1604, but performed as early as 1592), Goethe's *Faust* (1808, 1832), and Thomas Mann's *Doktor Faustus* (1947)

52–54 Poe / is still drowning / in Baltimore: American writer Edgar Allan Poe died four days after he was found delirious on a Baltimore street

58 Eureka: (ancient Greek) I have found [it]

59–60 Baudelaire's / passion: The publication in 1857 of French poet Charles Baudelaire's *Les Fleurs du mal* gave rise to controversy over its themes of decadence and eroticism. Baudelaire and his publisher were charged with insulting public decency, fined 300 francs, and six poems were banned until 1949.

63–64 Goethe / bathing in light: German writer Johann Wolfgang von Goethe wrote about colour theory in *Zur Farbenlehre* (Theory of Colours, 1810).

69–72 Chaucer / . . . / of sawdust horses: Geoffrey Chaucer's *The Canterbury Tales* (c1399), a collection of tales of pilgrims travelling from London to Saint Thomas Becket's shrine at Canterbury Cathedral, is made comical by the storytelling contest that provides the narrative framework for the text.

81–82 boatman left / to ferry you across: In Greek mythology, the boatman Charon ferries dead souls across the river Styx into Hades.

103 Orpheus: musician and poet in Greek mythology whose music was so compelling that he was able to persuade Hades and Persephone to return his recently deceased wife Eurydice to the living world

Circus Stuff

34–35 Lord Mayor's / procession: In many cities, the Lord Mayor is a ceremonial position. In London, England, the office is elected annually on or around Michaelmas (29 September), the Lord Mayor is sworn in in November, and a procession follows the next day.

35–37 Eaton's / Santa Claus parade in / Toronto: The Santa Claus Parade is an annual event held each November in Toronto. From 1905 until 1982, the parade was sponsored and organized by the T. Eaton Company (1869–1999), once Canada's largest department store retailer. By the 1950s, the parade was the largest in North America and was broadcast live on radio and television in Canada and the United States.

Dancing

4 Yorkshire: county located in northeast England

4 Kent: county located in southeast England

5 Warwick: The county town of Warwickshire in central England, Warwick lies on the River Avon.

5 Aberfoyle: village in the region of Stirling, Scotland, located forty-three kilometres northwest of Glasgow

Icons

21 Leningrad: Saint Petersburg, the Imperial capital of Russia (1713–1728; 1732–1918), was known as Leningrad from 1924 to 1991.

29 Piccadilly: major street in central London, England

48–49 un poco / amor: (Spanish) a little love

59 Birmingham: city in the West Midlands of England. Birmingham became a prominent manufacturing centre during the Industrial Revolution and is now the second most populous urban area in the United Kingdom.

63 Palma: the major port city on the island of Majorca and the capital city of Spain's Balearic Islands

Looking for Strawberries in June

59 Lenin: Vladimir Lenin (1870–1924), major figure of the Russian Revolution and first political leader of the Soviet Union

60 Karl Marx: German philosopher and economic historian. Karl Marx (1818–1883) and Friedrich Engels (1820–1895) significantly influenced twentieth-century political ideas, especially the rise of socialism and communism, with their books The Communist Manifesto (1848) and Das Kapital (1867).

60 Walt Whitman: influential American poet Walt Whitman (1819–1892), who established a new poetics rooted in personal issues and motifs

61 Chaucer: Middle English writer Geoffrey Chaucer (c1343–1400) significantly influenced English literature with The Canterbury Tales (c1399), Troilus and Criseyde (c1380s), and other works

61 Hopkins: British poet Gerard Manley Hopkins (1844–1889), little known in his lifetime but widely influential in the twentieth century because of his innovative use of sprung rhythm

62 Archibald Lampman: Archibald Lampman (1861–1899), one of Canada's Confederation Poets, along with Charles G. D. Roberts (1860–1943), Bliss Carman (1861–1929), and Duncan Campbell Scott (1862–1947)

Time II

5 Beersheba: Beersheba, the largest city in the Negev Desert of southern Israel, has been under Roman, Byzantine, Arab, and Ottoman rule. In 1948, Beersheba was taken by the Israeli Air Force through nighttime bombings.

12 Assyrian hill: Assyria, formerly a Semitic nation in northern Mesopotamia (present-day Iraq), also includes areas in the Assyrian empire

14 hamsin: (Arabic) fifty. Refers to a hot, dry, and dusty wind prevalent in North Africa and the Middle East that can blow for fifty days between February and June and can create debilitating sandstorms that interfere with vision and undermine compasses and other navigational equipment

24 Jaffa: ancient port city, also known as Joppa, now part of modern day Tel Aviv. Located on the Mediterranean Sea, Jaffa has been critical in military operations for thousands of years. The city is mentioned in the Bible and has been the site of ancient Egyptian and Roman incursions.

The Woman in the Blue Hat

19 New Statesman: British weekly magazine founded in 1913 by social reformers Beatrice Webb (1858–1943) and Sidney Webb (1859–1947)

Living Canadian: Words to Electronic Music 2

45 Clothilde: Saint Clotilde (475–545) (or Clothilde, Clotilda, Clotild), the second wife of Clovis I (c466–511), King of the Franks. She was venerated as a saint by the Catholic Church.

Flying with Milton

title Flying with Milton: an allusion to British poet John Milton's epic poem *Paradise Lost* (1667) when Satan and the rebel angels fly from the burning lake where they had been chained (I.225)

title ... he flew / With daring Milton through the fields of air / —Keats: lines from the poem "Written on the Day that Mr Leigh Hunt Left Prison" by British poet John Keats (1795–1821), based on Hunt's imprisonment for comments made against the Prince Regent, later George IV

Disguises

6 Gorky street in Moscow: now Tverskaya Street in Moscow. Named for social realist author Maxim Gorky (born Alexei Maximovich Peshkov, 1868–1936), the street resumed its former name after the demise of the Soviet Union.

12 **Museum of the Revolution:** now the State Museum of Contemporary Russian History on Tverskaya Street in Moscow. The museum showcases artifacts from the Soviet period (1917–1990).

15 **Moscow River:** The Moskva River flows through Moscow and lends the city its name.

24 **Hotel National:** Built in 1903 by Russian architect Alexander Ivanov, the Hotel National is a historic landmark located at the heart of Moscow's cultural and business centre, with views of the Kremlin and Red Square.

30–31 **Dreiser's / Sister Carrie:** In Theodore Dreiser's novel *Sister Carrie* (1900), a poor girl from Wisconsin travels to Chicago, finds wealth and fame through the men she attracts, but does not find happiness.

36–37 **Dizengoff Street in / Tel Aviv:** When this poem was first published, Tel Aviv's Dizengoff Street was considered fashionably upscale.

About How Hard It Is to Find New Words in an Outworn World when You Are Not a Magician

12 **panicles:** loosely branching clusters of flowers, e.g., oats or other grasses

Dream Telescope

22 **mosesmountain:** According to the Book of Exodus, Moses observed a bush that burned but was not consumed by fire while he was a shepherd on Mount Horeb. From this bush Moses heard the voice of God who instructed him to liberate his fellow Hebrews from bondage in Egypt.

25–26 **the dead sea and / scrolls:** the Dead Sea Scrolls, discovered between 1947 and 1956 on the shore of the Dead Sea in the present-day West Bank. These texts, in Hebrew, Greek, and Aramaic, are thought to be over two thousand years old and are the oldest known surviving copies of Biblical and related documents.

Cinderella Poems

title **Cinderella:** popular fairy tale figure derived from a folktale. *Cinderella; or, The Little Glass Slipper* is a folktale about a young woman whose unfortunate circumstances are suddenly transformed to remarkable fortune. Thousands of versions are known throughout the world, but one of the most popular is by Charles Perrault who introduced the fairy godmother, the pumpkin, and the glass slippers to the story in 1697.

95–96 hans andersen's / fairy tales: Danish writer Hans Christian Andersen (1805–1875) was noted for his fairy tales, particularly "The Emperor's New Clothes" (1837), "The Little Mermaid" (1837), and "The Ugly Duckling" (1843), which depict themes of beauty, goodness, and honesty. Andersen's birthday, 2 April, is now celebrated as International Children's Book Day.

A Drawing by Ronald Bloore
title Ronald Bloore: Canadian abstract artist Ronald Bloore (1925–2009), Waddington's colleague at York University in Toronto, where he taught from 1966 to 1990

Driving Home
1 ESSO: a brand of Imperial Oil gasoline sold across Canada. Its logo is a white oval with red lettering outlined in blue.

2 SHELL: a brand of gasoline sold across Canada. Its logo is a yellow shell outlined in red.

18 Volga: The Volga River, the longest and largest river in Europe, flows through central Russia.

21 Levitan: Isaac Levitan (1860–1900), Russian painter known for evocative landscapes

25–26 Chekhov's nineteenth-century / consumption: Russian author Anton Chekhov (1860–1904), best known for his plays *Uncle Vanya* (1897), *Three Sisters* (1900), and *The Cherry Orchard* (1904), died of tuberculosis (known as consumption in the nineteenth century).

29 Stanislavsky: Constanin Stanislavsky (1863–1938), Russian actor, theatre director, and father of method acting. In *My Life in Art* (1924), Stanislavsky writes about his professional collaboration with Chekhov on productions of *The Seagull* (1898) and *The Cherry Orchard* (1904).

33 Hitler: Adolf Hitler (1889–1945), chancellor of Germany from 1933 to 1945 who oversaw the rise of fascism in Europe. Intent on creating German hegemony, Hitler declared war on many European nations and orchestrated the persecution and mass genocide of the Jewish and Roma populations of Europe, as well as other oppressed groups, through the Holocaust.

90–91 the dead rabbis / of Lithuania: the Republic of Lithuania, a country in northern Europe and the largest of the three Baltic states (Estonia, Latvia, and Lithuania). Most of Lithuania's large Jewish population perished during the Holocaust.

111 **Mother Assiniboine:** A tributary of the Red River, the Assiniboine River is 1,070 kilometres long and runs through Saskatchewan and Manitoba. The name comes from the Assiniboine First Nation: "assine" (stone) and "bwan" (Sioux). Some believe the name reflects the practice of heating stones to cook food.

113 **Northwest Passage:** a sea route between the Atlantic and Pacific oceans, north of Canada. Between the sixteenth and nineteenth centuries, since trade routes in the eastern Mediterranean were blocked to much of western Europe, numerous European explorers searched for a route to Asia. Between 1903 and 1906, the Northwest Passage finally was navigated by Norwegian explorer Roald Amundsen.

A Man in Chicago

16 **Dostoevsky:** Fyodor Dostoevsky (1821–1881), Russian writer best known for his novels *Crime and Punishment* (1866), *The Idiot* (1869), and *The Brothers Karamazov* (1880)

37 **chequered taxi:** Checker Taxi, an American taxi company, used the Checker Taxi Cab produced by the Checker Motors Corporation of Kalamazoo, Michigan.

45–47 **the heads / of the lions   at / Michigan and State:** Michigan Avenue and State Street, two major north-south thoroughfares in Chicago. Although Waddington's poem suggests the streets converge at an intersection, they run mostly parallel through the city. Flanking the exterior Michigan Avenue entrance to the Art Institute of Chicago are two bronze lions by sculptor Edward Kemeys.

65 **Cinderella:** popular fairy tale figure derived from a folktale. *Cinderella; or, The Little Glass Slipper* is a folktale about a young woman whose unfortunate circumstances are suddenly transformed to remarkable fortune. Thousands of versions are known throughout the world, but one of the most popular is by Charles Perrault who introduced the fairy godmother, the pumpkin, and the glass slippers to the story in 1697.

65 **Rapunzel:** popular fairy tale figure derived from a folktale. The German fairy tale popularized by the Brothers Grimm in the nineteenth century was adapted from the French tale *Persinette* by Charlotte-Rose de Caumont de La Force originally published in 1698. Rapunzel is a beautiful maiden with long golden hair.

84–85 **59th / street:** Manhattan's 59th Street forms the southern border of Central Park. A few blocks north is the Central Park Zoo.

In London

32 leviathan: Leviathan, a Biblical sea monster described by Job; in the middle ages also used as an image of Satan

Sunday Evening Letters

1 Louis Aragon: Louis Aragon (born Louis Andrieux, 1897–1982), French writer active in the Dadaist, Surrealist, and Communist movements in 1920s Paris. Aragon married Elsa Triolet in 1939, served in the French military until Nazi occupation in 1940, and the couple then joined the French Resistance. Aragon was politically active after World War II and wrote numerous novels, short stories, and poems.

3 Elsa Triolet: Elsa Triolet (born Ella Kagan, 1896–1970), Russian-born French writer. Like her husband Louis Aragon, Triolet was active in the French Resistance and Communist movements in 1920s Paris. Encouraged by Russian writer Maxim Gorky to pursue a literary career, in 1944 Triolet was the first female writer to win the Prix Goncourt.

Eavesdropping

19–20 Governor / General's medal: Canada's Governor General's Literary Awards, established in 1937. Awarded annually in both English and French in seven categories: fiction, drama, poetry, non-fiction, children's literature (text and illustration), and translation.

32 who's who: a work of reference, published annually, containing biographical information on a particular group of people, i.e., *Canadian Who's Who* (1910–), which lists notable living Canadians

Language as I Used to Believe in It

28 CBC: The Canadian Broadcasting Corporation/Radio-Canada, a Canadian crown corporation, is the national public radio and television broadcaster.

The Nineteen Thirties Are Over

1–3 The nineteen thirties / . . . / the depression: The 1930s are often referred to as the Great Depression. From the stock market crash of 29 October 1929 to the start of World War II on 1 September 1939, the decade saw worldwide economic hardship.

3–4 Sacco- / Vanzetti: Ferdinando Sacco (1891–1927) and Bartolomeo Vanzetti (1888–1927), Italian immigrants to the United States, convicted of murdering two men during a 1920 armed robbery in South Braintree, Massachusetts and executed in 1927. The case is famous for the vehement protests against the executions and has become shorthand for the railroading of innocent men.

5 Tom Mooney: Thomas Joseph "Tom" Mooney (1882–1942), American political activist and labour leader convicted of the Preparedness Day bombing on 22 July 1916 in San Francisco. After serving twenty-two years in prison, Mooney was pardoned in 1939.

8 Eugene Debs: Eugene Victor "Gene" Debs (1855–1926), founding member of the International Labor Union and the Industrial Workers of the World and a frequent presidential candidate for the Socialist Party of America

10 the Winnipeg strike: The Winnipeg General Strike of 1919 was a landmark event in Canadian labour history. The impact of soldiers returning home after World War I and awareness of the Russian Revolution created social unrest. Municipal workers challenged Winnipeg city councillors for better wages, leading to a widespread strike and concerns that such action would spread to other cities. Violence erupted when the city government and the Northwest Royal Mounted Police attempted to end demonstrations. The strike ended after nearly six weeks with numerous arrests, including that of J. S. Woodsworth (1874–1942), whose seditious libel charges later were dropped; he went on to found the Co-operative Commonwealth Federation, forerunner of the New Democratic Party.

12 OBU: One Big Union, a trade union active in Western Canada. It was founded in Calgary on 4 June 1919 and merged with the Canadian Labour Congress in 1956. One Big Union organized strikes across Western Canada in support of the Winnipeg General Strike of 1919.

15–16 Josh / White's Talking Union: Joshua Daniel "Josh" White (1914–1969), American singer, guitarist, songwriter, actor, and civil rights activist. With the Almanac Singers, a group of folk musicians that included Sam Gary, Bess Lomax Hawes, Lee Hays, Millard Lampell, Pete Seeger, and Carol White, White recorded *Talking Union* (1941), a collection of six labour songs: "All I Want," "Get Thee Behind Me, Satan," "Talking Union," "The Union Maid," "Union Train," and "Which Side Are You On?" The album was reissued in 1955 and is still available today.

17 Prokofieff's Lieutenant Kije: Sergei Prokofieff (1891–1953), Russian composer who composed the score for the Soviet film *Lieutenant Kijé* (1934), based on the 1927 novel by Yury Tynyanov

21–22 Portage / and Main: Portage Avenue and Main Street, a major intersection in Winnipeg, often is referred to as the geographical midpoint of Canada and was the site of some of the events of the Winnipeg General Strike of 1919.

24–26 shores of Gimli where we / looked across to an Icelandic / paradise: rural municipality in south-central Manitoba on the western shore of Lake Winnipeg. Gimli is a cottage and resort town whose population swells each the summer as 100,000 tourists visit annually to swim, fish, and boat on Lake Winnipeg. The large number of Icelandic settlers in and around the area gave Gimli its name: home of the Norse Gods, Gimli is usually translated as "heaven." Since 1932, the town has hosted the annual Icelandic Festival.

The World on Easter Morning

1–2 The Thames is choked with daffodils / and Abraham's bridge is falling down: While the reference to "Abraham" is unclear, when this poem was first published, London Bridge had recently been dismantled because it was sinking into the River Thames. After it was sold and reassembled in Arizona, a new bridge was constructed and opened in 1973.

3 Golder's Green: area in north London which has had a significant Jewish population since the early twentieth century. Until 1923, Golders Green Tube station was the northern terminal of London Underground's Northern Line, which prompted rapid suburban development.

3 Whitechapel: area in east London. From the seventeenth to the twentieth century, Whitechapel was known primarily as an impoverished area and often featured in the novels of Charles Dickens, including *The Pickwick Papers* (1836–1837) and *Oliver Twist* (1838). When this poem was first published, Whitechapel was undergoing socio-demographic change.

6 red rover red rover we call you all over: Red Rover, a children's game believed to have originated in Britain. "Rover" is akin to the Norwegian word for "pirate," suggesting a reference to the Vikings who frequently invaded Britain during the eighth to the eleventh centuries.

8 Passover: Jewish holiday that commemorates the story of Exodus, in which the ancient Israelites were freed from slavery in Egypt. According to the Book of Exodus, the Israelites were aided by ten plagues, the last of which killed the first-born son of each Egyptian family. The Israelites were commanded to mark their doorposts with lamb's blood so God would know to "pass over" their homes.

9 Hampstead Heath: a park in north London

12 Red River: The Red River originates in North Dakota and Minnesota and flows north towards Lake Winnipeg. Once a key trade route for the Hudson's Bay Company, used by fur traders and the Metis community, it has also been the site of major floods in 1950, 1997, and 2009.

12 Galilee: large region in northern Israel that comprises Upper Galilee, Lower Galilee, and Western Galilee. Jesus is believed to have spent much of his life in Galilee.

13 Easter: Christian holiday that commemorates the resurrection of Jesus three days after his crucifixion. The name is thought to derive from the Old English "ostre," which the eighth-century monk Bede believed was a Germanic goddess associated with dawn. Easter and the Jewish holiday of Passover often take place at the same time.

The Land of Utmost

title The Land of Utmost: Buddhism refers to a land called "Utmost Bliss" where no one experiences affliction or pain, only pure immeasurable joy and happiness.

3 injuns: corrupted pronunciation of "Indians," considered an ethnic slur

4 arrivée: (French) arrived

5 ongekommen: (German) arrived

12 loup garou: (French) werewolf

13 Grossinger's Catskills: Grossinger's Catskill Resort Hotel in the Catskill Mountains in upstate New York, where working- and middle-class Jewish families (primarily from New York City) would spend their summer vacations from the 1920s to the 1960s

16 Rip-Van-Winkle: "Rip Van Winkle" (1819), short story by American writer Washington Irving, about a man living in the Catskill region of New York state who falls asleep for twenty years and wakes up to discover his wife has died and the American Revolution has taken place

17 United Jewish Appeal: United Jewish Appeal for Refugees and Overseas Needs, a philanthropic organization established in January 1939 to assist Jews in Europe and Palestine. In 1999, the United Jewish Appeal, the United Israel Appeal, and the Council of Jewish Federations merged to form United Jewish Communities.

21 stars and stripes: nickname for the flag of the United States of America

30–31 keeps our Miss Estelle from Pip / in a Chas. **Dickens' grip:** Estella and Pip, orphan characters in the novel *Great Expectations* (1860–1861) by Charles Dickens. They meet at the home of Miss Havisham, whom Pip believes is his secret benefactor.

Sad Winter in the Land of Can. Lit.
4 Nelly Sachs: Jewish German poet and playwright Nelly Sachs (1891–1970) fled Nazi Germany for Sweden in 1940. Her work probes the profound impact of the Holocaust. She was awarded the inaugural Nelly Sachs Prize in 1961 and the Nobel Prize in literature (with Shmuel Yosef Agnon) in 1966.

10 Madame Nathalie: Nathalie Sarraute (born Natalia/Natacha Tcherniak, 1900–1999), Russian-born French lawyer and writer, forced to stop practicing law during the Nazi occupation of France

61 duddy-kravitz: *The Apprenticeship of Duddy Kravitz* (1959), a novel by Canadian writer Mordecai Richler, about a poor but ambitious Jewish boy growing up in the Plateau neighbourhood of Montreal

65–66 cree / indian: The Cree are among the largest First Nations groups in Canada (with a current population of approximately 200,000), and are historically associated with the fur trade.

67 eskimo: a former term for indigenous peoples living in northern Canada. Today, "Eskimo" is considered pejorative in Canada and has been replaced by the term "Inuit."

Elijah
title Elijah: Hebrew prophet in the ninth century BCE. Elijah was believed to defend the worship of Yahweh, the god of Israel, over the more popular Baal, and to have raised the dead. According to the Book of Kings, Elijah ascended to heaven before his death. His expected return was interpreted as a harbinger of the Messiah. Elijah appears in the Babylonian Talmud, is compared to Jesus and John the Baptist in the Christian Scriptures, and is regarded as a righteous prophet in Islam.

2 William Blake, / his beard is as black as a chimney: British artist William Blake (1757–1827), seminal figure in the early Romantic period whose philosophical and mystical views were not always appreciated in his lifetime. Although deeply familiar with the Bible, Blake opposed all forms of organized religion and developed his own mythical iconography featured in his life's work that combined poetry and engraving. He is best known for writing and illustrating *Songs of*

Innocence (1789) and *Songs of Experience* (1794), and *The Marriage of Heaven and Hell* (1790). In his two poems "The Chimney Sweeper" (1789, 1794), Blake writes of poor boys, often as young as four or five, who are forced to work as chimney sweeps.

9–12 The Jewish seder is over / . . . / but Elijah's beaker is full: The Seder is a ritual feast that marks the beginning of the Jewish holiday of Passover and includes a retelling of the story of the liberation of the Israelites from slavery in ancient Egypt. The Cup of Elijah—a cup of wine poured for the prophet—is part of the Passover Seder.

Why Should I Care about the World
17 Kildonan: former rural municipality in Manitoba. Today, Old Kildonan, East Kildonan, and West Kildonan are suburban residential neighbourhoods of Winnipeg.

20 Galicia: historical region in Eastern Europe, currently divided between Poland and Ukraine

30 Lac du Bonnet: a town located northeast of Winnipeg, Manitoba

50 Bolshevik: (Russian) meaning "majority" from "bol'shinstvo." The Bolsheviks (originally Bolshevists) were a faction of the Marxist Russian Social Democratic Labour Party (unofficially the "Bolshevik Party"). The Bolshevik Party came to power during the October Revolution of 1917. In 1952, at the suggestion of Joseph Stalin, it was renamed the Communist Party of the Soviet Union. During the Cold War period, particularly the 1950s in North America and Western Europe, "Bolshevik" was used as a derogatory term. As a youth in Winnipeg, Waddington was once asked by a streetcar conductor if her father was a Bolshevik, which exacerbated her sense of being an outsider.

I Wish My Life Was a Movie
3 Jean-Luc Godard: French-Swiss film director, screenwriter, and film critic Jean-Luc Godard (1930–), often identified with the 1960s French film movement Nouvelle Vague (New Wave)

The Following
6 Amos: farmer and Hebrew prophet in the eighth century BCE who preached that the day of judgment was imminent to encourage the people of Israel to renew their religious faith

Leaves

16 Miriam: Biblical figure best known as elder sister to Moses, traditionally believed to have composed a victory song after Pharaoh's army was drowned in the Red Sea as the Israelites were leaving Egypt

Provincial

15 Elmwood: working-class residential area of Winnipeg, Manitoba, formerly part of Kildonan

22 St Vital: a district of Winnipeg, Manitoba, located in the south-central part of the city, once a predominantly French-speaking and Metis community

28 onion domes: St. Basil's Cathedral, located in Moscow's Red Square, is distinguished by its onion domes, sometimes thought to resemble burning candles. Constructed between 1555 and 1561 during the reign of Ivan IV, often referred to as Ivan the Terrible, the cathedral was secularized from 1929 to 1990. Ukrainian churches with onion domes are familiar sights in Manitoba, and Waddington would have grown up within easy sight of two of the most famous in Winnipeg: St. Ivan Suchavsky Sobor at 939 Main Street and St. Michael's Ukrainian Orthodox Church at 110 Disraeli Street.

32 Luxembourg Gardens: Jardin du Luxembourg, or Luxembourg Gardens, the second largest public park in Paris

Lights

11–12 the falling / towers of Avignon: Avignon, a city in southeastern France on the Rhône River. The residence of seven popes from 1309 to 1377, it often is referred to as the "City of Popes." The Palais des Papes, built during this period, has thick, impregnable walls and survives as the largest Gothic building in Europe.

My Kind of Internationalism

33 Eiffel tower: iron lattice tower located on the Champ de Mars in Paris. Named for its designer Gustave Eiffel and built as the entrance arch to the 1899 World's Fair, it is the tallest building in Paris and one of the most recognizable structures in the world.

Testing Free Enterprise

2 Domtar: a Canadian company, originally specializing in protecting timber from moisture and rot with coal tar

Transformations

8 St. Boniface: French-speaking district of Winnipeg, Manitoba. Originating as a Catholic mission in 1818, it was also the birthplace of Metis politician and activist Louis Riel (1844–1885). Incorporated as a city in 1908, St. Boniface amalgamated with Winnipeg in 1971.

20 Henry Hudson: British explorer Henry Hudson (c1560/70s–1611?) searched for a western passage to Asia around present-day New York City and north of Quebec. In June 1611, Hudson, his son, and a handful of loyal crew members were set adrift in a small boat by mutineers and never were seen again. The mutineers returned to England, were charged with and then acquitted of murder. Hudson Bay later was named for the explorer.

24 Mennonite: The Mennonites are followers of Menno Simons (1496–1596), a former Catholic priest who espoused anabaptism (adult baptism) and nonviolence. Manitoba has a significant Mennonite population.

Back at York University

title York University: Canada's third largest university, established in 1959 and located in the northern part of Toronto. In 1964, Waddington accepted a tenure-track position in the Department of English of York University.

3 Jackson Pollock: American painter Jackson Pollock (1912–1956), prominent during the abstract expressionist movement of the 1940s and 1950s. He is known particularly for departing from figurative representation by dripping paint onto a canvas laid out on the floor.

21 Central Square: student hub at York University, located in the northern part of Toronto

Gift: Venus 24 Degrees in Virgo

title Edmund Haines: American composer Edmund Thomas Haines (1914–1974), whose work includes *Concertino for Seven Solo Instruments* (1930). Over the course of his career, Haines received the Pulitzer Award (1941), two Fulbright grants, and five Guggenheim Fellowships.

New Religions

13 eskimo: a former term for indigenous peoples living in northern Canada. Today, "Eskimo" is considered pejorative in Canada and has been replaced by the term "Inuit."

Dreaming of Mister Never
7 **Besançon:** capital city of the Franche-Comté region in eastern France near the Alps

Finding Amos in Jerusalem
title **Amos:** farmer and Hebrew prophet in the eighth century BCE who preached that the day of judgment was imminent to encourage the people of Israel to renew their religious faith

41 **Damascus Gate:** the main entrance to the Old City of Jerusalem

45 **Nablus road:** Nablus Road begins at Damascus Gate and leads into the Old City of Jerusalem

Imitations
8 **towers of Avignon:** Avignon, a city in southeastern France on the Rhône River. The residence of seven popes from 1309 to 1377, Avignon often is referred to as the "City of Popes." The Palais des Papes, built during this period, has thick, impregnable walls and survives as the largest Gothic building in Europe.

Snowfences
22 **Mandeville:** the capital and largest town in the parish of Manchester in the county of Middlesex, Jamaica

Tapestry II
title **Helen Duffy:** Swiss-born Canadian curator and artist Helen Duffy (1923–2008) who painted floral and botanical watercolours

Dead Lakes
2 **Sudbury:** a city in northern Ontario, until the 1970s the world leader in nickel mining. Because of the concentration of mining activity (with initially no environmental controls; the Sudbury smelter was, for decades, the source of the highest sulfur dioxide emissions in the world), the area around Sudbury, including its numerous lakes, was significantly affected by acid rain.

22 **Flaubert:** French author Gustave Flaubert (1821–1880), best known for his novel *Madame Bovary* (1857). Although less prolific than some of his peers (such as Honoré de Balzac and Émile Zola), Flaubert is considered one of the greatest Western writers, acclaimed for his perfectionist style.

October 1970

title October 1970: Following the FLQ (Front de libération du Québec) kidnapping of Pierre Laporte (1921–1970) and James Cross (1921–) in October 1970, prime minister Pierre Elliott Trudeau (1919–2000) invoked the War Measures Act, which restricted civil liberties until April 1971—the only peacetime use of this federal power. Laporte was murdered a few days after his kidnapping, while Cross was released after sixty-two days in captivity. During this debacle, now known as the October Crisis, nearly five hundred people were arrested and detained without formal charges being laid.

Lot's Wife

title Lot's Wife: According to the Biblical story (Genesis 19), Lot fled Sodom with his family, but his wife defied the angels' orders, turned back to look at the burning city, and was turned into a pillar of salt.

Beau-Belle

2 Trois Rivières: a city in Quebec at the confluence of the St. Lawrence and Saint-Maurice rivers, about midway between Quebec City and Montreal

13 mauvaise anglaise: (French) poor English [woman]

20 Bleury and Pine: Bleury Street and Pine Avenue, an intersection in central Montreal

23–24 Madame / à votre service: (French) Madame, [I am] at your service

25–27 Monsieur / dis-moi tu, / tu es poupée: (French): Mister, tell me, I am [a] doll

Lovers III

2 Dior-Givenchy: Fashionable clothing from the design houses of Christian Dior (1905–1957) and Hubert de Givenchy (1927–)

Charlottetown

title Charlottetown: capital city of the province of Prince Edward Island. Named after Queen Charlotte, wife of George III, it was the site of the Charlottetown Conference of 1864, the first Confederation conference.

Spring III

title a loaf of bread / a jug of wine / and thou. . .: lines from The Rubáiyát of Omar Khayyám by Persian poet Omar Khayyám (1048–1131), translated by Edward FitzGerald (born Edward Purcell, 1809–1883)

Ten Years and More

1–2 When my husband / lay dying: Waddington's ex-husband, Patrick Waddington, died in 1973. He is best known for his short story "The Street That Got Mislaid" (1952).

27–28 Severn / River: a river in central Ontario, part of the Trent-Severn Waterway, an inland canal system that links Port Severn on Georgian Bay with Trenton on Lake Ontario via the Trent Canal

This Year in Jerusalem

title This Year in Jerusalem: The poem alludes to the Yom Kippur War (also known as the 1973 Arab-Israeli War, and coinciding with both Yom Kippur and Ramadan), which occurred in October 1973 and incurred thousands of casualties. The Passover Seder concludes with the phrase, "Next year in Jerusalem."

Two Trees

2 the tree of life: In Judaism, the tree of life is a metaphor for the Torah; in Christianity, it is related to but distinct from the tree of knowledge. According to the Book of Genesis, after Adam and Eve ate fruit from the tree of knowledge, they were cast out of Eden, but remaining in the garden—now eternally elusive— was the tree of life.

Friends II

title kibitzer: (Yiddish) a meddler who offers unwanted advice to others

3 Eaton's: The T. Eaton Company (1869–1999) was once Canada's largest department store retailer.

4 Volvo: Swedish-built automobile

6 Domtar: a Canadian company, originally specializing in protecting timber from moisture and rot with coal tar

13–15 since ever time began / and Adam was a man and Eve / was also-ran: According to the creation narrative in the Book of Genesis, Yahweh created Adam and Eve, the first human beings to inhabit earth.

36–37 uneasy only lies / the head that wears the crown: an allusion to Henry IV's speech in Shakespeare's *Henry IV, Part 2*, in which he refers to his own head and his inability to sleep peacefully: "Uneasy lies the head that wears a crown" (III.i.31)

47 Trilby: George du Maurier's 1894 novel about a girl who works as an artist's model in Paris, one of the most popular novels of its time. In stage adaptations, the main character, Trilby O'Ferrall, wears a trilby, a hat similar to a fedora.

By the Sea: For A. M. Klein
title A. M. Klein: A. M. (Abraham Moses) Klein (1909–1972), Ukrainian-born Canadian poet who suffered psychological distress and fell silent after the publication of his 1951 novel *The Second Scroll*. Waddington's *A. M. Klein* (Toronto: Copp Clark, 1970) was the first critical study of Klein's work

29 Apollo's golden ear: The son of Zeus and Leto, Apollo is one of the most important gods in Greek and Roman mythology, often associated with music, especially the lyre.

London Night
16–17 Blake's chimney- / sweeps: In his two poems "The Chimney Sweeper" (1789, 1794), British poet William Blake writes of poor boys, often as young as four or five, who are forced to work as chimney sweeps.

39 Caedmon: seventh-century monastery worker at Whitby Abbey in North Yorkshire, England, and the earliest known British poet. According to the eighth-century monk Bede, Caedmon learned to write sacred verse one night while he dreamed.

Artists and Old Chairs
title Helen Duffy: Swiss-born Canadian curator and artist Helen Duffy (1923–2008) who painted floral and botanical watercolours

The Dead
21–23 sinking hills / and rising rivers / of the Gatineau: The Gatineau Hills are a geological formation at the southern tip of the Canadian Shield that acts as the northern shoulder of the Ottawa Valley; the Gatineaus are also the foothills of the larger Laurentian Mountains to the east. Historically, the Gatineau River has been an important source of hydroelectricity; until 1991, it was used to transport logs to sawmills. In the spring of 1974, the area experienced extensive flooding.

Tallness and Darkness
11–12 my little brother / Moses: In the Hebrew Scriptures, Miriam is elder sister to Moses.

21 White Russia: traditionally refers to present-day Belarus, often specifically to the eastern part of Belarus

23 Point Pelee: Southwestern Ontario's Point Pelee National Park is the southernmost point of mainland Canada.

32 Mount Herman: In Biblical times, Mount Herman served as the northern boundary of the Promised Land (Deuteronomy 3:8). Today, the southern slopes of Mount Hermon extend to the Golan Heights in Israel, site of the Mount Herman Ski Resort, the country's highest elevation.

Naive Geography

4–7 Chicago is / . . . / 1000 miles to Winnipeg: The distance between Chicago and Winnipeg is just over 700 miles.

10 Metropolitan opera: The Metropolitan Opera, based in New York City, performs at Lincoln Center and has broadcast over the radio since 1931, on television since 1977, and online since 2006.

11 Wagner: influential German composer of opera Richard Wagner (1813–1883)

13–15 Eaton's charge account adding / to the music in a Henry Moore / skating rink: British sculptor Henry Moore (1898–1986), whose work *The Archer* (1965) is located in Nathan Phillips Square near Toronto City Hall's outdoor skating rink, which is across the street from the location of the former Eaton's department store

15–19 Montreal was / once an Iroquois city huddled / . . . / an Olympic dream: Montreal was built on the site of the Iroquois village of Hochelaga ("beaver dam"). The city was host to the 1976 Summer Olympic Games.

Winnipeg and Leningrad

title Leningrad: Saint Petersburg, the Imperial capital of Russia (1713–1728; 1732–1918), was known as Leningrad from 1924 to 1991.

Real Estate: Poem for Voices

Title Life begins enclosed, protected, all warm in the bosom of the house: from chapter three of Gaston Bachelard's 1958 seminal work, *La Poétique de l'Espace* (published in English as *The Poetics of Space*)

title Gaston Bachelard: French philosopher Gaston Bachelard (1884–1962), influential in the fields of poetics and the philosophy of science

55 LET THEM EAT GRASS: an allusion to "Let them eat cake" (originally French, "Qu'ils mangent de la brioche"), commonly attributed to the callous Queen Marie Antoinette who was supposed to have uttered the decree upon learning that the peasants lacked bread

What the Angel Said

1 **Caedmon:** seventh-century monastery worker at Whitby Abbey in North Yorkshire, England, and the earliest known British poet. According to the eighth-century monk Bede, Caedmon learned to write sacred verse one night while he dreamed.

Grand Manan Sketches

title **Grand Manan:** Grand Manan Island, located in the Bay of Fundy

An Unliberated Woman Seen from a Distance

5 **Tolstoy's Natasha:** Natasha Rostova, a major character in Leo Tolstoy's novel *War and Peace* (1869)

The Secret of Old Trees

title **Tobie Steinhouse:** Canadian printmaker and painter Tobie Steinhouse (1925–), based in Montreal

How I Spent the Year Listening to the Ten O'Clock News

29–33 **in the streets / of Chile or / how many poets / die of a broken / heart:** Chilean politician and poet Pablo Neruda (born Neftalí Ricardo Reyes Basoalto, 1904–1973) died of heart failure shortly after General Augusto Pinochet executed a military coup in September 1973.

Morning on Cooper Street

title **Cooper Street:** located a few blocks from Parliament Hill in Ottawa, Canada's capital city

12–13 **Sealtest / factory:** Sealtest Dairy, formerly a division of National Dairy Products Corporation (predecessor to Kraft Foods, Inc.) of Delaware

The Wind in Charlottetown

title **Charlottetown:** capital city of the province of Prince Edward Island. Named after Queen Charlotte, wife of George III, it was the site of the Charlottetown Conference of 1864, the first Confederation conference. The city's population is predominantly of European descent; Jewish and Muslim communities comprise less than one per cent of Charlottetown's populace.

Afternoon on Grand Manan

title **Grand Manan:** Grand Manan Island, located in the Bay of Fundy

9 **Swallow-Tail:** Swallowtail Lighthouse has operated in North Head, Grand Manan Island, since 1860.

The Price of Gold
2 Merida: Mérida, a city in Mexico

Horoscopes
3–4 December of / revolution: In December 1904, a series of labour strikes took place in Saint Petersburg, Russia. In January 1905, these strikes led to deathly violence at the Winter Palace, home of Czar Alexander II, an event that became known as Bloody Sunday and is usually considered the start of the Russian Revolution.

Certain Winter Meditations on Mister Never
22–25 Lohengrin of Leda / . . . / Elsa who waits / for a name?: Lohengrin is a character in German Arthurian literature. He first appears in Wolfram von Eschenbach's medieval romance *Parzival* (commonly dated to the first quarter of the thirteenth century) as a knight of the Holy Grail. Lohengrin is sent in a boat pulled by swans to rescue Elsa, the duke of Brabant's daughter, who must never ask his identity. Years after they marry, Elsa does ask and Lohengrin disappears forever. The story was adapted by Richard Wagner into the opera *Lohengrin* (1850).

26–28 Who launched their / letters like ships / on the waters: an allusion to the story of Helen of Troy. Seduced by the Trojan prince Paris—Helen is promised to Paris by Aphrodite—Helen abandons her husband Menelaus. Together with Helen's former suitors, from whom he has secured oaths, Menelaus sets sail for Troy to secure his wife's return. See the line in Christopher Marlowe's *Doctor Faustus* (1592): "Was this the face that launched a thousand ships?" (XIII.88).

43–45 three stems and / a flower two wings / and a seed: an allusion to the myth of Daphne, the nymph who was pursued by Apollo. In Ovid's *Metamorphoses*, Daphne seeks to elude Apollo and is transformed into a laurel tree.

Feasts
11–12 Feast of / the Tabernacles: also known as Sukkot, a Jewish holiday that commemorates the fragile dwellings that housed the Israelites during their forty year sojourn in the desert after leaving Egypt

24 Gatineau: a region in western Quebec just north of Ottawa that encompasses the city of Gatineau

Holiday Postcards
6–7 Mother / Goose: the imaginary author of a collection of fairy tales and nursery rhymes, often published as *Mother Goose Rhymes*

10 passé: (French) no longer current

54 Delphi: In Greek mythology, Delphi is the site of the ancient oracle, a sibyl or priestess who prophesied the future.

Lady in Blue: Homage to Montreal
30 calèches: (French) A calèche is a two-wheeled horse-drawn vehicle with or without a folding top and with the driver's seat on the splashboard.

32 Côte des Neiges: Côte-des-Neiges, a neighbourhood in Montreal

Letter from Egypt
30–31 Macbeth's / plunging hands: In William Shakespeare's *Macbeth* (1611), Macbeth soliloquizes on the bloody colour of his hands after stabbing Duncan to death (II.ii.58–61).

Mister Never in a Dream of the Gatineau
title Gatineau: a region in western Quebec just north of Ottawa that encompasses the city of Gatineau

40 La Verendrye: Pierre Gaultier de Varennes, sieur de La Vérendrye (1685–1749), Quebec-born military officer, fur trader, and explorer who travelled west of Lake Superior in search of a route to the Pacific Ocean

45 je me souviens: (French) I remember; the official motto of the province of Quebec since 1939

Postcard from Underground
14 Neptune: the Roman god of water

17 Orpheus: musician and poet in Greek mythology whose music was so compelling that he was able to persuade Hades and Persephone to return his recently deceased wife Eurydice to the living world

21 Bluebeard: *La Barbe bleue*, one of eight literary folktales published in 1697 by French author Charles Perrault in *Histoires ou Contes du temps passé*. The character Bluebeard kills a succession of wives.

Mister Never Shows Me How to Fall off the World
23–25 the rib of my / balance lost as / I walked Adamless: According to the Jewish book *The Alphabet of Ben-Sira*, God made Eve from Adam's rib.

The Big Tree
23 Lot: a Biblical figure, the nephew of Abraham. According to the Biblical story (Genesis 19), Lot fled Sodom with his family, but his wife defied the angels' orders, turned back to look at the burning city, and was turned into a pillar of salt.

South American Nights
7 Rose Red: In the 1889 German fairy tale *Schneeweißchen und Rosenrot* (*Snow-White and Rose-Red*), by the Brothers Grimm, sisters Snow White and Rose Red live with their widowed mother. Both the shy Snow White and the outspoken Rose Red eventually marry princes. This story is not related to the Grimm fairy tale *Snow White*, the basis for the 1937 American animated film *Snow White and the Seven Dwarfs* produced by Walt Disney.

Primary Colours
104 Tuwhit tuwhoo: an allusion to the opening of British poet Samuel Taylor Coleridge's *Christabel* (1816)

Selves
45 the Louvre: The Louvre in Paris is one of the largest and most visited museums in the world.

59–60 Kildonan / Park: located in north Winnipeg

67 Dead Man's Creek: in northern Manitoba

82 Selkirk avenue: in Winnipeg, Manitoba, near Kildonan Park

103 Red River: The Red River originates in North Dakota and Minnesota and flows north towards Lake Winnipeg. Once a key trade route for the Hudson's Bay Company, used by fur traders and the Metis community, it has also been the site of major floods in 1950, 1997, and 2009.

History: In Jordan
14 Jarash: or Jerash, a city north of Amman, Jordan, on the site of an ancient Greco-Roman city known as Gerasa

15 amphitheatre: one of the remains of Greco-Roman Jerash and a sign of the city's early prosperity

16 Nubian: the Nubians, an ethnic group originally from northern Sudan and southern Egypt who settled along the banks of the Nile River

Old Age Blues

48 just watch me: a phrase made famous by Canadian Prime Minister Pierre Elliott Trudeau (1919–2000), who offered this response to a news reporter just prior to invoking the War Measures Act, which suspended civil liberties during the October Crisis of 1970. When this poem was first published, Trudeau had been in office almost continuously for over a decade.

The Transplanted: Second Generation

2 Leningrad: Saint Petersburg, the Imperial capital of Russia (1713–1728; 1732–1918), was known as Leningrad from 1924 to 1991.

23 Peretz: I. L. (Isaac Leib) Peretz (1852–1915), Polish-born Yiddish-language author and playwright

24 Anski: Shloyme Zanvl Rappoport (1863–1920), known by his pseudonym S. Ansky (or An-sky), Jewish Russian author, playwright, and researcher of Jewish folklore who was influenced by I. L. Peretz. Initially, Ansky wrote in Russian, but from 1904 onward he became known as a Yiddish author.

36 glass museum-cases: the State Hermitage Museum, including the Winter Palace, in Saint Petersburg, Russia

The Visitants

20 Gabriel Dumont: Metis leader Gabriel Dumont (1837–1906) commanded the Metis forces in the Northwest Rebellion (1885). In 1884, Dumont persuaded Louis Riel to return to Canada from the United States, where Riel had fled in 1878. He sought Riel's support in presenting Metis grievances to the Canadian government.

The Secret-keeper

title Marvin Duchow: Canadian composer Marvin Duchow (1914–1979), an expert on Renaissance music and French music of the eighteenth century. The Marvin Duchow Music Library at McGill University in Montreal is named in his honour.

17–18 Yeats / who came to Montreal: Irish poet W. B. Yeats (1865–1939) visited Montreal during his North American tour of 1903–1904.

22 Mozart: prolific and influential composer of the Classical era Wolfgang Amadeus Mozart (1756–1791), born in Salzburg, Austria (then part of the Holy Roman Empire)

30 Bach: German composer, organist, harpsichordist, violist, and violinist Johann Sebastian Bach (1685–1750), prolific composer of sacred and secular music of the Baroque period

36 Beethoven: German composer and pianist Ludwig van Beethoven (1770–1827), among the most famous and influential composers of all time

44 Wagner: influential German composer of opera Richard Wagner (1813–1883) whose writings on race and anti-Semitism were embraced by Adolf Hitler

When We Met
17 Odessa: a port city on the northwest shore of the Black Sea in southern Ukraine

18 Volga: The Volga River, the longest and largest river in Europe, flows through central Russia.

In a Summer Garden
title Morris Surdin: Canadian composer Morris Surdin (1914–1979) composed more than two thousand scores for radio, television, and film.

Bulgarian Suite
4 Kopriv-shtitsa: historic town in central Bulgaria known for its nineteenth-century architectural monuments. The town was also the site of an uprising against the Ottoman Empire in April 1876.

6 St Trofim: possibly a reference to the legend of Trophimus, a Roman official during the reign of Emperor Probus (232–282 CE), who was horrified to witness torture against Christians in Antioch in Pisidia (in present-day Turkey) and was compelled to convert to Christianity, provoking his own torture and death

84 cyrillic alphabet: Cyrillic script is an alphabetic writing system developed during the tenth century in the First Bulgarian Empire, the basis of the alphabet used in the national language of Bulgaria and various Slavic-based languages.

Questions
3 Gatineau: a region in western Quebec just north of Ottawa that encompasses the city of Gatineau

14 Laurier Bridge: The Laurier Avenue Bridge crosses the Rideau Canal in Ottawa.

The Visitor I

1–9 the golden fleece / . . . / of Jason: In the Greek myth of Jason and the golden fleece, the Argonauts pursued the golden fleece to reclaim the throne seized by Jason's uncle.

Three Prose Poems: Little Allegories of Canada

4 Rouge hills with Pickering in its claws: Rouge Hill is a neighbourhood in northeastern Toronto near the Rouge River, which separates Rouge Hill from the city of Pickering.

5 Oshawa: a city located east of Toronto and north of Lake Ontario

5 lake of Kawartha: The Kawartha Lakes region is northeast of Toronto. The name is an anglicization of "Ka-wa-tha," believed to mean "land of reflections" in Anishinaabe, later adapted as "bright waters and happy lands" by the tourism industry.

31 Fullum street: located near Lafontaine Park in Montreal's Plateau Mont-Royal neighbourhood

54 Oranges and lemons the belles of Saint Clemens: an allusion to "Oranges and Lemons," a British nursery rhyme and singing game which refers to the bells of several London churches and begins with the lines, "Oranges and lemons, / Say the bells of St. Clements."

73 After many a summoner fades the swan: an allusion to British writer Aldous Huxley's 1939 novel *After Many a Summer*, published in the United States as *After Many a Summer Dies the Swan*

76–77 A peering pearson face a / diefening sound: allusions to Lester B. Pearson (1897–1972), Canada's fourteenth prime minister (1963–1968) and John Diefenbaker (1895–1979), Canada's thirteenth prime minister (1957–1963)

79–80 Mount / Pleasant road in Toronto and go walking in Edwards Gardens: Mount Pleasant Road is a major arterial road east of Yonge Street in Toronto, part of which has numerous commercial businesses. Edwards Gardens is a botanical park east of Mount Pleasant Road.

110 Red river: The Red River originates in North Dakota and Minnesota and flows north towards Lake Winnipeg. Once a key trade route for the Hudson's Bay Company, used by fur traders and the Metis community, it has also been the site of major floods in 1950, 1997, and 2009.

112–113 Red river / rover: Red Rover, a children's game believed to have originated in Britain. "Rover" is akin to the Norwegian word for "pirate," suggesting a reference to the Vikings who frequently invaded Britain during the eighth to the eleventh centuries.

The New Seasons: Light and Dark
33 Birnam Wood: In Shakespeare's *Macbeth* (1611), Macbeth is told that he "shall never vanquish'd be until / Great Birnam wood to high Dunsinane hill / Shall come against him" (IV.i.92–94). Macbeth acquires a false sense of security because he does not anticipate that Malcolm's army will approach camouflaged by trees cut from Birnam Wood.

Jacques Cartier in Toronto
title Jacques Cartier: French explorer of present-day Canada, Jacques Cartier (1491–1557) travelled as far west as the Ottawa River, but there is no extant evidence to suggest that he came to present-day Toronto.

23 Cathay: an alternative name for China in English, which obtained wide currency in Europe after the publication at the end of the thirteenth century of Marco Polo's travelogue *Il Milione*. For centuries, Europeans believed that Cathay and China were distinct nations with distinct cultures. By the late 1600s, however, they had come to recognize that Cathay and China were the same nation.

The Woman in the Hall
21 Guernica: a town in the Basque region of Spain, bombed by Nazi Luftwaffe on 26 April 1937, in support of Francisco Franco who sought to overthrow the Basque government. The devastation of the town and its enormous casualties were depicted by Pablo Picasso in his painting *Guernica* (1937), completed in two months and exhibited at the 1937 World's Fair in Paris.

23 Dieppe: a city in northern France, site of the Dieppe Raid of 19 August 1942 during World War II, in which more than one thousand Allied soldiers were killed and nearly two thousand Canadian soldiers were captured

25–26 sombre-eyed girls in Goya's / drawings: Spanish artist Francisco Goya (1746–1828), known for his *Maja* portraits and his print series *Los Desastres de la Guerra* (1810–1820)

39 Dead Sea: a salt lake that borders Jordan to the east and Israel and the West Bank to the west

The Snow Tramp
13 **Kildonan park:** located in north Winnipeg

Knives and Ploughshares
17 **Carmen:** George Bizet's French *opéra comique*, which premiered at the Opéra-Comique of Paris on 3 March 1875

The New Jasons
title **Jason:** In the Greek myth of Jason and the golden fleece, the Argonauts pursued the golden fleece to reclaim the throne seized by Jason's uncle.

Amos
title **Amos:** farmer and Hebrew prophet in the eighth century BCE who preached that the day of judgment was imminent to encourage the people of Israel to renew their religious faith

Ulysses Embroidered
title **Ulysses:** the Roman name for Odysseus, whose story Homer chronicles in the *Iliad* and, more extensively, in the *Odyssey*. After returning home to Ithaca after a twenty-year sojourn, Ulysses and his son Telemachus kill the suitors of wife and mother Penelope—nearly all had assumed Ulysses did not survive the journey home from the Trojan War.

16–17 **Charybdis / and Scylla:** sea monsters Ulysses and his sailors must overcome in their efforts to return home after the Trojan War. Ulysses confronts further challenges on his own as well.

34 **Penelope:** In Homer's *Odyssey*, Penelope fends off her suitors by telling them she is weaving a burial shroud for Laertes, elderly father to her husband Ulysses, and that she will choose her next husband when she completes the shroud. While the suitors see her weave by day, they do not know she undoes her stitches every night to defer completion of the shroud.

In the Hurly Burly Arcade
46 **Rogers Pass:** a high mountain pass through the Selkirk Mountains of British Columbia used by the Canadian Pacific Railway and the Trans-Canada Highway

49 **Crow's Nest Pass:** Crowsnest Pass is a high mountain pass across the continental divide of the Rocky Mountains on the border of Alberta and British Columbia.

53 **Gastown:** an area in the northeast end of downtown Vancouver

57 Victoria: capital city of British Columbia, located on the southern tip of Vancouver Island

58 Emily Carr: Canadian artist Emily Carr (1871–1945), who painted the landscape of the Pacific Northwest and the iconography of the area's indigenous peoples. Carr also ran a boarding house in Victoria, which she recalls in *The House of All Sorts* (1944).

74 McDonald's: McDonald's Corporation, the world's largest chain of hamburger fast food restaurants, founded in 1940 and headquartered in the United States

Mountain Interval II: Pow Wow at Bragg Creek
title Bragg Creek: a hamlet in southern Alberta, located thirty kilometres west of Calgary

Autumn
title Lyubomir Levchev: Bulgarian poet Lyubomir Levchev (1935–) whose numerous collections have been translated into many languages

Science and Literature
32 James Joyce: Irish novelist James Joyce (1881–1941) who influenced twentieth century literature, particularly through his innovative use of stream of consciousness in *Ulysses* (1922)

41 go and catch a falling star: the first line of "Song: Go and Catch a Falling Star" (1633) by British poet John Donne

Jacques Cartier in Winnipeg
title Jacques Cartier: French explorer of present-day Canada, Jacques Cartier (1491–1557) travelled as far west as the Ottawa River, but there is no extant evidence to suggest that he came to present-day Winnipeg.

4 Saint Malo: Saint-Malo, a port city on the northwest coast of France, birthplace and lifelong home of Jacques Cartier (1491–1557)

7–8 you sailed down / the broad Saint Lawrence: Jacques Cartier first sailed the St. Lawrence River in 1535.

18 Hiding-O-Seek: hide-and-seek (or hide-and-go-seek), a variant of the game of tag, in which several players conceal themselves in the environment, to be found by one or more seekers

19 Red Rover: a children's game believed to have originated in Britain. "Rover" is akin to the Norwegian word for "pirate," suggesting a reference to the Vikings who frequently invaded Britain during the eighth to the eleventh centuries.

Remembering Winnipeg

47 l'chaim: (Hebrew) to life (a toast)

55 bonne chance: (French) good luck

55 Louis Riel: Canadian activist Louis Riel (1844–1885). On behalf of Metis rights, Riel led the Red River Rebellion of 1869. In 1885, he participated in the Northwest Rebellion, was arrested and later tried. Convicted of treason, Riel was executed; his death intensified the antagonism between the Canadian government, the Metis community, and Quebec supporters that endured until well into the twentieth century.

58 Fort Garry: From 1822 to 1869, the Hudson's Bay Company trading post of Fort Garry was located at the confluence of the Red River and the Assiniboine River in what is now downtown Winnipeg. Today, Fort Garry is a residential district in the southwest part of Winnipeg, far from the site of the original fort. During Waddington's residency, the district of Fort Garry was on the outer edge of Winnipeg.

PREVIOUSLY UNPUBLISHED AND UNCOLLECTED POEMS

Reveille

title Reveille: (French) wake up; bagpipe, bugle, or trumpet call, primarily used to awaken military personnel at sunrise

Politics

5 The president's attaché: As a teenager, Waddington lived in Ottawa, Canada's capital city and the nation's political hub for visiting dignitaries.

9 Russia's two ambassadors: Britain controlled Canada's foreign diplomatic relations until 1931. Canada established formal diplomatic relations with the former Soviet Union in 1942.

Biology Room

title modern style: Modernism, a rejection of the aesthetic values of the Romantic and Victorian periods, dominated and influenced many areas of art in the first half of the twentieth century.

title Baroque: exaggerated style prevalent from the beginning of the seventeenth century to the early eighteenth century. Originating in Rome, it spread to much of Europe and was evident especially in painting, sculpture, architecture, and interior design.

21 spirogyra: filamentous green algae, named for its helical or spherical appearance

43 chanson modern: (French) modern song; French solo song characterized by a personal perspective and a distinctive vocal personality, developed in the sixteenth century and revived by notable practitioners such as Édith Piaf (1915–1963), Charles Aznavour (1924–), Serge Gainsbourg (1928–1991), and Jacques Brel (1929–1978)

What Is This Life
5 Jack be nimble, Jill be quick: a variation on the children's nursery rhyme: "Jack be nimble, / Jack be quick, / Jack jump over / The candlestick"

The Peasant's Revolt
title Revolt: This poem may be alluding to a number of uprisings that occurred during the 1930s, including the 1930 Salt March in India, the 1932 peasant uprising known as La matanza in El Salvador, and the 1937 workers' revolution known as Jornados de Mayo in Catalonia.

The Flying Weather
2 Lord, have mercy on my soul!: the Jesus prayer, an oft-repeated phrase during Christian sermons, especially in Eastern Catholicism

Envoi
6 star: The six-pointed Star of David, the universal symbol of Judaism, began appearing on tombstones in Europe in the eighteenth century.

6 cross: The cross, which symbolizes the crucifixion of Jesus Christ, has been in use as the universal symbol of Christianity since about the third century.

Medea
title Medea: In Greek mythology, the wife of Jason who helped him secure the golden fleece. Euripides's Greek tragedy *Medea* (first produced in 431 BCE) introduced the image of Medea as the mother who deliberately killed her children to exact revenge upon Jason after he abandoned her.

The Pattern

2 minuet: French social dance for two people, in 3/4 time characterized by short steps

Journey to Winnipeg: 1940

12 El Greco: (Spanish) El Greco (The Greek) was the nickname of Doménikos Theotokópoulos (1541–1614), an artist of the Spanish Renaissance. Born in Crete, then part of the Republic of Venice, El Greco moved first to Venice and then Rome in the tradition of Greek artists before him. In 1577, he moved to Toledo, Spain, where he developed his distinctive style considered a precursor to and inspiration for twentieth century Cubism and Expressionism.

22 Scheherazade: legendary Persian queen and storyteller of *One Thousand and One Nights*

26 Flin Flon: city on the Manitoba-Saskatchewan border where the mining of copper and zinc is the principal industry. The city is named for prospector Josiah Flintabbaty Flonatin, the main character in J. E. Preston Muddock's dime novel *The Sunless City* (1905).

31 Métis: Manitoba is home to many Metis and Waddington interacted with Metis children during her childhood in Winnipeg.

44 river Sambatyan: legendary river across which part of the ten "lost tribes" of Israel were exiled by the Assyrians. According to legend, it rages constantly except on the Sabbath, and so cannot be crossed.

55 Red River and Assiniboine: The Forks is a historic site and meeting place in downtown Winnipeg, located at the confluence of the Red River and the Assiniboine River. The Forks was an aboriginal camping site for over six thousand years and became a trading post for the European fur industry in the eighteenth and nineteenth centuries. Today, the area comprises the Forks Market, the Manitoba Theatre for Young People, and recreational facilities, including the world's longest skating rink.

Love

title John Sutherland: Canadian poet, literary critic, and editor John Sutherland (1919–1956) founded the literary magazines *First Statement* and *Northern Review* and established First Statement Press. He issued the anthology *Other Canadians: An Anthology of the New Poetry in Canada, 1940–46* and was the first publisher of the verse of Irving Layton. In the early 1940s, Sutherland and Waddington were lovers.

Who in Their Love
7 rivers into heaven: In Hinduism, the Ganges River is considered sacred. Pilgrims bathe in the Ganges to cleanse their sins and immerse the ashes of relatives in the river so their loved ones may enter heaven.

At Court
16 Daniel: In the Hebrew Scriptures, Daniel (whose name translates as "God is my judge") successfully interpreted the dreams of the Babylonian king Nebuchadnezzar and later had apocalyptic visions.

Man and Secretary
7 guillotine: first used in 1792 in France, its angled blade was considered a more humane and effective form of execution than the previous methods of axe or sword, which often caused bleeding and a slow death. Advocated (but not invented) by Joseph-Ignace Guillotin (1738–1814), a French physician who hoped the device eventually would end the need for the death penalty, the guillotine was in active use during the French Revolution's Reign of Terror (1793–1794) and was used in the 1793 execution of the deposed king and queen, Louis XVI and Marie Antoinette. It continued to be used in France and other countries until well into the twentieth century.

Some Notes on Our Time
15 red red light: In the nineteenth century, red lights were used in the American Old West to identify brothels. The red light developed as a traditional symbol for prostitution, especially in urban areas.

Untitled [Black doves in my cherry tree]
1 Black doves: Greek historian Herodotus (c484 BCE–425 BCE) recounts the legend of the Dodona prophetesses who were called "peleiades" (doves). Two black doves flew from Thebes in Egypt, one to Libya and one to Dodona. When the latter dove uttered human speech, an oracular shrine was established by the people of Dodona.

1 cherry tree: A popular but possibly apocryphal story about a young George Washington—who chopped down his father's cherry tree but admitted to the offence when questioned—was disseminated widely throughout the nineteenth century and much of the twentieth century to encourage children to emulate the demonstrated honesty of the inaugural president of the United States (1789–1797).

5 peace: The symbolic association of the dove and peace dates back to the Hebrew Scriptures. In the Book of Genesis, a dove bearing an olive leaf in its beak signalled to Noah the abatement of the Great Flood. Early Christians may have expanded upon this image, which did not specify the colour of the dove, but today it is the white dove that is symbolically identified with peace.

He Calls

5 raven: an allusion to the American writer Edgar Allan Poe's narrative poem *The Raven* (1845)

Doubles

2 sons who grow: a reference to Waddington's two sons, Marcus (1946–) and Jonathan (1951–)

Untitled [He who hobnobs]

2 Dobbs: Canadian writer Kildare Dobbs (1923–2013), born in India and educated in the United Kingdom. Dobbs's first book, *Running to Paradise* (1962), won the Governor General's Literary Award for fiction. He is a longtime literary broadcaster and journalist and a founding editor of the influential *Tamarack Review* (1956–1982).

5 Toye: William Toye (1926–), notable literary editor at Oxford University Press Canada from 1948 to 1991, and a founding editor of the influential *Tamarack Review* (1956–1982). Waddington published a total of nine books with Oxford University Press Canada.

6 McLure: Renaissance scholar Millar McLure (1917–1991), professor of English at Victoria College in the University of Toronto. McLure was a founding editor of the influential *Tamarack Review* (1956–1982) and, from 1960 to 1965, editor of the *University of Toronto Review*.

9 Anne Wilkinson: Canadian poet Anne Wilkinson (1910–1961) who, alongside Dorothy Livesay (1909–1996) and P. K. Page (1916–2010), gained literary prominence in the 1940s and 1950s. Wilkinson was a founding editor of the influential *Tamarack Review* (1956–1982).

11 Weaver: Robert Weaver (1921–2008), notable Canadian literary broadcaster and editor who worked at the CBC from 1948 to 1985, where he boosted the early careers of numerous Canadian authors, including Mordecai Richler (1931–2001), Alice Munro (1931–), and Margaret Atwood (1939–). Weaver was a founding editor of the influential *Tamarack Review* (1956–1982).

15 Smith: Canadian poet and anthologist A. J. M. (Arthur James Marshall) Smith (1902–1980) was a member of the Montreal Group, which included F. R. Scott (1899–1985), Leon Edel (1907–1997), Leo Kennedy (1907–2000), and A. M. Klein (1909–1972). As an undergraduate student at McGill University, Smith published verse in the *Dial*, an influential American literary journal that first published T. S. Eliot's *The Waste Land* (1922). Smith received the Governor General's Literary Award for *News of the Phoenix and Other Poems* (1943).

15 Scott: Canadian poet F. R. (Francis Reginald) Scott (1899–1985) was professor of law at McGill University and co-founder of the Co-operative Commonwealth Federation (forerunner of the New Democratic Party). Scott was a member of the Montreal Group, which included A. J. M. Smith (1902–1980), Leon Edel (1907–1997), Leo Kennedy (1907–2000), and A. M. Klein (1909–1972). In 1967, he was awarded the Molson Prize for outstanding achievement in the arts, humanities, and social sciences.

15 Frye: Northrop Frye (1912–1991), prominent and prolific Canadian literary critic and literary theorist, considered one of the most influential thinkers of the twentieth century. Frye was professor of English at Victoria College in the University of Toronto. His groundbreaking scholarly works include *Fearful Symmetry* (1947), which led to a reinterpretation of the poetry of William Blake, *Anatomy of Criticism* (1957), a work of literary theory, and *The Great Code* (1983), a study of Biblical typology.

16 Pie in The Sky: a phrase from "The Preacher and the Slave" (1911) by Swedish-born songwriter and labour activist Joe Hill. The phrase means "a promise of heaven, while continuing to suffer in life."

17 The Text: an allusion to New Criticism, a movement in literary theory that dominated North American literary criticism in the mid-twentieth century. New Criticism regarded literary works as aesthetically self-contained and emphasized the close reading of texts, especially poetry.

25 jack pine: North American pine tree (used in industrial applications, such as decking and utility poles), memorably depicted in the paintings of Tom Thomson (1877–1917), Canadian painter who influenced the group of artists now known as the Group of Seven

32 Laurels: The bay laurel traditionally symbolizes victory, especially in athletic and intellectual achievement. In Ovid's *Metamorphoses*, Daphne seeks to elude Apollo and is transformed into a laurel tree.

32 Tamarack: *Tamarack Review* (1956–1982), influential Canadian literary journal. Taking its name from the Algonquian word for "a kind of supple wood used for making snowshoes," the tamarack or North American larch is a deciduous conifer (that is, unlike most other conifers it sheds its needles each year) with short needles that turn bright yellow in the autumn before they fall. Tamarack wood is supple but strong and rot-resistant and is used for many purposes, including house frames, railroad ties, and fence posts, as well as more traditional uses such as toboggans, snowshoes, and canoes.

Untitled [the dandelion children]
1 dandelion children: psychological term describing children who are able to thrive under adverse conditions, including child abuse

Untitled [It's six o'clock]
2 Finch: Finch Avenue, a major east-west thoroughfare in northern Toronto, regularly affected by harsh winter conditions

In Jerusalem
5 eight-grush: coin valued at 1/100 of an Israeli lira

15 Amos: farmer and Hebrew prophet in the eighth century BCE who preached that the day of judgment was imminent to encourage the people of Israel to renew their religious faith

22 Little Sisters of Mercy: possibly a reference to the Religious Order of the Sisters of Mercy, founded by Catherine McAuley in Dublin in 1831 as a Catholic mission to serve impoverished women and children

23–24 thunderous dark forehead / of Moses glowers: Biblical figure significant in Judaism, Christianity, and Islam. Waddington's evocation of Moses invokes Michelangelo's sculpture *Moses* (c1513–1515) and José di Ribera's painting *St Moses* (1638).

26 Miriam: In the Hebrew Scriptures, Miriam is elder sister to Moses.

Swimming Away
10 Neptune: the Roman god of water

22 Milton's azure shores: a possible allusion to British poet John Milton's *Paradise Lost* (1667): "He walkt with to support uneasy steps / Over the burning Marl, not like those steps / On Heaven's Azure, and the torrid Clime / Smote on him sore besides, vaulted with Fire" (Book I, 295–298), describing Satan

23 ebony Egyptian cairn of kings: a possible allusion to the Valley of the Kings, located on the west bank of the Nile River where the tombs of the pharaohs were built, near the Theban hills

For Oliver Girling
title Oliver Girling: son of Harry Knowles Girling, Waddington's colleague in the Department of English at Toronto's York University. Today, Oliver Girling is a visual artist based in Toronto.

3 St. John's: capital city of Newfoundland and Labrador and the most easterly city in North America, settled before 1620

My Orphan Poems
title My Orphan Poems: Waddington once admitted: "Every poet has such unpublished poems somewhere in the back of a drawer. Sometimes poems are put aside until there is more time to finish them. Often that time never comes and those poems are orphaned and abandoned forever. Other times poems are put aside because they do not work, do not feel quite right to the poet, and so they are never really finished." Miriam Waddington, Foreword, *Archive for Our Times: Previously Uncollected and Unpublished Poems of Dorothy Livesay*, ed. Dean J. Irvine (Vancouver: Arsenal Pulp P, 1998) 9.

5–7 I've edited / the poems of a great / dead poet: Waddington edited *The Collected Poems of A. M. Klein* (Toronto: McGraw-Hill Ryerson, 1974).

Departure from Kashima
(After a Painting by an Unknown Artist on a 14th-Century Scroll)
title Kashima ... 14th-Century Scroll: Kashima is a port city in Ibaraki Prefecture, Japan, the site of Kashima Shrine, a Shinto temple. Scroll paintings in fourteenth-century Japan, known as the Muromachi period, were characterized by their monochromatic palette, reflecting the influence of Zen Buddhism and religious paintings from China, which were being imported into Japan at this time.

Happy New Year
7–8 leshona / tova: (Hebrew) Happy New Year (a greeting)

Cycles
2–3 monarch / butterflies return: The Monarch butterfly, perhaps the best known of all North American butterflies, migrates south to Mexico in the winter and returns north to Canada in the summer.

4–5 toad wakes up from / his hundred-year sleep: Toads have been known to live up to forty years, but in the wild they typically live ten to twelve years.

12 milkweed: herbaceous American plant with milky sap. Some milkweed attracts butterflies, some are grown as ornamental plants, and some yield a variety of useful products.

16–21 But the fireflies! / . . . / lamps are flaring again: Waddington's source for this reference to the disappearance and subsequent reappearance of fireflies is unknown, but some media reports of increasing urban density and concomitant light pollution suggest causes of a declining firefly population.

24 Bay of Quinte: on the northeastern edge of Lake Ontario

34 Beethoven: German composer and pianist Ludwig van Beethoven (1770–1827), among the most famous and influential composers of all time

A Garland for Terry

title Terry: Winnipeg-born Terry Fox (1958–1981), humanitarian, athlete, and cancer research activist. In 1980, after his right leg had been amputated, Fox undertook the Marathon of Hope, a cross-country run to raise money and awareness for cancer research. Although he was forced to end his run near Thunder Bay, Ontario, he completed more than 5,000 kilometres over 143 days and inspired several similar ventures. After his death, the Terry Fox Run was established in Canada and other countries. Today, it is the world's largest one-day annual fundraiser for cancer research.

3 a messenger on wings: Hermes in Greek mythology and Mercury in Roman mythology

7 Prometheus: In Greek mythology, Prometheus's theft of fire from Zeus allowed humans to cook and forge tools. To punish Prometheus for his crime, Zeus had him bound to a rock while an eagle devoured his liver each day, after it had regenerated during the night.

9 Zeus: in Greek mythology, the chief god among Olympian deities

19 St. John's: capital city of Newfoundland and Labrador and the most easterly city in North America, settled before 1620

30–31 Glovertown to Gambo, from Gander to South Brook Junction, from / Deer Lake to Cornerbrook: Newfoundland towns on the Trans-Canada Highway, and part of the first leg of Terry Fox's Marathon of Hope

32 Port aux Basques: town located on the southwestern tip of Newfoundland. Terry Fox was greeted by the entire town of Port aux Basques and given a donation of over $10,000, the first substantial expression of support for his Marathon of Hope.

41 Port Coquitlam: located east of Vancouver in British Columbia, the city where Terry Fox lived from age ten

45 Lupins: North American plant in the legume family, easily recognized by its palmate leaf and bright coloured spike-shaped flowers

49 the Plains of Abraham: historic site of the Battle of the Plains of Abraham of 13 September 1759, when the British defeated the French during the French-Indian War (1754–1763); now an area within Battlefields Park in Quebec City, named for Abraham Martin (1589–1664) who once owned a plot of land near the site of the present-day park

66 French River Trading Post: motel located on the northeast side of Georgian Bay where Terry Fox spent a night toward the end of his Marathon of Hope. The Ojibwa tribe named French River for its association with the seventeenth-century French explorers Samuel de Champlain (c1567–1635), Étienne Brûlé (c1592–1633), and Pierre-Esprit Radisson (1636–1710). Until the early nineteenth century, French River was a major canoe route in the European fur trade. In 1986, it was designated a Canadian Heritage River.

68 clouds of Black Flies: Black Fly season in Northern Ontario, mid-May to mid-June

75 Thunder Bay: Terry Fox was forced to abort his Marathon of Hope near Thunder Bay, Ontario. One year after his death, near the site where he ended his run, a nine-foot high bronze statue set on a granite base was erected in his memory.

To Manitoba Margaret on Her Sixtieth Birthday July 19/86
title Manitoba Margaret: Margaret Laurence (1926–1987), renowned Canadian writer and a friend of Waddington. This poem, which commemorates Laurence's sixtieth birthday, is dated less than six months before her death on 5 January 1987.

Untitled (For My Brother Alex)
title Alex: the poet's older brother

8 his brothers: the poet's younger twin brothers, Dave and Sol

19 O Sole Mio: (Italian) my sun; traditional Italian song written in 1898, widely sung and recorded, usually in the original Neapolitan language

20 Away to Rio: possibly the sailor song *Away Rio*

33 Ivory Coast: Côte d'Ivoire, a country in western sub-Saharan Africa

Untitled [Sometimes I imagine us]

4 Chopin: Polish-born composer and piano virtuoso Frédéric Chopin (1810–1849)

Untitled [I am addressed to you]

17 Passover: Jewish holiday that commemorates the story of Exodus, in which the ancient Israelites were freed from slavery in Egypt. According to the Book of Exodus, the Israelites were aided by ten plagues, the last of which killed the first-born son of each Egyptian family. The Israelites were commanded to mark their doorposts with lamb's blood so God would know to "pass over" their homes.

22 Haman: In the Book of Esther, Haman plots to kill all the Jews in Persia but is foiled by Queen Esther and is executed in place of Mordecai, whom he had intended to kill. The Jewish holiday of Purim commemorates the deliverance of the Jews in Persia and the defeat of Haman, who is regarded as an archetype of evil and the persecutor of Jews.

Ecology

3 hurben Yerushalyim: (Hebrew) the destruction of Jerusalem (Waddington's own note)

TRANSLATIONS—YIDDISH

Jewish Folk Song (Anonymous)

note This is Waddington's own note.

4 Rothschild: The Rothschild family, of Jewish German descent, established European banking and finance houses in the late eighteenth century. By the nineteenth century, the family possessed a vast fortune.

Yizkor (Jacob Glatstein)

title Yizkor: (Hebrew) remembrance; Judaism's memorial prayer for the dead

19 blind Samsons: The Biblical Samson was blinded by the Philistines.

28 machzor: (Hebrew) recitation; prayer book used by Jews during the High Holidays of Rosh Hashanah (Jewish New Year) and Yom Kippur (Day of Atonement)

36 yisgadal: (Aramaic) aggrandize; first word of the Kaddish (Jewish mourners' prayer)

37 hatikvah: (Hebrew) the hope; Israel's national anthem

Seven Brothers (Mani Leib)
34–35 Long / Island: island located in southeast New York, just east of Manhattan

49 yisgadal: (Aramaic) aggrandize; first word of the Kaddish (Jewish mourners' prayer)

Auld Lang Syne: New Year's Eve (Itsik Manger)
title Auld Lang Syne: Scots phrase which translates literally as "old, long ago"

Ballad of the Dying Christopher Marlowe (Itsik Manger)
title Christopher Marlowe: Elizabethan dramatist and poet Christopher Marlowe (1564–1593)

8 Barabbas: The Biblical Barabbas was released from prison over Jesus. Barabas is the title character in Christopher Marlowe's play *The Jew of Malta* (1633, but first performed in 1592).

28 Mammon: In the Christian Scriptures, Mammon denotes wealth or greed, often personified as a deity.

Fate (Itsik Manger)
2 Galilee: large region in northern Israel that comprises Upper Galilee, Lower Galilee, and Western Galilee

From An Elegy for Shlomo Mikhoels (Perets Markish)
title Shlomo Mikhoels: Shlomo Mikhoels (1890–1948), Jewish Soviet actor and artistic director of the Moscow State Jewish Theater, murdered on orders of Stalin

20 Levi Yitshak: Levi Yitshak (1740–1809) of Berdychiv, Ukraine, a rabbi, Chassidic leader, and composer of popular Chassidic folk songs

Aunt Dvorah (J. I. Segal)
3 Menorah: (Hebrew) candelabrum used in Jewish worship, especially one with eight branches and a central socket used at Chanukah

5 **Reb:** (Yiddish) short form of Rebbe, a Torah teacher

A Jew (J. I. Segal)

13 **Hasidim:** (Hebrew/Yiddish) those who follow the ways of Chassidism—the beliefs and practices of a sect of Orthodox Jews—and study its teachings

22 **Torah:** (Hebrew) The Torah, or Chumash, refers to the Five Books of Moses, also known as the Pentateuch.

22 **Haggadah:** (Hebrew) Jewish text that sets out the order of the Passover Seder and is read at the Passover table. The Seder is a ritual feast that marks the beginning of the Jewish holiday of Passover and includes a retelling of the story of the liberation of the Israelites from slavery in ancient Egypt.

Late Summer in Montreal (J. I. Segal)

1 **Mount Royal:** the mountain immediately west of downtown Montreal, which gave the city its name

16 **Mendelssohn:** Felix Mendelssohn (1809–1847), German composer, pianist, organist, and conductor of the early Romantic period

17 **Tehilim:** (Hebrew) The Book of Psalms

19–20 **St. Dominique / street:** Saint Dominique Street is located in the former Jewish quarter of Montreal.

Teaching Yiddish (J. I. Segal)

18 **Sholem Aleichem:** pen name of Solomon Naumovich Rabinovich (1859–1916), leading Yiddish author and playwright

23 **chumish:** (Hebrew) The Chumash, or Torah, refers to the Five Books of Moses, also known as the Pentateuch.

24 **gemorah:** (Aramaic) commentary on the collection of Jewish law known as the Mishna

29 **Motl Paisie the Cantor's son:** Sholem Aleichem's last novel *Motl Peyse dem Khazns* (1907)

Fragment from Ash (Zusman Segalovich)

13 **yahrzeit:** (Yiddish) in Judaism, the anniversary of the death of a relative, observed with mourning and the recitation of religious texts

Blood-stained Roses (Sholem Shtern)

10 **Reb:** (Yiddish) short form of Rebbe, a Torah teacher

10 **chassid:** (Hebrew) one who follows the ways of Chassidism—the beliefs and practices of a sect of Orthodox Jews—and studies its teachings

11 **Nu:** (Yiddish) Well? So? What's going on?

Spring Greetings (Moyshe Teyf)
17 **l'chaym brieder:** (Hebrew; Yiddish) to life, brothers (a toast)

18 **L'chaym chaverim:** (Hebrew) to life, friends (a toast)

TRANSLATIONS—GERMAN

School for Preparing (Otto Rank)
10 **Pegasus:** The offspring of Poseidon and Medusa, Pegasus is a fantastical creature, a winged divine horse, white in colour, and one of the best known creatures in Greek mythology.

Weltschmerz: Lines before Breakfast (Otto Rank)
title Weltschmerz: (German) world-pain or world-weariness. The term was coined by German author Jean Paul (born Johann Paul Friedrich Richter, 1763–1825) to denote the understanding that physical reality can never satisfy the demands of the mind. The modern meaning of the word is akin to anomie.

TRANSLATIONS—RUSSIAN

Under the Roof in My House (Rimma Fyodorovna Kazakova)
17 **Cossack:** A predominantly East Slavic people, Cossacks originally were members of democratic, semi-military communities in what is today Ukraine.

Springtime Girl (Robert Ivanovich Rozhdestvensky)
46 **Omsk:** a city in southwestern Siberia

47 **Biysk:** a city in southwestern Siberia

48 **Leningrad:** Saint Petersburg, the Imperial capital of Russia (1713–1728; 1732–1918), was known as Leningrad from 1924 to 1991.

49 **Krasnoyarsk:** third largest city in Siberia

50 **Varna:** a seaside resort and the third largest city in Bulgaria

51 **Karlsbad:** an administrative area in the district of Karlsruhe in Baden-Württemberg, Germany, situated in the northern Black Forest

96 Tashkent: capital of Uzbekistan and of Tashkent Province

98 Kharkov: second largest city in Ukraine

99 Weimar: German city renowned for its cultural heritage, located in the federal state of Thüringen

Appendix: Contents of Published Collections

Green World (1945)

The Second Silence (1955)

POEMS OF LOVE

Interval
Lullaby
You and Me
At Midnight
Problem
Novella
These Times
Lovers
Thou Didst Say Me
Circles
Three Poems for My Teacher
Three Poems to a Pupil
Uncertainties

POEMS OF CHILDREN

In the Park
Catalpa Tree
Wonderful Country
Worlds
Night in October
Fables of Birth
Childless

POEMS OF WORK

Investigator
Sorrow
Folkways
Foundling
Journey to the Clinic
Trip from the City
Charity

POEMS OF LIVING

New Year's Concert
The Bread We Eat
Poems about War
Growing
Erosion
St. Antoine Street
Time's Large Ocean
Prayer
Morning until Night
Getting Older
The Music Teachers
Adagio
City Street
Bird's Hill
Inward Look the Trees

The Season's Lovers (1958)

I POETS AND STATUES

Poets and Statues

II THE CITY'S LIFE

When World Was Wheelbarrow
The City's Life
Old Women of Toronto
Winnipeg
What Is Hard
The Young Poet and Me
People Who Watch the Trains
Traffic Lights at Passover
The Through Way

III TO BE A HEALER

In a Corridor at Court
Three Prison Portraits
My Lessons in the Jail
To Be a Healer
The Women's Jail
The Orator
The Thief

IV NO EARTHLY LOVER

Exchange
No Earthly Lover
Jonathan Travels
Did You Me Dream
You Are My Never
Song
The Honeymoon
The Exhibition: David Milne
The Artist
Semblances
In the Mountains

The Glass Trumpet (1966)

THINGS OF THE WORLD

Things of the World
The Land Where He Dwells In
From a Dead Poet's Book
The Bright Room
Saints and Others
Toronto the Golden-vaulted City
Sea Bells
Returning to Toronto
A Song of North York between Sheppard and Finch
The Terrarium
New Year's Day
Brotherly Love on Sherbrooke Street
Fortunes
Summer Letters
The Clearing
Saints and Bibliographers
The Gardeners
Children's Coloured Flags
The Far City
Goodbye Song
Prairie Thoughts in a Museum
Pictures in a Window
Hart Crane
The Glass Trumpet

CARNIVAL

Carnival
The Journeying
On My Birthday
Looking at Paintings
Remembering You
A Balkan Cemetery
Pleasures from Children
The Follower
The Mile Runner

Say Yes (1969)

Understanding snow
Living Canadian: Words to electronic music
Flying with Milton
The little fringes
Cape Cod
Waking
My travels
About free rides
Disguises
The magician
About how hard it is to find new words in an outworn world when you are not a magician
In my dream telescope
Looking for strawberries in June
The eight-sided white barn
How each one becomes another in the early world
Pont Mirabeau in Montreal
Memory box
Apollo tree
The wakened wood
You as real
How we are immortal in others
Sorrow song
From a train window
Women who live alone
Dark
Someone who used to have someone
All those who run in fields
Spring rain
Owning the world
Ukrainian church
Leaf
Summer
Laughter
Birch tree
Cinderella poems
Shakedown
Breaking with tradition

Swallowing darkness is swallowing dead elm trees
A drawing by Ronald Bloore
A morning like the morning when Amos awoke
Driving home
A man in Chicago
Circus stuff
A picture of O
Dancing
The woman in the blue hat
Transition
In London
Waking in London
Love poem
Waiting in Alberta
Time
Sunday evening letters
Icons

Dream Telescope (1972)
Dream Telescope
i Legend
ii Mysteries
iii Double Zero
iv Underground
v Singing
vi The Dream Telescope
vii Journey
viii Likeness
ix The Darkening
x Last Image
xi And Beyond

Leaves
The Landscape of John Sutherland
Runners
Snowfences
Elijah
The Bower
Eavesdropping

Driving Home (1972)

NEW POEMS

Voyagers
Transformations
Signs
A landscape of John Sutherland
Origins
I wish my life was a movie
The world on Easter morning
Between cities
Eavesdropping
Lights
The nineteen thirties are over
Fence post
Moscow roses
Advice to the young
Song: Elijah
Why should I care about the world
Sad winter in the land of Can. Lit.
Language as I used to believe in it
Song for sleeping people
Polemics
Anxious
In small towns
Imitations
Dead lakes
Lot's wife
Provincial
Gift: Venus 24 degrees in Virgo
New religions
Renunciations
Totems
Motions
The following
Tapestry
Finding Amos in Jerusalem

SELECTED POEMS

Wonderful country
Green world one
Lullaby
Morning until night
Thou didst say me
Unquiet world
In the big city
The music teachers
The bond
Portrait
West coast
Gimli
Summer in the street
Lovers
At midnight
Interval
Catalpa tree
In the sun
In the park
Inward look the trees
Seashell
Laughter
City street
The hockey players
Investigator
Getting older
Sympathy
Folkways
House of industry
Toronto the golden-vaulted city
Journey to the clinic
The thief
The women's jail
Old women of Toronto
Two prison portraits
My lessons in the jail
Christ in a loincloth

The season's lovers
The eight-sided white barn
The journeying
Waking
Canadians

The Price of Gold (1976)

1. RIVERS.

What the angel said
By the sea: for A. M. Klein
Little prairie picture
Grand Manan sketches
Rivers
Forest poem
Divinations
Legends
Ecstasy
Before I go
Leaves
Don't say anything
Profile of an unliberated woman
A space of love
London night
The dark lake
Someone who used to have someone
Quiet
Beau-belle
The things we talked about
Notes of summer
Harvest
The secret of old trees
Tallness and darkness
National treasures in Havana

2. LIVING CANADIAN

What is a Canadian
Snow stories
This year in Jerusalem
October
Déjà vu
How I spent the year listening to the ten o'clock news
The land of utmost
Husbands

Lovers
Friends
Back at York University
Putting on and taking off
Morning on Cooper street
Portrait: old woman
The wheel
In exile
Trumpets
Poets are still writing poems about spring
Spring on the Bay of Quinte
Popular geography
The wind in Charlottetown
Tourists
Charlottetown
Women
Artists and old chairs
Old chair song
I take my seat in the theatre
Afternoon on Grand Manan

3. THE CAVE

Two trees
The price of gold
Spring
Ten years and more
The dead
Wives' tales
Absences
The bower
A lover who knows
Ending
Downtown streets
The days are short
Where the north winds live
The cave

Mister Never (1978)
Prologue
Loving Mister Never
Mister Never in a Dream of the Gatineau
Dreaming of Mister Never
Mister Never in the Gardens of France
Mister Never in the Chekhov Museum in Moscow
Mister Never in London
Mister Never in Ottawa
Mister Never in Winnipeg
Mister Never on the Toronto Subway
Mister Never Shows Me How to Fall Off the World
A Monument for Mister Never
Mister Never Playing
Disposing of Mister Never as a Good Man
Fragments of Mister Never in My Dream Telescope
  Legends
  Mysteries
  Double Zero
  Underground
  Singing
  The Dream Telescope
  Journey
  Likeness
  The Darkening
  Last Image
  And Beyond
  Certain Winter Meditations on Mister Never

The Visitants (1981)

I CONSERVING

Playing
Conserving
The Big Tree
The Milk of the Mothers
Honouring Heroes
Feasts
South American Nights
Primary Colours
Selves
Prairie
Holiday Postcards
Unemployment Town
History: In Jordan
Letter from Egypt
Warnings
A Good Man and a Passionate Woman
Certain Winter
Horoscopes

II HOW OLD WOMEN SHOULD LIVE

Crazy Times
How Old Women Should Live
Old Age Blues
Portrait of the Owner of a Small Garbage Can
When the Shoe Is on the Other Foot for a Change
Real Estate: Poem for Voices
Past the Ice Age
Running Up and Down Mountains at Changing Speeds
Lady in Blue: Homage to Montreal
Old Woman in a Garden
Celebrating Mavericks

III THE VISITANTS

Collected Poems (1986)

GREEN WORLD (1945)

Green World
Gimli
Into the Morning
Portrait I
Unquiet World
Uncertainties
Ballet
Arabian
Investigator
Sympathy
The Sleepers
Lovers I
Tapestry
In the Big City
Who Will Build Jerusalem
The Bond
Dog Days
Circles
Integration
Girls
Summer in the Street
Cadenza
Where
Lullaby
Morning Until Night

THE SECOND SILENCE (1955)

POEMS OF LOVE
Interval
You and Me
At Midnight
Problems
Novella
These Times
Lovers II

II THE CITY LIFE
When World Was Wheelbarrow
The City's Life
Old Women of Toronto
Winnipeg
What Is Hard
The Young Poet and Me
People Who Watch the Trains
Traffic Lights at Passover
The Through Way

III TO BE A HEALER
In a Corridor at Court
Three Prison Portraits
My Lessons in the Jail
To Be a Healer
The Women's Jail
The Orator
The Thief

IV NO EARTHLY LOVER
Exchange
No Earthly Lover
Jonathan Travels
Did You Me Dream
You Are My Never
Song II
The Honeymoon
The Exhibition: David Milne
The Artist I
Semblances
In the Mountains
Islanded
An Elegy for John Sutherland
In the Sun
The Season's Lovers

THE GLASS TRUMPET (1966)

Christ in a Loincloth
The Midsummer Garden
Night on Skid Row
Second Generation
The Survivors
Incidents for the Undying World

THE FIELD OF NIGHT
The Field of Night
Green World Two
Seeing Beyond Brick
Camping
Selma
Falling Figure
Winter One
Winter Two
Committee Work
Night of Voices
Desert Stone
Losing Merrygorounds
A Man Is Walking
The Oracle
The Snows of William Blake

CALL THEM CANADIANS (1968)

What Is a Canadian
Trumpets
Child's Poem
Before I Go
The Children's Everlasting Tree
Laughter
Spring I
Spring II
Gossip
Friends
Crowds
In Exile
Jazz

SAY YES (1969)

Understanding Snow
Living Canadian: Words to Electronic Music
Flying with Milton
The Little Fringes
Cape Cod
My Travels
About Free Rides
Disguises
The Magician
About How Hard It Is to Find New Words in an Outworn World When You Are
not a Magician
Dream Telescope
Looking for Strawberries in June
The Eight-sided White Barn
How Each One Becomes Another in the Early World
Pont Mirabeau in Montreal
Memory Box
Apollo Tree
The Wakened Wood
You as Real
How We Are Immortal in Others
Sorrow Song
From a Train Window
Women Who Live Alone
Dark
Someone Who Used to Have Someone
All Those Who Run in Fields
Owning the World
Leaf
Birch Tree
Cinderella Poems
Shakedown
Breaking with Tradition
Swallowing Darkness Is Swallowing Dead Elm Trees
A Drawing by Ronald Bloore
A Morning Like the Morning when Amos Awoke
Driving Home
A Man in Chicago

Polemics
Anxious
In Small Towns
Imitations
Dead Lakes
Lot's Wife
Provincial
Gift: Venus 24 Degrees in Virgo
New Religions
Renunciations
Totems
Motions
The Following
Tapestry I
Finding Amos in Jerusalem

THE PRICE OF GOLD (1976)

1. RIVERS
What the Angel Said
By the Sea: For A. M. Klein
Little Prairie Pictures
Grand Manan Sketches
Rivers
Forest Poem
Divinations
Legends
Don't Say Anything
An Unliberated Woman Seen from a Distance
Profile of an Unliberated Woman
A Space of Love
London Night
The Dark Lake
Beau-Belle
The Things We Talked About
Notes of Summer
Harvest
The Secret of Old Trees
Tallness and Darkness
National Treasures in Havana

MISTER NEVER (1978)

Prologue
Mister Never in a Dream of the Gatineau
Dreaming of Mister Never
Mister Never in the Gardens of France
Mister Never on the Toronto Subway
Mister Never Shows Me How to Fall Off the World
A Monument for Mister Never
Mister Never Playing
Disposing of Mister Never as a Good Man
Certain Winter Meditations on Mister Never

THE VISITANTS (1981)

I CONSERVING
Conserving
The Big Tree
The Milk of the Mothers
Honouring Heroes
Feasts
South American Nights
Primary Colours
Selves
Prairie II
Holiday Postcards
Unemployment Town
History: In Jordan
Letter from Egypt
Warnings
Horoscopes

II HOW OLD WOMEN SHOULD LIVE
Crazy Times
How Old Women Should Live
Old Age Blues
Portrait of the Owner of a Small Garbage Can
When the Shoe Is on the Other Foot for a Change
Real Estate: Poem for Voices
Past the Ice Age

Committees
Running Up and Down Mountains at Changing Speeds
Lady in Blue: Homage to Montreal
Old Woman in a Garden
Celebrating Mavericks

III THE VISITANTS
The Transplanted: Second Generation
Managing Death
The Visitants
The Secret-keeper
When We Met
The Green Cabin
In a Summer Garden
Elegies for a Composer
Bulgarian Suite
Wake-up Song

UNCOLLECTED POEMS

The Exiles: Spain
Magic
The Returner
Unheard Melodies
The Parting
Night Wanderer
Of Dreams
Out of Season
Struggle to Free the Spirit
The Old Sailor
Early Snow
Organization
Starch
The Zoo
Alone
Song I
Woman at Evening
Experience in Loneliness
Dream Not of Heroes

In Our Time
Contemporary
Ladies
Branching from Golder's Green
I Love My Love with an S
Now We Steer
Two Poems
Contrasts
Indoors
Poem
Rocky Mountain Train
People I
Festival
Fragments from Autobiography
Lake Superior
Strange Country
Partisans I
Partisans II
Snow-whorls
The Hub
Avenues
Windfalls: Bastard Country
Letter to Margaret
Oasis
Changes
Museum
The Heart Cast Out
A Ballad for the Peace
Stillness
Noon Hour Downtown
Soft Midnight of Summer
Dahlias
Quiet Go to Midnight
The Prison Worker
Faces
Portrait II
Studio on Ste. Famille Street
Departure
Housing Development

The Last Landscape (1992)
The Snow Tramp
The Woman in the Hall
Instead of Lovers
Futures
Reflections
The Life of a Woman
Knives and Ploughshares
The Angels Who Sweep I
The Angels Who Sweep II
Living with Rumours of War
The Last Landscape
The New Jasons
Amos
Ulysses Embroidered
Gardens and Us
Paper Boats
Questions
Languages
Mechanics for Women
The Summer Girls
In the Hurly Burly Arcade
Klara and Lilo
Mountain Interval I: Studio
Mountain Interval II: Pow Wow at Bragg Creek
Places
A Few Things
Aspects of Owls I
Aspects of Owls II
Freedom Games
A Man and His Flute
Orchestra
Autumn
Science and Literature
The Writer
Spring Night at Home
Jacques Cartier in Toronto
Jacques Cartier in Winnipeg
The Bouquet

Remembering Winnipeg
Mysteries
The Visitor
The Archivist
Peace Notes

Index of Poem Titles

PREVIOUSLY PUBLISHED POEMS

PREVIOUSLY UNPUBLISHED AND UNCOLLECTED POEMS

Index of Translation Titles

Under the Ruins of Poland (Itsik Manger)
What More Do You Want (Melekh Ravitch)
Yizkor (Jacob Glatstein)

TRANSLATIONS—GERMAN

School for Preparing (Otto Rank)
Weltschmerz: Lines before Breakfast (Otto Rank)

TRANSLATIONS—RUSSIAN

Springtime Girl (Robert Ivanovich Rozhdestvensky)
Under the Roof in My House (Rimma Fyodorovna Kazakova)